PASSWORD 5

THIRD EDITION

A READING AND VOCABULARY TEXT

Lynn Bonesteel

Password 5: A Reading and Vocabulary Text
Third Edition

Pearson Education, 221 River Street, Hoboken, NJ 07030

Staff credits: The people who made up the Password team, representing editorial,
production, design, and manufacturing, are Pietro Alongi, Claire Bowers, Tracey Cataldo,
Mindy DePalma, Dave Dickey, Warren Fischbach, Pam Fishman, Niki Lee, Amy McCormick,
Robert Ruvo, Kristina Skof, and Joseph Vella.

Development Editor: Penny Laporte
Cover image: © S. Parente - Travel - RF / Alamy Stock Photo
Text composition: ElectraGraphics, Inc.

Library of Congress Cataloging-in-Publication Data
A catalog record for the print edition is available from the Library of Congress.
ISBN-10: 0-13-439939-0   ISBN-13: 978-0-13-439939-3

Printed in the United States of America
16 2023

CONTENTS

SCOPE AND SEQUENCE

Unit/ Chapter	Developing Reading Skills	Learning Target Vocabulary	Building on the Vocabulary	Using Critical Thinking	Practicing Writing
Unit 1 ARTISTIC INNOVATIONS					
Chapter 1: What is Anime? page 2	• Understanding topics and main ideas • Understanding cause and effect	*beauty, challenge, complex, evil, fascinated, get one's start, involved, moral, originality, popularity, provide, rapid, related, reportedly, talented* **Guessing Strategy:** Using context to guess word meaning	• Using the target vocabulary in new contexts • Word Families: Suffixes *-ity, -al, -ly* • Word Grammar: Collocations – Adjectives + Prepositions	• **Determining** figurative meaning • **Analyzing** the writer's use of words • **Determining** the author's point of view • **Citing** evidence in the text to support opinions	• Writing a paragraph or short essay about a comic book or cartoon character • Writing a paragraph or short essay about a film or television show
	Tips • Finding the topic in the title • Being an active reader		**Tips** • Using new words without worrying about making mistakes	**Tips** • Introducing critical thinking	**Tips** • Using a dictionary to find word families
Chapter 2: The Scientist and the Stradivarius page 13	• Understanding topics and main ideas • Scanning for information • Understanding inference	*announcement, belief, brilliant, chemical, due to, heavenly, illiterate, knowledge, laboratory, mystery, proof, remarkable, stand by, theory, threatened* **Guessing Strategy:** Using context to guess positive, negative, or neutral meaning of adjectives	• Using the target vocabulary in new contexts • Word Families: Suffixes for parts of speech • Word Grammar: Cause and Effect with *due to, because, so*	• **Analyzing** the structure of the text • **Analyzing** the effect of the writer's choice of words on meaning and tone • **Citing** evidence in the text to support opinions	• Writing a summary of Dr. Nagyvary's theory • Writing a paragraph or short essay about using science to solve a mystery
	Tips • Finding the main idea • Finding support for inferences		**Tips** • Using word cards to learn different forms of words	**Tips** • Noticing unusual phrasing	**Tips** • Using adjectives to make writing clearer and more interesting
Chapter 3: The History of Rap page 25	• Understanding topics and main ideas • Scanning	*call for, characteristic, clever, compete, contribute, equipment, expression, grow out of, interact, live, performer, personality, rhyme, scratch, spinning, stand out, technique* **Guessing Strategy:** Using the signal word *or* to guess word meaning	• Using the target vocabulary in new contexts • Word Families: Suffixes *-ion, -tion, -ance* • Word Grammar: Phrasal verbs	• **Determining** the author's point of view • **Summarizing** and paraphrasing main ideas in the text • **Citing** evidence in the text to support your opinions	• Writing an essay about a type of music that you like • Writing a letter to a performer that you admire
	Tips • Reading without a dictionary • Identifying the topic of each paragraph		**Tips** • Recognizing when changes in word form change meaning	**Tips** • Supporting your opinions with information from the text	**Tips** • Putting information into your own words • Identifying sources
Unit 1 Checkpoint page 36	• Look Back • Extra Reading: *Pablo Picasso* • Expanding Vocabulary: *Guessing Strategy: Phrasal Verbs Word Families: Suffixes* • Playing with Words: *Crossword Puzzle* • Building Dictionary Skills: *Finding Phrasal Verbs*				
Unit 2 THE CHALLENGES OF YOUTH					
Chapter 4: Sleepy Teens page 44	• Distinguishing major points from supporting details	*absence, at least, complaint, concern, depressed, dropout, experiment, expert, in tears, lack, likely, official, pattern, reduce, stay up* **Guessing Strategy:** Identifying synonyms to guess meaning	• Using the target vocabulary in new contexts • Word Families: Recognizing the different forms of a word • Word Grammar: Participial adjectives	• **Analyzing** the structure of the text • **Making** inferences • **Applying** concepts from the text • **Citing** evidence in the text to support your ideas	• Writing a letter to a school official • Writing an essay about a problem that affects teenagers
	Tips • Annotating a text	**Tips** • Using a dictionary for meaning and usage		**Tips** • Questioning a text	**Tips** • Putting information into your own words • Improving your writing by reading
Chapter 5: Growing Up Gifted page 55	• Understanding major points • Understanding inference	*achieve, burn out, championship, concentrate on, critical, despite, gifted, injustice, literature, peers, perfectionist, pressure, publish, sensitive, survive, tend to* **Guessing Strategy:** Using context to guess positive or negative meaning of words	• Using the target vocabulary in new contexts • Word Families: Related Words • Word Grammar: Gerunds after prepositions	• **Analyzing** the author's point of view • **Making** inferences • **Applying** the information from the text • **Citing** evidence in the text to support your opinion	• Writing an opinion essay based on the chapter reading • Writing an essay about a child prodigy
	Tips • Understanding text features: Bullet points	**Tips** • Learning frequently used words		**Tips** • Reconsidering an opinion based on new information	**Tips** • Supporting an opinion essay with factual information

Unit/Chapter	Developing Reading Skills	Learning Target Vocabulary	Building on the Vocabulary	Using Critical Thinking	Practicing Writing
Chapter 6: *School Bullies* page 67	• Understanding main ideas and major points • Understanding relationships between ideas: Semicolons	*aggression, anxiety, attitude, background, based on, bully, conduct, data, economic, examine, harmful, humiliation, insult, intentional, physical, pick on, self-esteem, survey, victim, violent* **Guessing Strategy:** Understanding semicolons	• Using the target vocabulary in new contexts • Word Families: Using a dictionary to find related words • Word Grammar: Collocations with verb + noun **Tips** • Recognizing words inside of words	• **Considering** an issue from various perspectives before forming an opinion • **Analyzing** the writer's use of words • **Applying** information from the text • **Citing** evidence in the text to support your opinion **Tips** • Highlighting new information • Learning about a topic from multiple sources	• Writing a report based on a survey about teenagers • Writing a story about a school bully **Tips** • Considering point of view when writing a story

Unit 2 *Checkpoint* page 78	• Look Back
	• Extra Reading: *The Teenage Brain*
	• Expanding Vocabulary: *Word Grammar: Compound Words*
	                     Word Grammar: Phrasal Verbs
	                     Word Families: The Suffix -ize
	• Playing with Words: *Word Search Puzzle*
	• Building Dictionary Skills: *Finding the Correct Meaning*				

Unit 3   THE SCIENCE OF WHO WE ARE

Unit/Chapter	Developing Reading Skills	Learning Target Vocabulary	Building on the Vocabulary	Using Critical Thinking	Practicing Writing
Chapter 7: *The Science of Genetics* page 86	• Scanning • Summarizing **Tips** • Highlighting information in a text	*cell, come out, cure, desirable, determine, disease, gender, gene, generation, get rid of, illness, individual, inherit, instruction, prevent, realize, replace, trait* **Guessing Strategy:** Recognizing in-text definitions to understand meaning of unfamiliar words	• Using the target vocabulary in new contexts • Word Families: Adjectives ending in -able • Word Grammar: Collocations with verb + direct object + preposition **Tips** • Recognizing suffixes that change word meaning	• **Applying** information from the text to new situations • **Explaining** your opinion • **Citing** evidence in the text to support your opinion **Tips** • Expressing your opinions	• Writing an essay about the advantages and disadvantages of genetic testing • Writing a letter to the editor about one of the issues raised in the chapter reading **Tips** • Understanding a topic by writing about it
Chapter 8: *Designing the Future* page 98	• Making inferences • Summarizing **Tips** • Making reasonable inferences	*acceptable, actually, advantage, appearance, approaching, athletic, biologist, bring up, convince, feature, historically, humanity, identify, in short, lead to, restrict, risk, shortage* **Guessing Strategy:** Understanding dashes	• Using the target vocabulary in new contexts • Word Families: Adjectives ending in -ous • Word Grammar: Adverbs **Tips** • Using an English-English Dictionary	• **Analyzing** the writer's use of language • **Recognizing** the purpose of a paragraph • **Summarizing** and analyzing the writer's point of view • **Citing** evidence in the text to support your opinion **Tips** • Answering questions raised in the text	• Writing a letter to your future child • Writing an essay supporting your point of view on genetic engineering **Tips** • Writing a summary from memory
Chapter 9: *A Terrible Inheritance, A Difficult Decision* page 110	• Interpreting a diagram **Tips** • Annotating a text that compares and contrasts people or things	*benefit, complication, diet, effective, factor, fortunate, in charge of, intend, operation, poison, prescribe, progress, recover, severe, suffer* **Guessing Strategy:** Using antonyms to guess meaning **Tips** • Learning a word and its antonym	• Using the target vocabulary in new contexts • Word Families: Target words • Word Grammar: Collocations-specialized vocabulary	• **Making** inferences • **Summarizing** key points in the text • **Identifying** problems • **Citing** evidence in the text to support your opinion **Tips** • Imagining yourself in the same situation described in the text	• Writing an essay based on issues raised in the chapter reading • Writing about an imaginary future **Tips** • Using collocations when you write
Unit 3 *Checkpoint* page 120	• Look Back • Extra Reading: *GM Food* • Expanding Vocabulary: *Word Grammar: Transitive and Intransitive Verbs* *Word Families: Prefixes* • Playing with Words: *The Game of Concentration* • Building Dictionary Skills: *Finding Collocations*				

Unit/Chapter	Developing Reading Skills	Learning Target Vocabulary	Building on the Vocabulary	Using Critical Thinking	Practicing Writing
Unit 4 GETTING EMOTIONAL					
Chapter 10: *Can You Translate an Emotion?* page 130	• Paraphrasing • Applying information **Tips** • Answering a question posed in the title	*associate, cheerfulness, disgust, honor, in contrast, indeed, grief, guilt, observe, particularly, recognize, reveal, shame, translate, universal* **Guessing Strategy:** Recognizing words with similar meanings	• Using the target vocabulary in new contexts • Word Families: Emotions • Word Grammar: Verb patterns **Tips** • Paying attention to verb patterns	• **Explaining** the writer's use of language • **Making** comparisons • **Inferring** meaning • **Applying** information from the text to other situations • **Citing** evidence in the text to support your opinion **Tips** • Answering questions posed in the text	• Writing an essay about emotion **Tips** • Deciding when to paraphrase specific words
Chapter 11: *Catching an Emotion* page 142	• Understanding figurative language • Understanding reference words **Tips** • Recognizing when quotation marks are used to indicate figurative language • Finding the referent for the pronoun *it*	*artificial, choosy, conscious, facial expression, frown upon, greet, humorous, imitate, make up, mood, muscle, out loud, proper, virtue* **Guessing Strategy:** Recognizing word families to guess meaning	• Using the target vocabulary in new contexts • Word Families: Adjectives ending in –y • Word Grammar: Phrasal verbs - *Make Up* **Tips** • Using word cards for different meanings of the same word	• **Interpreting** words and phrases in the text • **Applying** information in the text to other situations • **Making** inferences and drawing logical conclusions • **Citing** evidence in the text to support your opinion **Tips** • Recognizing a writer's suggestions • Checking comprehension by applying an idea to a new situation	• Writing an essay about expressing emotions • Writing an essay about reading emotions in a professional setting **Tips** • Paraphrasing figurative language • Using figurative language to make your writing more interesting
Chapter 12: *Reading Faces* page 153	• Understanding figurative language • Paraphrasing complex ideas **Tips** • Testing your comprehension by paraphrasing • Understanding the writer's attitude	*accuse, attempt, calculate, detect, flash, gesture, incident, injury, interpret, legal, motivation, rage, range, security, tool, tragedy, vehicle* **Guessing Strategy:** Asking questions to guess meaning	• Using the target vocabulary in new contexts • Word Families: The prefix *micro-* • Word Grammar: Collocations- Compound nouns **Tips** • Using prefixes to guess the meaning of unfamiliar words	• **Analyzing** key structural features used in the text • **Drawing** logical conclusions • **Expressing** and supporting opinions • **Citing** evidence in the text to support your opinion **Tips** • Creating personal examples to deepen understanding of an idea	• Writing an opinion essay about ideas raised in the chapter reading **Tips** • Changing both words and sentence structure when paraphrasing
Unit 4 *Checkpoint* page 166	• Look Back • Extra Reading: *Chronic Blushing* • Expanding Vocabulary: *Word Grammar: Collocations* *Word Families: Spelling* • Playing with Words: *Word Categories Game* • Building Dictionary Skills: *Finding words in the same word family*				
Unit 5 MAN AND BEAST					
Chapter 13: *Is Music Universal?* Page 174	• Using an outline **Tips** • Identifying what a descriptive phrase modifies	*ancient, appreciation, auditory, bond, damage, drum, endless, evidence, hollow, journal, key, make sense of, precise, scale, species, structure, system, the deaf theme, visual* **Guessing Strategy:** Using descriptive phrases to guess meaning	• Using the target vocabulary in new contexts • Word Families: Word roots • Word Grammar: Collocations with *system* **Tips** • Learning the meaning of word roots	• **Analyzing** text development • **Examining** the writer's opinion • **Comparing** findings in two texts • **Citing** evidence in the text to support your opinion **Tips** • Quoting rather than paraphrasing	• Writing a short research report on animal songs • Writing a letter about life without music **Tips** • Writing a summary from an outline • Researching topics
Chapter 14: *Man's Best Friend* page 185	• Understanding the main idea • Using an outline • Summarizing **Tips** • Finding the main idea	*companion, distinguish, establishment, evolve, frequency, gaze, measure, mutual, pleasurable, raise, regardless, release, resemble, striking, sustained, task* **Guessing Strategy:** Finding words with similar meanings	• Using the target vocabulary in new contexts • Word Families: The prefix *co-*	• **Inferring** meaning from the text • **Interpreting** words and phrases in the text • **Summarizing** key details • **Evaluating** the conclusions in the text • **Citing** evidence in the text to support your opinion **Tips** • Making good inferences	• Writing a report based on interviews about pet ownership • Writing an opinion essay about the value of the research in the reading **Tips** • Using words with similar meanings but different forms when paraphrasing

Unit/Chapter	Developing Reading Skills	Learning Target Vocabulary	Building on the Vocabulary	Using Critical Thinking	Practicing Writing
Chapter 15: *The Mind of the Chimpanzee* page 196	• Understanding major points, supporting details, and the main idea • Summarizing **Tips** • Understanding negative statements	*analyze, bitterly, combine, controversy, eventually, imply, infant, intellectual, meaningful, out of sight, pile, possess, protest, puzzled, stretch, the wild* **Guessing Strategy:** Using sentence structure to guess meaning	• Using the target vocabulary in new contexts • Word Families: Adding variety to your writing • Word Grammar: *The +* adjective **Tips** • Becoming more flexible in your use of vocabulary	• **Applying** ideas from the text • **Summarizing** key details • **Citing** evidence in the text to support your opinion **Tips** • Applying what you have learned	• Writing a report on Jane Goodall's life and work • Writing an essay on what distinguishes humans from other animals **Tips** • Using quotations
Unit 5 *Checkpoint* page 208	• Look Back • Extra Reading: *Little Joe* • Expanding Vocabulary: *Guessing Strategy: Collocations with* bitter *Word Families: Suffixes and Word Meaning* • Playing with Words: *A Crossword Puzzle* • Building Dictionary Skills: *Finding the Correct Meaning*				

Unit 6   THE PEOPLE BEHIND THE SCIENCE

Unit/Chapter	Developing Reading Skills	Learning Target Vocabulary	Building on the Vocabulary	Using Critical Thinking	Practicing Writing
Chapter 16: *A Woman's Fate* page 218	• Understanding text organization • Making inferences • Summarizing **Tips** • Paying attention to time words to determine chronological order	*agricultural, come up with, confirm, determined, fate, former, function, glove, interfere, prestigious, resist, see the big picture, slip, stain, suitable, sweat, unique, well-being* **Guessing Strategy:** Using the signal word *or* to guess meaning	• Using the target vocabulary in new contexts • Word Families: The prefix *Inter-* • Word Grammar: Phrasal verbs with *come* **Tips** • Using both prefixes and context to guess word meaning	• **Analyzing** the writer's choice of words • **Explaining** the author's development of ideas • **Applying** information from the text • **Citing** evidence in the text to support your opinion **Tips** • Understanding euphemisms	• Writing a persuasive letter to a potential investor • Writing an essay about an important invention **Tips** • Including all major points when summarizing
Chapter 17: *The Father of Vaccination* page 230	• Understanding reference • Understanding major points and important details • Summarizing **Tips** • Recognizing references to previously introduced information • Using the reporting questions (*who, what, when, where, why* and *how*) to check your understanding of a text	*abuse, contagious, deliberately, free of, ignore, infect, means, mild, permission, physician, practice, procedure, request, review, surgery, turn down, vaccination* **Guessing Strategy:** Recognizing signal words for contrast **Tips** • Learning the most common signal words	• Using the target vocabulary in new contexts • Word Families: • Words with a root and a prefix • Word Grammar: Collocations with *mild* and *severe*	• **Summarizing** key details • **Applying** information from the text • **Examining** your response to the text • **Citing** evidence in the text to support your opinion **Tips** • Looking for evidence for a writer's claims	• Writing a report about current research on vaccines • Writing an opinion essay about using human subjects in medical research **Tips** • Preparing to write a summary by answering reporting questions
Chapter 18: *A Nose for Science* page 242	• Understanding purpose • Summarizing **Tips** • Inferring the writer's purpose	*access, discount, entertain, focus, fragrance, fraud, investment, legend, obsessed, path, perfume, physics, poetic, royalty, scent, secretive, standard, tale* **Guessing Strategy:** Using signal words for cause and effect to guess word meaning	• Using the target vocabulary in new contexts • Word Families: Adjective suffixes • Word Grammar: Reflexive pronouns **Tips** • Recognizing common suffixes for different parts of speech	• **Determining** the writer's point of view • **Exploring** the writer's use of figurative language • **Synthesizing** information • **Citing** evidence in the text to support your opinion **Tips** • Identifying a writer's attitude toward her subject	• Writing a report on a well-known scientist • Writing a description of a memory associated with a particular smell **Tips** • Deciding which information to include in a summary
Unit 6 *Checkpoint* page 255	• Look Back • Extra Reading: *A New Way of Teaching Science?* • Expanding Vocabulary: *Guessing Strategy: Phrasal Verbs with* turn *Word Families: Prefixes, Suffixes, and Roots* • Playing with Words: *Word Categories Game* • Building Dictionary Skills: *Idioms*				

THE THIRD EDITION OF THE *PASSWORD* SERIES

Welcome to the third edition of *Password*, a series designed to help learners of English develop their English-language reading skills and expand their vocabularies. The series offers theme-based units which include:

- engaging nonfiction reading passages,
- a variety of activities to develop reading and critical thinking skills, and
- exercises to help students understand, remember, and use new words and phrases.

Each book in the *Password* series can be used independently of the others, but when used as a series, the books will help students reach the 2,000-word vocabulary level, at which point, research has shown, learners can begin to read unadapted texts.

The *Password* approach to reading skill development for English-language learners is based on the following ideas:

1. The best way for learners to develop their English reading skills is to read English-language materials at an appropriate level.

Attractive, high-interest materials will spark learners' motivation to read, but to sustain that motivation, "second language reading instruction must find ways to avoid continually frustrating the reader."[1] Learners of English need reading materials at an appropriate level of difficulty, materials that do not reduce them to struggling to decipher a puzzle. Materials at an inappropriate level will not allow learners to develop reading strategies but rather will discourage them from reading.

The level of difficulty of ELT materials is determined by many factors, such as the learner's familiarity with the topic, the learner's L1 reading skills, the length and structure of the words, sentences, and paragraphs, and the structure of the text as a whole. These are among the factors that influence the construction of all good ELT reading materials and the way they gradually increase in difficulty. However, an additional, critical factor in determining the difficulty of a text for English language learners is the familiarity of the vocabulary. Note that:

> There is now a large body of studies indicating that poor readers primarily differ from good readers in context-free word recognition, and not in deficiencies in ability to use context to form predictions.[2]

Learners of English must be able to recognize a great many words on sight so that they can absorb, understand, and react to the text much as they would to a text in their first language.

The *Password* series is distinguished by its meticulous control and recycling of vocabulary so that the readings consistently maintain an appropriate level of difficulty. When learners can recognize enough of the words in their reading materials, they can then develop and apply reading skills and strategies. The result is an authentic reading experience, the kind of experience learners need to become proficient readers of English.

2. An intensive reading program is essential to prepare English language learners for the demands of college and careers.

An intensive reading program means students engage in the careful reading of nonfiction texts with the goal of understanding them in detail, under the guidance of the teacher. A well-designed textbook can play a critical role in helping students not only meet that goal but acquire reading skills and strategies they can apply to further reading. Course materials should provide practice with the types of thinking skills that students need, not only to comprehend explicitly stated information but to interpret texts, draw inferences, analyze the language, make comparisons, and cite evidence from the text to support their views. The materials should also facilitate collaboration with classmates throughout the process. When their classroom discussions are stimulating and rewarding, students are motivated to do the assigned readings, and thus get the reading practice they need.

3. An ELT reading textbook should teach the English vocabulary that will be most useful to learners.

Corpus-based research has shown that the 2,000 highest-frequency words in English (as identified in Michael West's classic *General Service List*) account for about 80 percent of the running words in academic texts.[3] The *New General Service List*, with 2,368 high-frequency "word families," goes even further, providing 90 percent coverage of the words in most general English texts.[4] Clearly, the highest-frequency words are highly valuable words for students of English to learn.

The *Password* target word lists are based on analyses of high-frequency word data from multiple sources, including the Longman Corpus Network. Also taught in the series are common collocations and other multiword units, such as phrasal verbs, while a few target words have been chosen for their value in discussing a particular topic. With the

---

[1] Thom Hudson, *Teaching Second Language Reading* (Oxford, UK: Oxford University Press, 2007) 291.

[2] C. Juel, quoted in *Teaching and Researching Reading*, William Grabe and Fredericka Stoller (Harlow, England: Pearson Education, 2002) 73.

[3] I. S. P. Nation, *Learning Vocabulary in Another Language* (Cambridge, England: Cambridge University Press, 2001) 17.

[4] "A New General Service List (1.01)." (n.d.) Retrieved December 15, 2015, from http://www.newgeneralservicelist.org

increasing interest in corpus-based research in recent years, a wealth of information is now available as to which words are the highest-frequency, be it in US and/or British academic contexts, in written English of various types, in spoken English, and so on. Teachers may worry about how to choose from among the various lists, but at the level of the 2,000 highest-frequency words in general use—the level of the *Password* series—the lists are far more alike than they are different.

While becoming a good reader in English involves much more than knowing the meanings of words, there is no doubt that vocabulary knowledge is essential. To learn new words, students need to see and understand them repeatedly and in varied contexts. They must also become skilled at guessing the meaning of new words from context, but they can do this successfully only when they understand the context.

Research by Paul Nation and Liu Na suggests that "for successful guessing [of unknown words] . . . at least 95% of the words in the text must be familiar to the reader."[5] For that reason, the vocabulary in the readings has been carefully controlled so that unknown words should constitute no more than five percent of any reading passage. The words used in each reading are limited to those high-frequency words that the learner is assumed to know, or has studied in previous chapters, plus the new vocabulary being taught. New vocabulary is explained and practiced in exercises and activities, encountered again in later chapters, and reviewed in the Unit Checkpoints and Self-Tests. This emphasis on systematic vocabulary acquisition is a highlight of the series.

The chart below shows the number of words that each *Password* book assumes will be familiar to the learner, and the range of the high-frequency vocabulary targeted in the book.

The five books in the series vary somewhat in organization, to meet the diverse needs of beginning to high-intermediate students, as well as in the increasing complexity of the reading materials and exercises. All five books will help learners make steady progress in developing their reading, critical thinking, and vocabulary skills in English. Please see the Overview in each book for detailed information about that book's organization and contents, including the exciting new features the third edition has to offer.

Linda Butler, creator of the Password *series*

Additional References

Grabe, William. *Reading in a Second Language: Moving from theory to practice.* Cambridge: Cambridge University Press, 2009.

Liu, Dilin. "The Most Frequently Used Spoken American English Idioms: A Corpus Analysis and Its Implications," *TESOL Quarterly 37* (Winter 2003): 4, 671-700.

Nation, I.S.P. *Teaching Vocabulary: Strategies and techniques.* Boston: Heinle, Cengage Learning, 2008.

Schmitt, Norbert, and Cheryl Boyd Zimmerman. "Derivative Word Forms: What Do Learners Know?" *TESOL Quarterly 36* (Summer 2002): 145–171.

Highest-frequency words	Password 1	Password 2	Password 3	Password 4	Password 5
2,000					**target words** *absence, acceptable, advantage,...*
1,500				**target words** *appear, attach,...*	**words assumed** *a/an, able, about, active, address, adult, agree, almost, amount, appear, attach,...*
1,200			**target words** *active, amount,...*	**words assumed** *a/an, able, about, active, address, adult, agree, almost, amount,...*	
900		**target words** *able, adult,...*	**words assumed** *a/an, able, about, address, adult, agree, almost,...*		
600	**target words** *agree, almost,...*	**words assumed** *a/an, about, address, agree, almost,...*			
300	**words assumed** *a/an, about, address,...*				

[5] Nation 254

OVERVIEW OF *PASSWORD 5*, THIRD EDITION

Password 5 is intended for students who need to build a solid foundation for reading in English, whether for academic purposes or for their careers. Each of the 18 chapters features an engaging nonfiction reading passage as the basis for a variety of activities to help students develop their reading, critical thinking, speaking, writing, and vocabulary skills.

The book assumes students start out with a vocabulary of about 1500 words in English, and it teaches over 300 more of the high-frequency words and phrases and academic vocabulary that students most need to know. In each chapter, from 14 to 20 words and phrases are highlighted in the reading passage and taught in the exercises. All are recycled in readings and exercises in later chapters. Because of the systematic building of vocabulary, as well as the progression of the skills work, it is best to do the chapters in order.

The target vocabulary consists primarily of words found among the 2000 highest-frequency words in English and the *Academic Word List*. Other, lower-frequency words and phrases are targeted for their usefulness in discussing a particular theme, such as *gene* and *trait* in Unit 3: Genetics: The Science of Who We Are.

Organization of the Book

Password 5 contains six units, each with three chapters and a *Checkpoint* chapter. Vocabulary *Self-Tests* are found after Units 3 and 6. The answers to the Self-Tests and the Index to the Target Vocabulary are at the end of the book.

THE UNITS   Each unit is based on a theme, includes three chapters, and is built around a reading about a real person, situation, phenomenon, or event.

★ **New in this edition:** Each unit opens with a *Think about This* question, designed to activate prior knowledge of the unit theme. It will get students thinking and talking about the topic from the start.

THE CHAPTERS   Each of the three chapters in a unit is organized as follows:

Getting Ready to Read—The chapter opens with a photo and pre-reading tasks. The tasks are often for pair or small-group work. *Getting Ready to Read* improves students' reading comprehension by activating schema. The tasks get them to connect with the topic before they read by raising questions, eliciting what students already know, asking for their opinions, and introducing key vocabulary.

★ **New in this edition:** The new, color photo will spark interest in the topic. The *Learning Outcome* tells students the content objective of the chapter: what they will be reading, talking, and learning about by working through the chapter. Then, at the start of the Reading section, they will find the new Read to Find Out question to give direction to their reading.

Reading—This section begins with the reading passage for the chapter. The passages progress from about 500 to about 900 words over the course of the book. Students should do the reading the first time without stopping to look up or ask about new words. Careful control of the vocabulary in each passage means that students will not get derailed by too many new words and can have the authentic reading experience they need to build their reading skills.

An audio program, with recordings of the readings, is included in the Essential Online Resources. Students may wish to play the audio while they reread the passage, as listening while reading can aid comprehension, retention, and pronunciation.

★ **New in this edition:** The readings and materials in Chapters 6, 12 and 14 are entirely new, and the reading and materials in Chapter 8 have been substantially revised. All other readings have been updated, and the material in many chapters has been expanded upon substantially.

The reading passage is followed by *Quick Comprehension Check*, a brief true/false/can't determine the answer from the text exercise to help students monitor their general understanding of the text. At this point, students focus only on comprehension of the major points in the reading. Vocabulary study and an in-depth examination of the text will follow.

★ **New in this edition:** Students must locate and cite evidence from the reading to support their answers and to make corrections to the false statements. These are essential skills for academic reading.

Exploring Vocabulary—This section teaches the target vocabulary from the reading. In *Thinking about the Target Vocabulary*, first students learn and practice a *Guessing Strategy* that develops their ability to guess the meaning of unfamiliar words from context. Next, students look at a list of target words and phrases and circle those that are new to them. Students then return to the reading to see what they can learn about the words from the context in which they are used. Finally, students complete a chart with the target words and phrases from the reading organized according to parts of speech. Students can do the vocabulary independently or in pairs, but they may benefit from working on this first as a whole class, with the teacher's guidance.

Understanding the Target Vocabulary follows, with one or two exercises to help students understand the meanings of the target words and phrases as they are used in the reading. The exercises can be done in class, by students working individually or in pairs, or for homework. When taken as a whole, *Understanding the Target Vocabulary* is actually a summary of the most important information from the text.

★ **New in this edition:** *Vocabulary Tips* teach strategies for learning and using new vocabulary.

Developing Your Reading Skills—In this section are tasks that require students to delve back into the reading. Re-reading is a vital part of the reading process, and the tasks in this section motivate students to do that re-reading and thereby deepen their understanding of the text. The tasks include work on recognizing or stating topics of paragraphs, identifying or stating the main ideas of entire texts, scanning for specific information, recognizing or stating cause and effect, understanding reference words, identifying the writer's purpose, tone, and point of view, making inferences, understanding text organization, paraphrasing, outlining, and summarizing. Developing these skills is essential preparation for academic reading in English.

★ **New in this edition:** *Reading Tips* teach reading strategies, offer advice on good reading habits, and raise awareness of text structure.

Building on the Vocabulary—In this section, students move from understanding the vocabulary to actively acquiring it. First, they practice using the target words in new contexts. Next, students build on their knowledge by learning related items that are in the same word families as the target vocabulary. Finally they learn more about phrasal verbs, collocations, or the word grammar associated with the target vocabulary. After working through the exercises in *Building on the Vocabulary*, students can turn to their dictionaries for further information, if needed.

Critical Thinking—This new section for the third edition adds rigor to the discussion of the reading passages by requiring students to analyze and evaluate what the writer is saying before they offer personal opinions and reactions to the reading. Students are guided to examine the text, make inferences, draw comparisons, determine author purpose, cite evidence--in short, to apply a range of vital thinking skills and demonstrate a thorough understanding of the text. Still included from previous editions are community-building questions, inspired by the readings, that get students to use their imaginations and share their own experiences and ideas.

In this section, students are also instructed to use the target vocabulary (including the derived forms that were introduced in the chapter). The words that are most likely to be useful when responding to the questions are listed. You may want to specifically assign someone from each group to keep track of how many times the words were used in their group's discussion. You can then ask the class which vocabulary they had difficulty using, and provide additional instruction as needed.

★ **New in this edition:** Questions for discussion promote the critical thinking skills expected and required for success in college and careers in the 21st century. *Critical Thinking Tips* help students to develop those skills and become more aware of them.

Writing—This section contains a choice of two topics related to the content of the reading. Writing in response to reading is a way for students to not only to develop writing and vocabulary skills, but also deepen understanding of the reading and make connections to the unit theme. Students respond to one of the two topics, using at least five of the target words in their writing.

★ **New in this edition:** *Writing Tips* provide strategies to help students become more successful writers.

UNIT CHECKPOINT   Each unit ends with a Checkpoint chapter, which is designed to help students review and expand on the content of the unit. Students see the vocabulary in new contexts and have the chance to test what they remember and can use. The Checkpoint begins with a *Look Back* section, in which students are asked to recall and reflect on what they learned (*Think about This*) and think about their own response to each of the reading passages (*Remember the Readings*). *Reviewing Vocabulary* gives students another point of interaction with the target vocabulary from the unit; *Expanding Vocabulary* teaches students about word families and word parts; and *Playing with Words* puts target vocabulary into a game or a crossword or word search puzzle. The final section, *Building Dictionary Skills*, provides practice based on excerpts from Longman dictionaries of American English. Knowing how to use a dictionary effectively is an essential skill for the independent language learner.

★ **New in this edition:** A *Learning Outcome* introduces each Checkpoint chapter. The *Look Back* section provides a valuable follow-up to the students' reading experiences in each unit.

THE VOCABULARY SELF-TESTS   Two multiple-choice vocabulary tests appear in the book, the first covering Units 1,2, and 3, and the second covering Units 4, 5 and 6 . The answers are given at the back of the book, as these tests are intended for students' own use so that they can review the target vocabulary and assess their progress.

★ **New in this edition:** The Self-Tests have been updated to include the new target vocabulary.

NEW Essential Online Resources

A new set of resources is available online for *Password 5*. It contains:
- Audio recordings of each reading
- Bonus activities for extra practice in timed reading and study skills
- The Teacher's Manual, containing:
  - The answer key for all exercises in the book, updated to be much more extensive in this edition. It contains explanations for each of the Quick Comprehension questions, as well as extensive answers for the Critical Thinking section. Teachers can use these answers to encourage more discussion of the readings and expand on the chapter theme.
  - Five unit tests with answers, updated for this edition
  - Quick Oral Reviews, sets of prompts to use in class for rapid drills of the target vocabulary for each chapter. These drills can be an important part of the spaced repetition of vocabulary—repeated exposures to newly learned words and phrases at increasing intervals—that helps students remember the vocabulary. The Introduction to the Teacher's Manual contains tips on how to use the prompts.

To the Student

Welcome to *Password 5*! This book will help you learn many new words and improve your reading skills as you learn about a wide range of topics. I hope you will enjoy using it.

ACKNOWLEDGMENTS, CREDITS, AND ABOUT THE AUTHOR

Acknowledgments

I would like to first thank Dr. Jeong-Wha Choi, who graciously agreed to allow me to use her story. I would also like to thank Samuela Eckstut for being so generous with her time, advice, and encouragement.

I would also like to thank the reviewers whose comments on early drafts of the first edition of this book were very helpful: Christina Cavage, Atlantic Cape Community College, Atlantic City, NJ; Leslie Corpuz, Tidewater Community College, Virginia Beach, VA; Anthony Halderman, Cuesta College, San Luis Obispo, CA; Martha Hall, The New England School of English; Steve Horowitz, Central Washington University, Ellensburg, WA; Susan Jamieson, Bellevue Community College, Bellevue, WA; Kathy Sherak, San Francisco State University, San Francisco, CA; Julie Un, Massasoit Community College, Brockton, MA; Jo Dee Walters, formerly affiliated with San Diego State University, San Diego, CA.

I'd also like to extend my gratitude to Linda Butler, whose vision and concept for the series were a constant source of guidance and inspiration as I worked on this project.

A great many people helped in the making of this book, most of all my development editor, Penny Laporte, and the Pearson English team, which includes Pietro Alongi, Tracey Cataldo, Mindy DePalma, Dave Dickey, Warren Fischbach, Pam Fishman, Niki Lee, Amy McCormick, Robert Ruvo, Kristina Skof, and Joseph Vella.

Finally, I would like to thank my mother and father for introducing me at a very early age to the wonder of reading. It is the most precious of gifts.

Illustration Credits

ElectraGraphics, Inc.

Photo Credits

Page 1: Gino Santa Maria/Fotolia; **2 (top):** Manga Entertainment/Everett Collection; **2 (bottom):** Universal/Everett Collection; **13:** Mihalec/Shutterstock; **25:** Wenn Ltd/Alamy Stock Photo; **36:** Gino Santa Maria/Fotolia; **43:** Syda Productions/Shutterstock; **44:** Image Source/Alamy Stock Photo; **55:** Olaf Speier/Fotolia; **67:** asiseeit/ E+/Getty Images **78:** Syda Productions/Shutterstock; **85:** Adimas/Fotolia; **86:** Photo Researchers, Inc/Alamy Stock Photo; **98:** JGI/Jamie Grill/Blend Images/Alamy Stock Photo; **120:** adimas/Fotolia; **129:** william87/Fotolia; **130:** Takke mei/Fotolia; **142:** Antonio balaguer soler/Stock Photo/123RF; **153 (top):** Master1305/Shutterstock; **153 (bottom):** Master1305/Shutterstock; **166:** william87/Fotolia; **173:** Alena Ozerova/Shutterstock; **174:** ead72/Fotolia; **185:** Taka/Fotolia; **196:** Kay/Karl Ammann/Avalon/Bruce Coleman Inc/Alamy Stock Photo; **208:** Alena Ozerova/Shutterstock; **217:** PhotoSky/Shutterstock; **218:** Zoran Simin/Alamy Stock Photo; **230:** Stefano Bianchetti/Corbis Historical/Getty Images; **242:** David Parker/Science Source; **255:** PhotoSky/Shutterstock.

Text Credits

Page 3: "What is Anime?" by Bryan Pfaffenberger. Used with permission of the author; **14:** The Scientist and the Stradivarius, *Ottawa Citizen*, Postmedia Network Inc.; **45:** Adapted from "Sleepy Teens," *Boston Globe*, January 5, 2003. Used with permission of Laura Pappano; **68:** Fiona Smith, How Norway Deals with Bullies, *Irish Times*, 1994, Irish Times; **209:** Jane Goodall, *The Mind of the Chimpanzee, Through a Window*, Houghton Mifflin, 1990

About the Author

Lynn Bonesteel has been teaching ESL since 1988. For much of her teaching career, she has been a full-time senior lecturer at the Center for English Language and Orientation Programs at Boston University. She writes materials for learning and teaching English, and is the author of a number of ESL/EFL textbooks, including *Center Stage*, Books 2, 3, and 4 (co-authored with Samuela Eckstut), Books 1 and 3 of the *Real Reading* series, and Book 1 of the *From Reading to Writing* series.

ARTISTIC INNOVATIONS

Gino Santa Maria, Woman and Guitar

THINK ABOUT THIS

Do you enjoy these activities? Rank your answers:

1 = very much   2 = some   3 = not very much

_____ looking at paintings and sculpture

_____ listening to music

_____ watching dance performances

_____ watching movies

_____ Other (Add an activity related to art that you enjoy doing)

_____

CHAPTER 1

What is Anime?

#1: From "Perfect Blue"

#2: From "The Secret Life of Pets"

LEARNING OUTCOME

❯ Learn about a Japanese style of animation

GETTING READY TO READ

Talk in a small group.

1. Did you watch cartoons or read comic books when you were a child? Which ones? Do you ever watch cartoons or read comic books now? Which ones?

2. Compare the two movie posters. Check (✓) the words that you think describe the posters. Explain your answers to your classmates.

	BEAUTIFUL	CREATIVE	INTELLIGENT	FUNNY	SERIOUS	INTERESTING	SIMPLE
Poster #1: Anime (Japanese-style animation)							
Poster #2: Disney-style animation							

READING

Read the definitions beside the reading. Then read "What is Anime?" If you see a new word, circle it, but don't stop reading. Instead, try to understand the sentence without it. You can learn the word later.

What Is Anime?

1   *Anime* is a special style of Japanese animation.[1] You can immediately see the difference between anime and other styles of animation. This is because of the high quality of the artwork and the style of anime; such as characters with large, childlike eyes. In addition, you will see that anime is strongly influenced by Asian, and especially Japanese, religious and cultural traditions. Specifically, in anime you can see the influences of Shinto, a Japanese religion; Zen Buddhism, another religious tradition that is practiced throughout Asia; and the martial arts, such as karate and judo, that have been an important part of Japanese culture for a very long time. You could say that anime **provides** a window into Japanese culture.

2   Anime is closely **related** to Japanese style comic books, which are called manga. Many anime television shows and videos **got their start** as popular manga. Just as anime is different from American animated films and television shows, manga are quite different from American comic books. Manga usually include fewer words, but more **complex** drawings than American comic books. Such complex drawings can tell the stories themselves, without very many words. Manga are also much more popular among adults in Japan than comic books are in the United States. In fact, manga is a multi-billion[2] dollar business in Japan, and more than one-half of all printed material sold there is manga.

3   Like manga, anime is popular with Japanese of all ages. In fact, a large percentage of manga and anime is made for adults only. Their **popularity** helps explain why the quality of anime is so high—anime and manga are big business. A recent anime film **reportedly** cost $45 million to make. Some of Japan's most **talented** artists and musicians are **involved** in creating manga and anime.

4   But it is not just the quality of the artwork that makes anime so popular. Many anime stories deal with complex subjects and characters that change as the stories develop. The "bad guy" of Disney cartoons—completely **evil** and not very believable[3]—is not common in anime. Rather, in anime it is not always clear who the "good guys" and "bad guys" are. Also, death is shown as a natural part of life much more often in anime than in Disney movies and cartoons. If your only experience with animation is Disney, anime might surprise or even shock you at first. However, many people soon become **fascinated** by this Japanese form of animation.

[1] *animation* = a technique made by photographing pictures or by drawing a series of pictures by hand or with a computer, used in animated movies and television programs

[2] *multi* = many

5   Some of the most interesting anime deal with modern technology. In this type of anime, the differences between machines and people, males and females, and good and evil are not always clear. Anime often looks at the **challenges** of life and culture in a world of **rapid** technological change. The characters in this type of anime deal with deep **moral** questions, such as the possible negative effects of technology on human relationships. This is very different from the simple way that Hollywood films and cartoons usually deal with the same subjects.

6   With the **beauty** of the artwork and the complexity and **originality** of the stories and characters, it should not be surprising that the popularity of anime is growing rapidly all over the world. Anime has also had an influence on Hollywood. Some animated films made in the United States today are more complex than they were in the past, and are fascinating not only to children but also adults.

[3] *believable =* easy to believe because it seems possible and real

Quick Comprehension Check

A. Read these sentences **about the reading**. Circle T (true), F (false), or ? (can't determine the answer from the reading). If you circle T or F, write the number of the paragraph with the answer on the line.

1. Anime and Disney cartoons are quite similar.   T   F   ?   _____

2. Anime can teach you a lot about Japanese culture.   T   F   ?   _____

3. Manga is a special kind of anime.   T   F   ?   _____

4. Anime is "big business" because it is not very
   expensive to make.   T   F   ?   _____

5. Most anime is made for children.   T   F   ?   _____

6. Anime often deals with serious subjects.   T   F   ?   _____

7. Important characters rarely die in anime.   T   F   ?   _____

8. Anime will probably become more popular than
   Disney movies.   T   F   ?   _____

9. Anime has influenced American animation.   T   F   ?   _____

B. Work with your class. Share your answers from part A. Go back to the reading to find the reason why a sentence is true or false. Correct the false sentences.

EXPLORING VOCABULARY

Thinking about the Target Vocabulary

Guessing Strategy: Using Context

Learning how to figure out what a new word means is an important skill. In every chapter of this book, you will practice a strategy to help you guess the meaning of a word from its **context**. The context of a word is the words and sentences before and after it. These other words help you to guess a word's meaning. For example, look at the context of the word *complex*.

> *Many anime stories deal with **complex** subjects and characters that change as the stories develop.*

The context tells you that something that is complex changes and is not always clear. Therefore, you could conclude that *complex* subjects and characters are not simple.

Don't worry if your guesses are not very specific. To understand the sentence, often it is enough to get a general idea of the meaning of an unfamiliar word. Also, in some cases there is not enough context to help you with the meaning of an unfamiliar word. In that case, you should just skip the word and focus on the meaning of the sentence without it.

A. Read the sentences. Circle the words that help you understand the **boldfaced** words. Then write a definition or explanation of the **boldfaced** target word.

1. The **popularity** of anime is growing. Millions of people all over the world are starting to watch it.

   Popularity probably means _____.

2. The "bad guy" of Disney cartoons—completely **evil** and not very believable—is not common in anime. Rather, in anime it is not very clear who the "good guys" and "bad guys" are.

   Evil probably means _____.

3. Anime often looks at the **challenges** of life in a world where technology is always changing. The characters in anime face difficulties that many people deal with in their own lives.

   Challenge probably means _____.

B. Look at the target words. Which ones are new to you? Circle them here and in the reading. The numbers in parentheses ( ) help you find the words in the paragraphs.

Target Words

provides (1)	popularity (3)	evil (4)	moral (5)
related (2)	reportedly (3)	fascinated (4)	beauty (6)
got their start (2)	talented (3)	challenges (5)	originality (6)
complex (2)	involved (3)	rapid (5)	

C. Read "What is Anime?" again. Look at the context of the new words. Can you guess their meanings?

D. Look at the word-form chart below. It shows the parts of speech (noun, verb, adjective) of the target words. Note that verbs are listed in their base form, and nouns in their singular form. The one verb phrase is listed under *Verbs*. Where would you put the two missing target words, *complex* and *beauty*? Add them to the correct columns in the shaded parts of the chart.

NOUNS	VERBS	ADJECTIVES	OTHER
popularity	provide	related	reportedly
evil	get one's start		
challenge		talented	
		involved	
originality		fascinated	
		rapid	
		moral	

> **Vocabulary Tip:**
> To use a new word correctly, you need to know not only what it means, but also its part of speech. This is an important part of the grammar of the word.

Understanding the Target Vocabulary

A. These sentences are **about the reading**. Complete them with the words in the box. Circle the words in the sentences that help you understand the meanings of the target words.

beauty	involved	related
challenges	moral	reportedly
evil	popularity	
got their start	rapid	

1. Anime is closely _____ to Japanese comic books. They are connected because they have some of the same characters and a similar style of artwork.

2. Anime is popular with people of all ages in Japan. Because of its _____, anime is big business in Japan.

3. According to newspaper reports, anime films usually cost millions of dollars to make. One recent film _____ cost $45 million to produce.

4. Many talented Japanese artists and musicians work on anime. Hundreds or even thousands of artists might be _____ in just one anime film.

5. In most Hollywood films, it is easy to tell who is good, and who is bad. The

_____ characters do bad things, and the good ones try to stop

them.

6. The stories in anime are complex, and the characters often have to deal with

difficult _____ choices. That is because .the differences between

good and evil and right and wrong are often not very clear.

7. Because of technology, life is changing very fast, and many people have

difficulty accepting all the changes. Some of the most interesting anime deal

with the _____ of living in a world of _____ change.

8. People enjoy watching anime because of its artistic quality and

_____.

9. Many of the artists who work on anime are now _____ working

on manga (Japanese comic books).

B. Read the sentences and circle the words or phrases that help you understand the meanings of the **boldfaced** target words. Then circle the correct answers.

1. Some of the best, most **talented** artists in Japan work in anime. Someone who is *talented*

   a. has a lot of money.   b. has a very good natural ability.

2. Anime deals with **complex** characters and situations. The stories are usually not simple. A *complex* story

   a. has many parts and is   b. usually has a sad ending.
   difficult to understand.

3. The **originality** of the stories is wonderful. The people who write them have great imaginations. *Originality* means the quality of

   a. being new and completely   b. being a talented writer of stories.
   different from anything else.

4. Both children and adults are **fascinated** by anime, and enjoy watching it together. *Fascinated* means

   a. very scared.   b. very interested.

5. Watching anime can **provide** you with a lot of information about Japanese culture. *Provide* means

   a. make (something) available   b. make (someone) happy

DEVELOPING READING SKILLS

Understanding Topics and Main Ideas

What is the Topic? What is the Main Idea?

A reading is about someone or something. That person or thing is the **topic** of the reading. The **main idea** of a reading is the most important information about the topic. The main idea of a reading is usually written in a full sentence.

Answer these questions.

1. What is the topic of "What Is Anime?" _____

2. What is the main idea of "What Is Anime?"

   a. Anime is a Japanese style of animation that is popular because of its beauty, originality, and complexity.
   b. Anime got its start in Japan as manga, or comic books, and is big business in Japan because of its popularity.
   c. Anime is much better than Hollywood style animation because of the complexity of the characters.

> **Reading Tip:**
> Often, the title of a reading will tell you what the topic is.

Understanding Cause and Effect

Cause and Effect

When you read, it is important to understand the connections between ideas. For example, you must be able to tell the difference between the cause of something and the effect. Often, writers use words like *so, because,* and *therefore* to show cause and effect.

Complete these sentences using information from "What Is Anime?"

1. Makers of anime spend a lot of money producing it because *anime is big business in Japan* _____.

2. When people who watch only Disney cartoons first watch anime they might be

   shocked because _____

   _____.

3. Anime contains beautiful artwork and fascinating, complex stories and characters.

   Therefore, _____

   _____.

4. Anime is gaining worldwide popularity, so _____

   _____.

BUILDING ON THE VOCABULARY

Using the Target Vocabulary in New Contexts

Complete the sentences with the target words in the box. Be careful. There are two extra words.

beauty	involved	rapid
challenges	moral	related
fascinated	popularity	reportedly
got his start	provide	talented

1. The president is _____ traveling to China tomorrow. That's what I read in the newspaper this morning, anyway.

2. She has faced many difficult _____, but she has always been successful.

3. Parents have a _____ responsibility to teach their children right from wrong.

4. The owner of this restaurant _____ as a waiter here.

5. Because of the rock star's _____, he was paid $500,000 to play one show. He's not a great musician, but young people all over the world love him.

6. You usually need a visa to study or work in another country. To get a visa, you must _____ the government with the information that they request.

7. We look alike, so many people think that we are sisters. However, we are not _____.

8. We were all _____ in the discussion, but our boss made the final decision.

9. His English is good, but he still has trouble understanding _____ speech.

10. She visits Costa Rica every year because she loves the natural _____ of the rain forest.

Expanding Vocabulary

Word Families: Suffixes

Words often belong to **word families**. Word families contain different forms of a word. One common way to change the form of a word is to add a suffix, or word ending, to it. Suffixes often change the part of speech of the original word.

- *-ity* is a noun suffix, for example *originality*
- *-al* is an adjective suffix, for example *original*
- *-ly* is an adverb suffix, for example *originally*

Complete the sentences with the words in the chart. Make sure you use the correct part of speech of the word. Be careful. Three words will not be used.

NOUNS	ADJECTIVES	ADVERBS
complexity	complex	complexly
morality	moral	morally
originality	original	originally
rapidity	rapid	rapidly

1. _____, his work was very simple. Over time, however, it became more complex.

2. This is not the _____ painting. It is a copy.

3. Is it best to be honest in every situation? For example, is there any _____ in lying to protect someone else from danger?

4. It can be confusing to live in a world in which technology is changing so _____.

5. Stealing is _____ wrong.

6. Because of the _____ of the issue, there are no easy or obvious solutions.

7. Many people find it difficult to deal with the _____ of change in the modern world. They would prefer slower or fewer changes.

8. It is not necessary to answer so _____. I just want a simple response.

> **Writing Tip:** If you know only one form of the word, use your dictionary to find the other parts of speech that belong to the same word family.

Word Grammar: Collocations—Adjectives & Prepositions

Collocations are words we often put together. Prepositions (for example, *in, on, of, to*) often go together with adjectives. Some prepositions can go with certain adjectives, and some cannot. Look at the examples.

Correct: *He is not related to her.*

Incorrect: *He is not related with her.*

A. Read these sentences. Circle the prepositions that go with the **boldfaced** adjectives.

1. My son is **fascinated** by cars. He can tell you the name of almost every car he sees.
2. He didn't decide alone. Many people were **involved** in the decision.
3. Dogs are closely **related** to wolves. A long time ago, there were no dogs, just wolves.
4. She's very **talented** in music. Someday, she would like to be a famous musician.

Vocabulary Tip: To learn a new word, you must see it and use it many times. Don't worry about making mistakes. The more times you use a new word, the fewer mistakes you will make.

B. Write four sentences about yourself or people that you know. Use the **boldfaced** adjectives + prepositions from part A.

1. _____ .
2. _____ .
3. _____ .
4. _____ .

CRITICAL THINKING

A. Discussion

Share your ideas in a small group. As you talk, try to use the vocabulary below. Each time someone uses a target word, put a check (✓) next to it.

challenge	moral/morality/morally
complex/complexity	original/originality
fascinated	rapid/rapidly/rapidity
involve	

Critical Thinking Tip: In this book, you will be able to practice critical thinking. Using critical thinking will help you read with more understanding.

1. In paragraph 1, the writer says that anime "provides a window into Japanese culture." Look at the information that comes before that phrase in the paragraph. Then explain how anime (a movie or television show) is similar to a window. What kinds of things can you see through that window? Use specific examples from the text in your answer.

2. The writer uses the word *complex* a number of times when referring to anime and manga. In what ways are anime and manga complex, according to the writer? Refer to information from paragraphs two, four, five, and six.

3. Do you agree with the writer that animated films and television shows can be complex? Explain your answer by referring to the writer's explanation of complexity (see question 2) and applying it to animated movies or television shows that you have watched.

4. What is the writer's opinion on anime and Hollywood style animated films? Does he prefer one to the other, or does he remain neutral, with no opinion on the subject? Use specific sentences from the text to support your answer.

5. Have you ever watched Japanese anime? If so, is your point of view similar to or different from that of the writer? If you have never watched anime, after reading this text, do you think you would like to watch it? Why or why not?

6. Some people consider anime to be an art form. When you think of art, what do you think of? Do you consider anime to be art? Is Hollywood animation art? Explain your answer.

Reading Tip: Be an active reader. Pay attention to which statements are facts, and which express the writer's opinion. If the writer has an opinion, think about whether you agree with it or not.

B. Writing

Complete one or both of these writing topics. When you write, use at least five of the target words from the chapter. Underline the target words in your paper.

1. Write a paragraph or short essay describing a comic book or cartoon character that you liked when you were a child. Explain why you liked the character.

2. Write a paragraph or short essay about a film or television show that taught you something about another culture. Explain what you learned.

CHAPTER 2

The Scientist and the Stradivarius

GETTING READY TO READ

Talk in a small group.

1. Do you play a musical instrument? If so, which one? How long have you been playing? If you don't know how to play a musical instrument, would you like to learn? Which instrument would you choose?

2. Scientists often try to answer questions about the past with modern science. Check (✓) the questions that scientists have been able to answer.

   ☐ a. How were the Egyptian pyramids built?

   ☐ b. How old is the earth?

   ☐ c. What killed the dinosaurs?

   ☐ d. How was our universe formed?

READING

Read the definitions beside the reading. Then read "The Scientist and the Stradivarius." If you see a new word, circle it, but don't stop reading. Instead, try to understand the sentence without it. You can learn the word later.

The Scientist and the Stradivarius

1   When Regina Buenaventura walks onto the stage, all eyes are on her violin. In the fifth row, Joseph Nagyvary closes his eyes and listens. He has spent years in a **laboratory** studying the sound of the most famous instrument of all time. Nagyvary believes that he has finally solved the centuries-old **mystery** behind the **remarkable** sound of the Stradivarius violin.

2   This young musician holds the result of Nagyvary's scientific efforts under her chin—the Nagyvarius. She begins playing and the violin makes a clear, **brilliant**, **heavenly** sound. Creator Nagyvary opens his eyes. Could this be the magical Stradivarius sound?

3   For 150 years, violin makers, musicians, and scientists have tried to solve the mystery of the Stradivarius. Antonio Stradivari lived in Cremona, a small northern Italian city. Before his death in 1737, he had made over 1,000 violins, violas,[1] cellos,[2] and guitars. Two sons followed him into the business, but they died soon after. The details of how their father and other violin makers from Cremona made their remarkable instruments died with them.

4   How could an **illiterate** man with no education produce instruments with such a heavenly sound? Did Stradivari and the other violin makers from Cremona have a secret?

5   Joseph Nagyvary's laboratory in the United States at Texas A&M University is a world away from Cremona. Nagyvary began teaching biochemistry[3] at the university in the late 1960s. A number of years ago he began making violins. Using his **knowledge** of chemistry, Nagyvary believes that he has found the answer to the Stradivarius puzzle.

6   In 1977, Nagyvary provided the Violin Society of America with the results of his research. He claimed that the high quality of Stradivari's instruments was not **due to** his artistic talent. Rather, the remarkable sound was a result of the materials Stradivari used, specifically the **chemical** properties[4] of the wood and varnish.[5] Stradivari himself probably did not understand the importance of these materials. In other words, Stradivari was certainly talented, but he probably owed much of his success to luck.

7   Nagyvary's **announcement** shocked violin makers and dealers.[6] His **theory** was a direct challenge to the way that violins had been made for years. It also challenged violin makers' **belief** in the importance of their artistic talent.

[1] *a viola =* a wooden musical instrument shaped like a violin but larger and with a lower sound

[2] *a cello =* a large wooden musical instrument, shaped like a violin but much larger, that you hold between your knees and play by pulling a bow (a special stick) across wire strings

[3] *biochemistry =* the scientific study of the chemistry of living things

[4] *a property =* a quality that belongs naturally to something

[5] *a varnish =* a clear liquid that is painted onto wood to protect it

[6] *a dealer =* someone who buys and sells a particular product, especially an expensive one

8   Nagyvary **stands by** his theory. "The pieces of the puzzle have been around and I have not invented anything new. But I put the pieces, well, together while the others could not. I am the first chemist of good international standing[7] . . . who, obviously, has a much better understanding of the effects of these natural chemicals."

9   The best **proof** of Nagyvary's theory may be the instruments he makes. By using what he has learned from his research, Nagyvary claims to produce violins with a sound quality very similar to that of a Stradivarius. This is demonstrated in *The Stradivarius Puzzle*, a thirteen-song CD recorded by well-known professional violinist Zina Schiff. On it, Schiff plays both a Nagyvarius and her 1697 Stradivarius, reportedly worth $3,000,000. Schiff says, "I sent *The Stradivarius Puzzle* to a friend of mine who is a conductor[8] and he had no idea . . . . He just could not tell . . . . The truth is, I would rather be playing on one of Dr. Nagyvary's instruments."

10 Isaac Stern, one of the most respected violinists of the 20th century, is quoted as saying, "Dr. Nagyvary's knowledge . . . makes his work of special value to us all today."

11 So, why do violin makers and dealers refuse to even discuss Nagyvary's theory? Nagyvary's website suggests that because many violin makers consider themselves artists, they have a personal interest in focusing on the art, not the science, of violin production. And Schiff believes that violin makers and dealers feel **threatened** by the fairly low cost ($10,000 to $25,000) of a Nagyvary instrument.

12 Schiff came from a poor family, so she feels very strongly that people who cannot afford Stradivari violins should still be able to have high-quality instruments. According to Schiff, Dr. Nagyvary's violins have made this possible, without having a negative effect on the beauty and value of a Stradivarius.

[7] *standing* = someone's position in a system or organization, based on what other people think of him or her

[8] *a conductor* = someone who stands in front of a group of musicians and directs their playing

Quick Comprehension Check

A. Read these sentences **about the reading**. Circle T (true), F (false), or ? (can't determine the answer from the reading). If you circle T or F, write the number of the paragraph with the answer on the line.

1. Dr. Nagyvary is not sure why Stradivari instruments sound so good.   T   F   ?   _____

2. Dr. Nagyvary is both a scientist and a violinist.   T   F   ?   _____

3. Dr. Nagyvary is both a university professor and a violin maker.   T   F   ?   _____

4. Dr. Nagyvary believes that chemistry can explain why Stradivari instruments produce such an excellent sound.   T   F   ?   _____

5. According to Dr. Nagyvary, Stradivari knew why his violins had such a remarkable sound.   T   F   ?   _____

6. Nagyvary violins sound better than Stradivari violins.   T   F   ?   _____

7. People who make and sell violins are excited by Dr. Nagyvary's work.   T   F   ? _____

8. Professional violinists are interested in Dr. Nagyvary's work.   T   F   ? _____

B. Work with your class. Share your answers from part A. Go back to the reading to find the reason why a sentence is true or false. Correct the false sentences.

EXPLORING VOCABULARY

Thinking about the Target Vocabulary

Guessing Strategy: Adjectives—Positive or Negative Meaning?

If an unfamiliar word is an **adjective** (a word that describes a noun), think about whether it has a positive (good) or negative (bad) meaning. Look at the example.

I will never forget the first time that I heard the remarkable, clear sound of a Stradivarius.

Because the writer describes the sound as *clear* (a positive quality), and says that she will never forget the first time she heard it, you can guess that the adjective *remarkable* probably has a positive meaning.

A. Find these target words in the reading. Do they have a positive or a negative meaning? Write P (positive) or N (negative).

_____ brilliant   _____ heavenly   _____ illiterate   _____ threatened

B. Look at the target words. Which ones are new to you? Circle them here and in the reading. The numbers in parentheses help you find the words in the paragraphs.

Target Words

laboratory (1)	illiterate (4)	belief (7)
mystery (1)	knowledge (5)	theory (7)
remarkable (1)	due to (6)	stands by (8)
brilliant (2)	chemical (6)	proof (9)
heavenly (2)	announcement (7)	threatened (11)

C. Read "The Scientist and the Stradivarius" again. Look at the context of the new words. Can you guess their meanings?

D. Look at the word-form chart below. It shows the parts of speech (nouns, verbs, adjectives, etc.) of the target words. Note that verbs are listed in their base form, and nouns in their singular form. The one prepositional phrase is listed under *Other*. Where would you put the four missing target words, *heavenly*, *chemical*, *belief*, and *proof*? Add them to the correct columns in the shaded parts of the chart.

NOUNS	VERBS	ADJECTIVES	OTHER
laboratory	stand by	remarkable	due to
mystery		brilliant	
knowledge			
announcement		illiterate	
theory			
		threatened	

Understanding the Target Vocabulary

These sentences are **about the reading**. Complete them with the words in the box. Circle the words in the sentences that help you understand the meanings of the target words.

announcement	illiterate	mystery	stands by
beliefs	knowledge	proof	theory
brilliant	laboratory	remarkable	threatened
due to			

1. Dr. Joseph Nagyvary is a scientist who worked out of his _____ at Texas A&M University.

2. Antonio Stradivari was an 18th century violin maker who could not read or write. He was _____.

3. Stradivari violins have a very special sound. Dr. Nagyvary has spent many years of his life trying to solve the _____ of why they have such a _____ sound.

4. Stradivari violins make a sound that is so clear and _____ that it shines like a light.

5. Dr. Nagyvary believes that the remarkable sound of the Stradivari instruments is _____ the materials Stradivari used.

6. Dr. Nagyvary made an _____ about his discoveries during a speech to the Violin Society in 1977.

7. Violin makers and dealers were shocked. Dr. Nagyvary's _____ challenged every tradition of violin making.

8. If Dr. Nagyvary is right, a lot of what violin makers have always believed is wrong. His theory challenges all of their _____ about what is important in violin making.

9. They feel _____ by Dr. Nagyvary's ideas.

10. Many people do not agree with Dr. Nagyvary's theory, but that doesn't bother him. He _____ his theory because he is sure that he is right.

11. One way that Dr. Nagyvary is trying to prove his theory is by making his own violins using his _____ of chemistry.

12. Many professional musicians cannot tell the difference between his violins and Stradivari violins. Dr. Nagyvary claims that this is _____ that his theory is correct.

DEVELOPING READING SKILLS

Understanding Topics and Main Ideas

Answer these questions.

1. What is the topic of "The Scientist and the Stradivarius"? _____
   _____

2. What is the main idea of the reading? (Remember, write the main idea in a full sentence.) _____
   _____

Reading Tip: The main idea is often (but not always) stated in the last sentence of the introduction to a reading.

Scanning for Information

Scanning

Sometimes you need to find a specific piece of information in a reading. To do this, you **scan** the reading. *Scan* means to read rapidly and look for just the information you need. Here are some suggestions to help you scan effectively.

If you are looking for . . .	*scan for . . .*
the name of a person or place ⟶	capital letters
when something happened ⟶	a time or date
an amount or a date ⟶	a number
a reason or an effect ⟶	cause/effect words: *because, so, due to, therefore, thus, cause, result*

Read these questions about "The Scientist and the Stradivarius." Scan the reading and write short answers. Write the paragraph number where you found the information on the line next to your answers.

1. Who made the famous Stradivarius instruments? _____ _____

2. When did Dr. Nagyvary first make a speech about his theory? _____ _____

3. How many and what kind(s) of violins does Zina Schiff play on *The Stradivarius Puzzle*? _____ _____

4. How much do Nagyvary violins cost? _____ _____

5. What is the name of the world-famous violinist who is quoted on Nagyvary's website? _____ _____

6. Why does Schiff believe so strongly in what Dr. Nagyvary is doing? _____ _____

Understanding Inference

Making Inferences

Some information cannot be found by scanning. This is because the information is not written directly in the text. Instead, you have to think about what the text says, and then make a logical conclusion, or **inference**.

A. What is the best way to complete each sentence? Circle *a* or *b*.

1. At the beginning of the text, when Regina Buenaventura walked onto the stage, everyone was looking at her violin rather than at her because they probably knew

   a. that she would be playing a very valuable violin.

   b. about Dr. Nagyvary's theory.

Reading Tip: Although inferences are not stated directly in a text, they must be supported by something that is written in the text.

2. According to Dr. Nagyvary, Stradivari never told anyone his secret because

    a. he didn't know he had a secret.   b. he wanted his secret to die with him.

3. Traditionally, violin makers believed that the most important thing in violin making was

    a. their own artistic talent.   b. the materials they used.

4. Stradivari's sons and other violin makers from Cremona made violins using

    a. the same kinds of materials that Stradivari used.   b. different kinds of materials than Stradivari.

5. If Dr. Nagyvary is able to prove his theory, Stradivari instruments might become

    a. more difficult to find.   b. less valuable.

B. Work with a partner. Look back at the reading on pages 14–15. Write the number of the question from exercise A next to the paragraph where you can find support for your inferences.

BUILDING ON THE VOCABULARY

Using the Target Vocabulary in New Contexts

Complete the sentences with the target words and phrases in the box. Be careful. There are two extra words or phrases.

announcement	due to	mystery	stand by
belief	illiterate	proof	theory
brilliant	laboratory	remarkable	threatened
chemical			

1. If he's _____ and can't sign his name, he can just make an X on the

signature line.

2. _____ the bad weather, our flight arrived late.

3. You can't be sure that he stole the money. You don't have any _____.

4. Everyone thought that he loved his job. We were all shocked by his

_____ at the meeting that he was going to quit.

5. Anna got her start working in a research _____. Then she decided to

go to medical school.

6. Due to my father's strong _____ in the importance of education, he

   has decided to give $1,000,000 to help illiterate people learn how to read and write.

7. It doesn't matter what my children do. I feel that I have a moral responsibility to

   _____ them.

8. Fifty years after the crime, the police still do not know who was involved. It will

   probably remain a _____ forever.

9. A _____ is an idea or a set of ideas that explain something about life

   or the world.

10. Look at the _____ color of those roses. I've never seen such a

    bright red.

11. This essay is _____. It is one of the most original essays I have

    ever read.

Expanding Vocabulary

Word Families: Suffixes

As you saw in Chapter 1, a suffix can tell you if a word is a noun, adjective, or adverb. Pay attention to suffixes. They contain information that can help you to use the word correctly when you write.

A. Study the chart and answer the questions.

NOUN (PERSON)	NOUN (THING)	VERB	ADJECTIVE
announcer	announcement	announce	
chemist	chemistry		chemical
	remark	remark	remarkable

1. Which two suffixes show that a word refers to a person? _____,

   _____

2. Which two suffixes show that a word refers to a thing? _____,

   _____

3. Which two suffixes show that a word is an adjective? _____,

   _____

4. Which two words in the chart do not have a suffix? _____ and

_____

B. Complete the sentences with words from the chart. Be careful. You will not use all the words.

1. Who told you? Did he _____ it, or did his boss?

2. The radio _____ lost his job because he made too many mistakes when he was reporting the news.

3. He lost his job because he made an impolite _____ to a coworker about his boss.

4. That _____ company develops products that are used in making new drugs.

5. He studied _____ in college, and now he works for a company that develops new drugs.

6. Tomorrow, they are going to make an _____ about who has won the grand prize.

Vocabulary Tip:
To learn new word forms, write the familiar form on one side of an index card. On the other side, write the other forms of the word with the part of speech next to each one. Review your cards frequently.

Word Grammar: Expressing Cause and Effect

There are many words and phrases that describe why something happens. Look at the sentences from the reading.

- *He claimed that the high quality of Stradivari's instruments was not **due to** his artistic talent.*

- *Schiff believes that it's **because** the dealers are threatened by the fairly low cost ($10,000 to $25,000) of a Nagyvary violin.*

- *Schiff came from a poor family, **so** she feels very strongly that people who cannot afford Stradivari violins should still be able to have high-quality instruments.*

***Due to**, **because**, and **so** are connecting words that explain why something happens. However, the grammar that follows each one is different. **Due to** is followed by a noun or a noun phrase. **Because** is followed by a full clause (subject + verb). **So** is also followed by a full clause, but it introduces an effect, or result, rather than a cause. Also there is always a comma in front of **so**.

A. Complete these sentences with *due to*, *because*, or *so*.

1. She is successful _____ she has worked hard.

2. Her success is _____ her hard work.

3. She has worked hard, _____ she is successful.

4. _____ a family emergency, Frank will not be in this afternoon.

B. Write three sentences about your life. Use *due to*, *because*, and *so*.

1. _____

2. _____

3. _____

CRITICAL THINKING

A. Discussion

Share your ideas in a small group. As you talk, try to use the vocabulary below. Each time someone uses a target word or phrase, put a check (✓) next to it.

☐ belief	☐ knowledge	☐ theory
☐ brilliant	☐ laboratory	☐ threatened
☐ chemical/chemistry	☐ proof	
☐ due to	☐ remarkable	

1. Look back at paragraphs one and two of the reading on pages 14–15. How does the author begin the reading?

   a. With historical facts
   b. With a short biography
   c. With an anecdote (a short story)
   d. With scientific research

   What effect does this type of introduction have on you? How does it make you feel? For example, does it make you feel curious?

2. In paragraph 5 of the reading, the author says "Joseph Nagyvary's laboratory in the United States at Texas A&M University is a world away from Cremona." What does the author mean by "a world away"? What is the author trying to emphasize with that particular choice of words?

   > **Critical Thinking Tip:** Sometimes authors say things in an unusual way. Pay special attention to the words they choose. They are probably emphasizing something important.

3. In paragraph 9 of the reading, the author says, "The best proof of Nagyvary's theory may be the instruments he makes." What does the author mean? How can a modern instrument be proof of a theory about instruments that are hundreds of years old?

4. Do you think that the author believes in Dr. Nagyvary's theory? Support your answer by referring to specific parts of the reading.

5. Are you convinced by Dr. Nagyvary's theory? Why or why not? If not, what might convince you?

6. Do you know of a historical mystery that has been solved with modern technology? If so, tell your group about it.

B. Writing

Complete one or both of these writing topics. When you write, use at least five of the target words from the chapter. Underline the target words in your paper.

1. Write a short summary of Dr. Nagyvary's theory and how he is testing it. Put the summary in your own words. Do not copy any sentences or phrases from the reading.

2. Write a paragraph or short essay describing a mystery that you think science will solve in the near future. Explain how science will be used to solve the mystery.

> **Writing Tip:** Use adjectives to make your writing clearer and more interesting. Don't limit yourself to general words such as *nice, good,* or *bad*. Use more specific words, such as *remarkable, heavenly,* or *threatening*.

CHAPTER 3

The History of Rap

DJ Grand Master Flash

GETTING READY TO READ

Talk in a small group.

1. What kind of music do you like? What kind of music don't you like? Who is your favorite musician or singer?

2. Do you like to sing? Have you ever sung or done some other type of performance (for example, acting or dancing) in front of people? If so, tell your group about it.

3. What do you know about rap music? Tell your group.

READING

Read to Find Out: How and where did rap music get its start?

Read the definitions beside the reading. Then read the "The History of Rap." If you see a new word, circle it, but don't stop reading. Instead, try to understand the sentence without it. You can learn the word later.

The History of Rap

1   Rap is a spoken form of musical **expression**. It involves words spoken in **rhyme** with a recorded or **live** rhythm section.[1] Many people use the terms "hip-hop" and "rap" to mean the same thing. In fact, hip-hop is the culture that modern rap **grew out of**. Hip-hop is a culture with its own language, clothing styles, music, and ways of thinking, and it is constantly growing and changing. It includes several different art forms, including visual art,[2] dance, and music. Rap is just one part of hip-hop culture.

2   Although there is a lot of disagreement about exactly where and how rap began, most people agree that it got its start in the mostly African-American[3] neighborhoods of the Bronx in New York City in the 1960s. At that time, large outdoor street parties called *block parties* were becoming popular. Young people who could not afford expensive musical instruments or **equipment** took simple turntables[4] and microphones[5] out onto the streets. But instead of just playing the music, they moved the **spinning**, or turning, records with their hands. At the same time, they **scratched** them with the needles of the turntables. The changes in the sound of the music became known as *cutting*, or *scratching*. The young people who played the music were called *disc jockeys*. These disc jockeys, or *DJs*, used their turntables as instruments to create a new musical form.

3   Other **performers** working with the DJ **interacted** with the crowd by talking louder than the music, often in rhyme. These performers were called *emcees*, or *MCs*, and their interaction with the crowd became known as *rapping*. Later, the MCs became known as *rappers*. Interaction between the performers and the crowd is an important **characteristic** of rap.

4   Among the many people who **contributed** to the development of rap, artist Grandmaster Flash **stands out**. The **techniques**, or methods, that he invented have become an important part of hip-hop culture. Flash was one of the first DJs to begin using a turntable as a musical instrument, rather than just a piece of equipment that played records. First, he would find a short section of a song that he liked. This was called the *break*. Then he would use two copies of the same record and two turntables to invent creative ways to play the break over and over without stopping.

5   In the 1970s and 1980s rap's popularity grew, and the rhymes became more complex and **clever** as the performers **competed** with each other. The music that they rapped to included recordings of famous African-American musicians and breaks from popular disco[6] and rock music of the time. Many rappers also performed with live musicians.

---

[1] *a rhythm section* = the part of a band that provides a strong beat using drums and other similar instruments

[2] *visual art* = art such as painting that you look at

[3] *an African-American* = a Black American of African ancestry

[4] *a turntable* = the round flat surface on a record player that you put records on

[5] *a microphone* = a piece of equipment that you hold in front of your mouth when you are singing, giving a speech, etc., in order to make your voice sound louder

[6] *disco music* = a type of dance music with a strong repeating beat that was popular in the 1970s

6   Today, hip-hop culture is popular all over the world, and young people everywhere listen to rap. There are many reasons for rap's popularity. It offers young people the chance to express themselves freely. It is an art form that can be performed without a lot of money, training, or equipment. Rapping involves verbal[7] skills that many people already have or can develop. You can rap slowly, or you can rap fast. All of this allows rappers with very different **personalities** or ideas to express themselves.

7   This does not mean that rapping is easy, however. It **calls for** a quick mind, an ability to use language well, originality, and an excellent sense of rhythm.[8] It presents the performer with many challenges, but only two rules: rhyme to the beat of the music, and be original.

[7] *verbal* = spoken, rather than written

[8] *rhythm* = a regular repeated pattern of sounds or music

Quick Comprehension Check

A. Read these sentences **about the reading**. Circle T (true), F (false), or ? (can't determine the answer from the reading). If you circle T or F, write the number of the paragraph with the answer on the line.

1.	Hip-hop is a kind of rap music.	T	F	?	_____
2.	Many people confuse rap and hip-hop.	T	F	?	_____
3.	Rap got its start in Africa.	T	F	?	_____
4.	The first rappers didn't have a lot of money.	T	F	?	_____
5.	Rappers sometimes perform to live music.	T	F	?	_____
6.	To be a good rapper, you need to be able to sing well.	T	F	?	_____

Reading Tip: Reading and learning vocabulary are different processes. When you read, first try to understand the main points. Do not stop to look up words in a dictionary. If you stop, you might forget the main points. You can learn the vocabulary later.

B. Work with your class. Share your answers from part A. Go back to the reading to find the reason why a sentence is true or false. Correct the false sentences.

EXPLORING VOCABULARY

Thinking about the Target Vocabulary

Guessing Strategy: The Signal Word *or*

The signal word **or** can help you guess the meaning of unfamiliar words. Look at the examples.

*But instead of just playing the music, they moved the **spinning**, or turning, records with their hands.*

*Young people could not afford expensive musical instruments or **equipment**.*

In the first sentence, *or* signals that what follows it—*turning*—is a definition or synonym for *spinning*. Notice the use of commas (**spinning**, *or turning*) when *or* signals that the words have the same meaning.

In the second sentence, **or** shows that the word that follows it—*equipment*—is different in meaning from *musical instruments*. Note that commas are not used when **or** signals additional or different information.

A. Read the sentences with *or* and the target words in bold face. Circle *the same as* or *different from* in the statement that follows.

1. Rappers can perform to **live** or recorded music.

   Live music is   the same as / different from   recorded music.

2. One of rap's **characteristics**, or special qualities, is that the performers speak to the beat of the music.

   A **characteristic** is   the same as / different from   a special quality.

3. The **techniques**, or methods, that he invented have become an important part of hip-hop culture.

   A **technique** is   the same as / different from   a method.

4. All of this allows rappers with very different **personalities** or ideas to express themselves.

   Personality is   the same as / different from   an idea.

B. Look at the target words. Which ones are new to you? Circle them here and in the reading. The numbers in parentheses help you find the words in the paragraphs.

Target Words and Phrases

expression (1)	scratched (2)	techniques (4)
rhyme (1)	performers (3)	clever (5)
live (1)	interacted (3)	competed (5)
grew out of (1)	characteristic (3)	personalities (6)
equipment (2)	contributed (4)	calls for (7)
spinning (2)	stands out (4)	

C. Read "The History of Rap" again. Look at the context of the new words. Can you guess their meanings?

D. Look at the word-form chart below. It shows the parts of speech (noun, verb, adjective) of the target words. Note that verbs are listed in their base form, and nouns in their singular form. The verb phrases are listed under *Verbs*. Where would you put the four missing target words and phrases, *grow out of, call for, rhyme,* and *live*? Add them to the correct columns in the shaded parts of the chart.

NOUNS	VERBS	ADJECTIVES
expression		
	scratch	spinning
equipment	interact	clever
performer	contribute	
characteristic	stand out	
technique	compete	
personality		

Understanding the Target Vocabulary

These sentences are **about the reading**. Circle the meaning of each **boldfaced** word. Then circle the words in the sentences that help you understand the meanings of the target words.

1. Rap is a special type of musical **expression**. Rappers show who they are and what they feel through their music. *Expression* means

   a. something you say, write, or do that shows what you feel.
   b. an instrument that you play with great feeling.
   c. something that is becoming very popular.

2. Rap involves words spoken in **rhyme**, like in some poems. *Rhyme* means

   a. a very loud or very soft voice.
   b. two words ending in the same sound, like "hit" and "sit."
   c. a slow, soft, musical sound like "shhhh."

3. In rap music, there are often a number of different **performers**: a DJ, an MC, and one or more musicians. *Performers* are

   a. actors, musicians, dancers, etc., whom people watch.
   b. people who listen to rap or other types of music.
   c. writers who write songs for rappers.

4. Hip-hop culture existed before rap, so we can say that rap **grew out of** hip-hop culture. *Grew out of* means

   a. had an effect on.
   b. developed from.
   c. created.

5. Rap artists **interact** with the crowd. The crowd shouts things out, and the performers answer them in rhyme. *Interact* means

   a. argue.
   b. communicate.
   c. sing.

6. Grandmaster Flash **contributed** a lot to the development of rap. *Contributed* means

   a. sang.
   b. gave.
   c. spent.

7. Grandmaster Flash wasn't the only person who was involved in rap's development, but his work **stands out**. It was very important to rap's popularity. *Stands out* means

   a. is a lot faster.
   b. is much harder.
   c. is very significant.

8. Flash invented several techniques. For example, he **scratched** the records with the needle on the turntable. This made a special sound, but also left a mark on the record. *Scratched* means

    a. changed from one to another very quickly.
    b. made a shallow, or not deep, cut with something sharp.
    c. played many times, over and over again.

9. Rappers are good at using language, so their rhymes are often very **clever**. *Clever* means

    a. fast and difficult to understand.
    b. unusual and interesting.
    c. loud and funny.

10. Rap artists **compete** with each other to make the best rhymes. *Compete* means

    a. try to be stronger than someone else.
    b. try to be better than someone else.
    c. try to be kinder than someone else.

11. Every rapper has a different way of performing. That's because each rapper has his or her own special **personality** and way of expressing himself or herself. *Personality* means

    a. person who helps them in their work.
    b. people who like their way of performing.
    c. character and way of behaving.

12. Rapping is not easy. It **calls for** many different skills. *Calls for* means

    a. teaches.
    b. makes.
    c. needs.

13. Sometimes rappers perform to **live** music, and sometimes they perform to recorded music. *Live* means

    a. performed with other singers or musicians.
    b. performed for people who are present and watching or listening.
    c. performed in a new or different way.

14. The basic **equipment** needed for early rap music included two turntables, a microphone, and speakers. *Equipment* means

    a. the best technology available to performers at the time.
    b. the musical instruments that were used when rap started to become popular.
    c. the special things (for example, machines) that you need for a specific activity or type of work.

DEVELOPING READING SKILLS

Understanding Topics and Main Ideas

Answer this question.

What is the main idea of "The History of Rap"? Write a full sentence.

_____

Scanning

A. Where is the information about these topics in "The History of Rap"?
Scan the reading, and write the paragraph number (1–7).

_3_   a. MCs and rappers

____   b. how rap and hip-hop are related

____   c. the development of rap in the 1970s and 1980s

____   d. why rap is popular

____   e. Grandmaster Flash's contributions to rap

____   f. how rap got its start

____   g. the challenges of rap

B. Write a sentence or two about each of the seven topics from paragraphs
1–7. Use information from the reading, but do not copy. Use your own words.

Paragraph 1: _Hip-hop is a culture that includes several different_
art forms. One of the art forms is rap.

Paragraph 2: _____

_____

Paragraph 3: _____

_____

Paragraph 4: _____

_____

Paragraph 5: _____

_____

Paragraph 6: _____

_____

Paragraph 7: _____

_____

> **Reading Tip:** When you finish reading each paragraph, pause and think about the topic. How is it related to the main idea of the reading? Write the topic in the margin. If you are not sure, write a question mark (?) so that you remember to ask your teacher.

BUILDING ON THE VOCABULARY

Using the Target Vocabulary in New Contexts

Complete the sentences with the target words in the box. Be careful. There are two extra words.

calls for	contributes	live	spinning
characteristics	expression	performers	stands out
clever	grew out of	personality	technique
competing	interact	rhyme	

1. I love his _____. He's so clever, funny, and kind.

2. We need somebody really special for this job. The job _____ someone who is artistic, smart, and ready to work hard.

3. Police officers who work in big cities have to _____ with all different kinds of people every day.

4. He is one of the most brilliant students I've ever had. He really _____.

5. That artist uses a special _____ to make his colors look very bright.

6. What a _____ idea! You have a great imagination.

7. Stories for very young children are often written in _____. Little children like them because they sound like songs.

8. The two brothers are always _____ for their parents' attention. It's really sad.

9. She _____ $5,000 a year to a children's hospital. The money allows the hospital to provide patients with non-medical items such as toys.

10. She plays the piano with wonderful _____. She hasn't been playing for a long time, but she knows how to communicate her feelings through her playing.

11. One of the most important _____ of a musical performer is talent.

12. It is much more exciting to go to a _____ performance than to watch it on TV.

13. His desire to become an artist _____ his fascination with color as a child.

Word Families: Suffixes

In Chapters 1 and 2, you learned that the suffixes *-ity*, *-ry*, and *-ment* show that a word is a noun, and the suffixes *-er* and *-ist* show that a word is not only a noun but also a person. Other common suffixes for nouns are *-ion*, *-tion*, and *-ance*. Often, these suffixes are added to verbs to change them to nouns. Sometimes you need to change the spelling of the main part of the word before you add the suffix. For example the spelling of the noun form of *provide* is *provision*.

A. Add the correct suffix to make the noun form. Use your dictionary to check your answers.

VERBS	NOUNS
provide	provision
express	
perform	
interact	
compete	
contribute	
fascinate	

Vocabulary Tip: Sometimes changing a word from one form to another also changes the meaning of the word. Check the meanings of new word forms in your dictionary.

B. Complete the sentences with the nouns from exercise A.

1. He's usually a great actor, but his _____ in that movie was not very good.

2. Our basketball team won the _____ .

3. I think that babies should have _____ with a lot of different kinds of people, not just their mothers or fathers.

4. Your _____ to the work of the team was very important. Thank you!

5. She wrote him a poem as an _____ of her love.

6. Under a special _____ approved by the president of the company, workers will no longer be required to work on holidays.

7. I don't understand your _____ with cars. What is so interesting about them?

Word Grammar: Phrasal Verbs

Stand out and *call for* are **phrasal verbs**. Phrasal verbs have two or more parts: a verb (such as *stand* or *call*) and one or more particles (such as *out* or *for*). The meaning of a phrasal verb is different from the meaning of just the verb alone. In Chapter 2, you learned the phrasal verb *stand by*.

C. Rewrite the underlined part of these sentences using the phrasal verbs *stand by*, *stand out*, and *call for*. You may need to change the form of the verb to fit the sentence.

1. Many of the musicians have some talent, but only two of them <u>are really remarkable</u>. _____

2. If you really believe in something, you should <u>defend</u> it. _____

3. That job <u>requires</u> someone who is very strong. _____

CRITICAL THINKING

A. Discussion

Share your ideas in a small group. As you talk, try to use the vocabulary below. Each time someone uses a target word, put a check (✓) next to it.

☐ call for

☐ characteristic

☐ clever

☐ compete/competition

☐ contribute/contribution

☐ express/expression

☐ interact/interaction

☐ performer/perform/performance

☐ personality

Critical Thinking Tip: When you express your opinion about a reading, you should be able to support it with specific information from the reading.

1. Read paragraph six of "The History of Rap" again. What is the writer's opinion about why rap music is so popular? Restate it in your own words. Do you agree or disagree? Be specific about which parts you agree with and which parts you disagree with. You can also add your own ideas about rap's popularity.

2. What is the writer's attitude toward rap music and hip-hop culture in general? Is it positive, negative, or neutral? Find sentences in the article to support your answer. Do you share the writer's attitude? Explain why or why not.

3. Ask each other these questions about music. Have one person write down everyone's responses. Tell the class a few of the most interesting things you found out.

   a. How much time on average do you spend listening to music every day?
      1. none or almost none
      2. about 15 minutes
      3. 30 minutes
      4. an hour or more

   b. How many concerts do you go to a year?
      1. none
      2. 1 or 2
      3. 3–5
      4. 6 or more

   c. How often do you go out to listen to live music?
      1. once a week
      2. once a month
      3. a few times a year
      4. once a year (or less)

   d. How do you usually listen to music?
      1. on my computer
      2. on the radio
      3. on my smart phone
      4. on my tablet

e. Check (✓) all of the statements that are true for you.

☐ I listen to music while I study or work.

☐ I listen to music when I feel sad.

☐ I listen to music when I feel happy.

☐ I like to dance when I listen to music.

☐ I listen to music when I want to relax.

☐ Listening to music helps me fall asleep.

B. Writing

Complete one or both of these writing topics. When you write, use at least five of the target words from the chapter. Underline the target words in your paper.

1. Choose a type of music that you like, and do some research on it. Then, write an essay about it. Your essay should include the following information:

   - A description of the music (for instance, the instruments used)
   - The history of this type of music (where, when, and how it got its start)
   - Well-known performers of this type of music
   - Why you like it

2. Choose a performer (living or dead) that you like, and write a letter to that performer. Explain why you like that person, and ask some questions about his or her life and work.

> **Writing Tip:** When you research a topic and then write about it, do not copy sentences from the research. Instead, put the ideas in your own words. Follow your teacher's instructions on how to identify the sources you used for your research.

Checkpoint

LEARNING OUTCOME

❯ Review and expand on the content of Unit 1

LOOK BACK

A. Think About This

Think again about your ranking of activities in the *Think About This* exercise on page 1.

Do you want to add any other activities?

B. Remember the Readings

What do you want to remember most from the readings in Unit 1?

For each chapter, write one sentence about the reading.

Chapter 1: What is Anime?

_____

Chapter 2: The Scientist and the Stradivarius

_____

Chapter 3: The History of Rap

_____

Read the text. Do not use a dictionary.

Pablo Picasso

1 Among the many talented artists of the twentieth century, Spanish painter Pablo Ruiz Picasso stands out. Due to his brilliant talent and originality, he is considered by many to be the most important artist of his time.

2 Picasso was born in 1881 in Málaga, Spain. His father was an art teacher, and he knew very early that his son Pablo was remarkably talented. At the age of fourteen, Picasso entered the Academy of Fine Arts in Barcelona, Spain. In one day, he completed the entrance test that traditionally took students a month to finish.

3 From 1900 to 1904, Picasso lived in both Spain and France. During that time, he worked in a completely original style, which became known as his Blue Period. The name came from Picasso's use of only the color blue in his paintings of the time. In 1904, Picasso moved to France, where he began working in a variety of modern artistic styles.

4 One of Picasso's many contributions to the history of art was the invention of the artistic technique of collage—using materials such as letters, cloth, or pieces of newspaper to make a piece of art. He was also involved in the development of cubism—a new style of modern art in which people and things are painted using shapes such as triangles and squares. In fact, many people consider Picasso's 1907 painting *Les Demoiselles d'Avignon* the first cubist painting.

5 Picasso's popularity today might make one forget that throughout his lifetime, he challenged Western European artistic traditions. Picasso died in 1973, but the beauty, complexity, and originality of his artistry live on in the many works he left behind.

Quick Comprehension Check

A. Read these sentences **about the reading**. Circle T (true), F (false), or ? (can't determine the answer from the reading). If you circle T or F, write the number of the paragraph with the answer on the line.

1.	Picasso had a great influence on modern art.	T	F	?	____
2.	Picasso's father taught him how to paint.	T	F	?	____
3.	*Les Demoiselles d'Avignon* was painted during Picasso's Blue Period.	T	F	?	____
4.	Picasso was not the only painter to contribute to the development of cubism.	T	F	?	____
5.	Picasso did most of his work in a traditional style.	T	F	?	____

B. Go back to the reading to find the reason why a sentence is true or false. Correct the false sentences.

Guessing Meaning from Context

Answer this question.

What is the meaning of *Academy* in paragraph 2?

_____

_____

Understanding Inference

Check (✓) the sentences that you can infer from the text. Remember, an inference is not written directly in the text. You have to think about what the text says, and make a logical conclusion.

☐ 1. Picasso began to paint before the age of fourteen.

☐ 2. In his lifetime as a painter, Picasso used the color blue more than any other color.

☐ 3. Collage is a technique that is still used by artists today.

☐ 4. Picasso was not a popular artist when he was alive.

☐ 5. Picasso knew how to paint in a traditional style.

Scanning

Scan the reading to find the information to complete the sentences.

1. Pablo Picasso is considered one of the greatest painters of modern times because

_____.

_____.

2. The years from 1900 to 1904 were called Picasso's Blue Period because

_____.

_____.

3. *Les Demoiselles d'Avignon* is a very important painting because

_____.

_____.

4. Picasso's contributions to art did not end with his death because

_____.

_____.

EXPANDING VOCABULARY

Guessing Strategy: Phrasal Verbs

As you learned in Chapter 3, a **phrasal verb** has a verb and one or more particles. *Stand by* and *stand out* are phrasal verbs. It is often difficult to figure out the *exact* meaning of a phrasal verb, but you can get a *general idea* of the meaning by thinking about the meaning of the verb and the particle(s). The context will help you gain a more complete understanding of the meaning.

A. Read these sentences. Match the phrasal verbs to their definitions.

1. Why are you just **standing around**? Don't you have any work to do?

2. His name is Philip J. Johnson. The "J" **stands for** his middle name, Jackson, which was his grandfather's name.

3. I don't understand why you let him treat you so badly. Why don't you **stand up for** yourself?

4. He's my boss. I don't like the way he treats me, but if I **stand up to** him, I might lose my job.

Phrasal Verb	Definition
_____ 1. stand around	a. support or defend a person or idea that is being attacked
_____ 2. stand for	b. refuse to accept bad or unfair treatment from a person or organization
_____ 3. stand up for	c. stand somewhere and not do anything
_____ 4. stand up to	d. represent a word, name, or idea, especially in a short form

B. Write your own sentences with the phrasal verbs from Part A.

1. _____

2. _____

3. _____

4. _____

Word Families: Suffixes

As you learned in Chapters 1–3, different word forms have different suffixes. These suffixes can change the part of speech of a word, for example from a verb to a noun or adjective.

A. Put each suffix in the box into the correct category in the chart.

-al	-er	-ion	-ity	-ry
-ance	-ic	-ist	-ment	-tion

NOUN (PERSON)	NOUN (NOT A PERSON)	ADJECTIVE

B. Complete these sentences with the words in the chart. All of the words are related to target words from the unit.

complexity	involvement	provider	relevance	theorist

1. He got into trouble because of his _____ in criminal activity.

2. How is that point connected to what we are discussing? What is its

   _____ to the topic?

3. The _____ of that chemistry problem makes it very difficult to solve.

4. She studies how different cultures are related, and then writes about her ideas.

   She is a cultural _____ .

5. She is a good _____ . She works hard, and is able to give her

   children everything they need: food, housing, clothing, and a good education.

PLAYING WITH WORDS

Complete the puzzle with words you studied in Chapters 1–3.

ACROSS

2. talk to other people, work together with them, etc.
6. something you say, write, do, or make that shows what you think or feel
10. very, very bad
11. facts, information, papers, etc., that prove that something is true
12. connected in some way
13. something that is difficult, especially in a way that is interesting
14. a quality that things, places, or people have that makes them attractive to look at

DOWN

1. the place where scientists or researchers do their work
3. produced first (for example, a movie); not copied or based on anything else
4. the feeling that something is definitely true or definitely exists
5. something important that someone says
7. make a thin mark on a hard surface with something sharp or rough
8. according to what people say or report
9. very fast

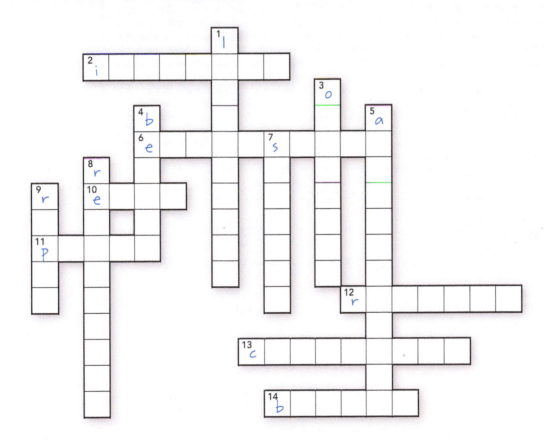

BUILDING DICTIONARY SKILLS

Finding Phrasal Verbs

Dictionary Entries for Phrasal Verbs

Phrasal verbs do not have their own entries in most dictionaries. They are part of the entry for the verb. Usually, the phrasal verbs are listed at the end of all the definitions for the verb.

A. Look at the dictionary entry for the verb *call*. Circle the phrasal verbs and read the definitions. Then, complete the sentences with the correct particles. Be careful: you will not use all of the phrasal verbs listed.

> **call**[1] /kɔl/ *v* **1 TELEPHONE** [I,T] to telephone someone: *I called about six o'clock.* | *He said he'd call me tomorrow . . .* **9 CALL IT A DAY** *spoken* said when you want to stop working, either because you are tired or because you have done enough: *Come on, guys, let's call it a day.* **call (sb) back** *phr v* to telephone someone again, or to telephone someone who tried to telephone you earlier: *Okay, I'll call back around three.* | *Can I call you back later?* **call for** sth *phr v* **1** to ask publicly for something to be done: *Parents are calling for a return to basics in education.* **2** to need or deserve a particular type of behavior or treatment: *a situation that calls for immediate action* **3** to say that a particular type of weather is likely to happen: *The forecast calls for more rain.* **call in** *phr v* **1 call** sb ↔ **in** to ask or order someone to come and help you with a difficult situation: *The governor called in the National Guard to deal with the riots.* **2** to telephone the place where you work, especially to report something: *Jan called in sick this morning.* **3** to telephone a radio or television show to give your opinion or ask a question **call** sb/sth ↔ **off** *phr v* **1** to decide that a planned event will not happen or will not continue: *The game had to be called off due to bad weather.* **2** to order a dog or person to stop attacking someone: *Call off your dog!* **call on** *phr v* **1** to formally ask someone to do something: *The UN has called on both sides to observe the cease fire.* **2** to visit someone for a short time: *a salesman calling on customers* **call out** *phr v* **1 call** (sth ↔) **out** to say something loudly: *"Phone for you," Rosie called out.* **2 call** sb/sth ↔ **out** to ask or order someone to come help you in a difficult situation: *The Army has been called out to help fight the fires.* **call up** *phr v* **1 call** (sb ↔) **up** to telephone someone: *Dave called me up to tell me about it.* **2 call** sth ↔ **up** IT to make information appear on a computer screen

1. She called _____ to him in the crowd, but he didn't hear her.

2. Look how late it is! I'd better call my boss _____ and tell him I'll be late.

3. The baseball game was called _____ due to the rain.

4. The teacher always calls _____ me to answer the most challenging questions.

B. Write your own sentences with the phrasal verbs from part A.

THE CHALLENGES OF YOUTH

THINK ABOUT THIS

Read the title of the unit. Check ☑ the topics that you think you might read about in this unit.

- ☐ diseases that affect both the young and the old
- ☐ young people with remarkable talent
- ☐ how children's personalities change as they become teenagers
- ☐ how much easier it is to be a teenager today than in the past
- ☐ challenges that young people face in school

CHAPTER 4

Sleepy Teens

LEARNING OUTCOME

❯ Learn about the sleeping habits of teenagers

GETTING READY TO READ

1. Walk around the class, and ask your classmates about their sleeping habits. Write their names in the chart. Try to find at least one person for each category.

Gets enough sleep	Doesn't get enough sleep	Falls asleep during class	Sleeps less than 6 hours a night	Sleeps more than 8 hours a night	Likes to take naps	Usually goes to bed before 12:00 midnight

2. Ask your classmates if they are happy with their sleep habits. If not, what would they like to change?

READING

Read to Find Out: How are the sleep patterns of teenagers different from those of adults?

Read the definitions beside the reading. Then read "Sleepy Teens." If you see a new word, circle it, but don't stop reading. You can learn the new word later.

Sleepy Teens

1   When school superintendent[1] Russell Dever enters the local coffee shop at around 7:20 a.m., it is crowded with students. "The line is out the door because our high school kids are getting coffee," he said.

2   And they are not standing in line for the decaf[2]—they need the caffeine[3] to stay awake in class. Talk to American high school students and you hear the **complaints** about how late they **stay up**, how little they sleep—and how early they must be in class.

3   These days, there is increasing **concern** in schools across the United States about students who are not completely awake in morning classes. School **officials** in some states have even changed start times so teenagers can sleep later.

4   According to sleep **expert** Mary Carskadon, the fact that many teenagers work long hours outside of school and have computers and televisions in their bedrooms contributes to a serious **lack** of sleep. But, she said, the problem is also due to biology.[4] As the bodies of teenagers develop, their brains also change. These changes make teens more **likely** than adults to have trouble sleeping at night.

5   Teenagers need **at least** eight to nine hours of sleep a night, but the average teen gets a lot less. Carskadon's study, completed in the fall of 2001 with researcher Amy Wolfson, showed that nearly 30 percent of students in the tenth grade slept less than six hours on school nights. Less than 15 percent got more than eight hours of sleep each night. Eighth-graders averaged eight hours of sleep a night, although that age group, she said, needs at least nine hours a night.

6   Even more remarkable are the results of a 1997–1998 school year study. In that study, 12 out of 24 U.S. high school students who were part of an **experiment** at a sleep laboratory had brain wave **patterns** similar to those of someone with narcolepsy, a serious condition that affects sleep. "What's going on is that at 8:30 in the morning these kids … , would normally be in school sitting in a classroom, but . . . their brain is still in the middle of the night," said Carskadon.

7   Parent Dawn Dow says her son just cannot go to bed before 10 p.m. "Last year he was trying to put himself to bed at 8:30 and was coming in at 9:30 and 10:00 **in tears** saying, 'I just can't go to sleep.' It is not a case of children wanting to be up late . . . . It is a change in his chemistry."

[1] *a school superintendent* = someone who is responsible for all of the schools in a particular area of the United States

[2] *decaf* = short form of the phrase *decaffeinated coffee*, coffee that has had the caffeine removed

[3] *caffeine* = the chemical substance in coffee, tea, and some other drinks that makes people feel more active

[4] *biology* = the scientific study of living things

8 So would letting teenagers wake up later make a difference? Kyla Wahlstrom of the University of Minnesota in the United States studies the effects of changing school start times. She has looked at students in Edina and Minneapolis, two cities in Minnesota, where public school officials have moved high school starting times past 8:30 a.m. In Minneapolis, the middle school begins at 9:30 a.m. She said the later starting times have **reduced** student **absences**. They have also lowered **dropout** rates by eight percent over four years. In addition, she said, teachers report that students are not sleeping at their desks during the first two hours of class anymore. She said 92 percent of parents from Edina reported that their teenagers were easier to live with. The students reported that they were feeling less **depressed** and were getting better grades.

9 Big changes in school start times may not be possible in some areas. However, Wahlstrom said her research shows that even small changes can contribute to a solution to this serious problem.

Notes

1. At the time this article was written, Mary Carskadon was professor of psychiatry[5] and human behavior at Brown University in Providence, Rhode Island, U.S.A., and director of sleep and chronobiology[6] at Bradley Hospital in East Providence, Rhode Island, U.S.A.

2. Amy Wolfson was a researcher at the College of the Holy Cross in Worcester, Massachusetts, U.S.A.

3. Kyla Wahlstrom was associate director[7] of the Center for Applied Research and Educational Improvement at the University of Minnesota, U.S.A.

[5] *psychiatry* = the study and treatment of mental illness

[6] *chronobiology* = the study of the effects of time on living things

[7] *an associate director* = someone who assists the director

Quick Comprehension Check

A. Read these sentences **about the reading**. Circle T (true), F (false), or ? (can't determine the answer from the reading). If you circle T or F, write the number of the paragraph with the answer on the line.

1. Teenagers drink a lot of coffee because without it they might fall asleep in class.   T   F   ?   ____

2. Some schools start their classes later so that teenage students can get more sleep in the morning.   T   F   ?   ____

3. Most teenagers sleep more than they should.   T   F   ?   ____

4. There are scientific reasons that explain why teenagers have difficulty sleeping at night.   T   F   ?   ____

5. The brains of teenagers are the same as the brains of adults.   T   F   ?   ____

6. Teenagers can do their best schoolwork in the early morning.   T   F   ?   ____

7. Many parents do not want high school officials to change school start times.   T   F   ?   ____

Reading Tip:
Get into the habit of annotating a text as you read. *Annotate* means to take notes in the margins or on the reading itself. For example, write '?' next to something confusing, or '!' next to something interesting.

B. Work with your class. Share your answers from part A. Go back to the reading to find the reason why a sentence is true or false. Correct the false sentences.

EXPLORING VOCABULARY

Thinking about the Target Vocabulary

Guessing Strategy: Synonyms

Often, writers don't want to repeat a word, so they use a **synonym**. Synonyms are words that have similar meanings. If you don't know a word, look at the sentences nearby to see if there is a synonym. Look at the example.

> *Some students who don't get enough sleep get **depressed***. *And because they feel so unhappy, they can't concentrate on their schoolwork.*

Based on the context, you can guess that the words *depressed* and *unhappy* are similar in meaning.

A. Read the sentences. Circle the word or words in the second sentence that are synonyms for the **boldfaced** target word(s).

1. She said the later starting times have **reduced** student absences. They have also lowered dropout rates by eight percent over four years.

2. Her son came out of his bedroom **in tears**. He was crying because he couldn't fall asleep.

3. These days, there is increasing **concern** about students who are not completely awake in morning classes. Both parents and teachers are worried that teenagers are not getting enough sleep.

4. A **lack** of sleep is related to many health problems. For example, not enough sleep can cause headaches.

> **Vocabulary Tip:**
> Synonyms have similar meanings, but often cannot be used in the same way. A learner's dictionary such as the *Longman Advanced American Dictionary* includes helpful information on word usage.

B. Look at the target words. Which ones are new to you? Circle them here and in the reading. The numbers in parentheses help you find the words in the paragraphs.

Target Words

complaints (2)	expert (4)	experiment (6)	absences (8)
stay up (2)	lack (4)	patterns (6)	dropout (8)
concern (3)	likely (4)	in tears (7)	depressed (8)
officials (3)	at least (5)	reduced (8)	

C. Read "Sleepy Teens" again. Look at the context of the new words. Can you guess their meanings?

D. Complete the word form chart. Fill in the shaded areas of the chart with the target words from the reading. Write the base form of the verbs and the singular form of the nouns.

NOUNS	VERBS	ADJECTIVES	OTHER
complaint			

Understanding the Target Vocabulary

These sentences are **about the reading**. Complete them with the words in the box. Circle the words in the sentences that help you understand the meanings of the target words.

absences	concern	experts	patterns
at least	dropout	lack	reduced
complaint	experiment	likely	stay up

1. High school students _____ late at night, so they have trouble waking up early to go to school.

2. A common _____ from young people is that they don't get enough sleep. They are unhappy that school begins so early.

3. Some parents and school officials are worried that many high school students are too tired to learn. Because of their _____, school officials in several cities have decided to change the time when high school classes start.

4. Researchers did an _____ with teenagers at a sleep lab to find out about their sleep _____.

5. Researchers say that teenagers get much less sleep than they really need. According to these _____, there are many reasons for this serious _____ of sleep.

6. Teens' bodies are changing. That's the main reason they are more _____ to have trouble sleeping than adults.

7. Most teenagers need _____ eight hours of sleep a night. In fact, it's even better if they get nine or ten hours.

8. When teenagers don't get enough sleep, they are more likely to miss class. In one school where start times were changed from 8:30 a.m. to 9:30 a.m., there are now fewer _____. The later start times seem to have _____ the number of students who don't go to class because they can't wake up in the morning.

9. The later start times have also lowered the _____ rate. This means that fewer students are quitting school.

DEVELOPING READING SKILLS

Distinguishing Major Points from Supporting Details

Main Ideas, Major Points, and Supporting Details

A reading generally has one **main idea**, with several **major points** to support it. Those major points are supported by **supporting details**. For example, in "Sleepy Teens" there is one main idea, three major points to support it, and many supporting details to illustrate the major points.

Answer these questions.

1. What is the main idea of "Sleepy Teens"?
   a. Some schools in the United States are experimenting with later school start times because experts say that teenagers will be happier and do better in school if they get more sleep.
   b. Many teenagers have difficulty falling asleep at night because of the biological changes in their brains and because they have televisions and computers in their rooms.
   c. Most American teenagers are depressed because they do not get enough sleep.

2. Match the major points and their supporting details. Be careful. Some of the major points have more than one supporting detail.

Major Points

_b_ 1. There are many reasons that teenagers have trouble sleeping at night.

____ 2. Research shows that many teenagers do not get enough sleep.

____ 3. Schools that are experimenting with later start times are happy with the results.

Supporting Details

a. Thirty percent of students in the tenth grade sleep less than six hours on school nights.

b. Many teenagers work long hours outside of school.

c. There are biological changes in the brains of teenagers that make it difficult for them to fall asleep at night.

d. In one school that changed its start time from 8:30 to 9:30 a.m., the number of student absences has gone down.

e. The students feel less depressed and get better grades when they get enough sleep.

BUILDING ON THE VOCABULARY

Using the Target Vocabulary in New Contexts

Complete the sentences with the target words in the box. Be careful. There are two extra words.

absences	depressed	lack	patterns
at least	dropout	likely	reduce
complaint	expert	official	stay up
concerns			

1. She has written more than ten books on education. She is an _____

   on the subject.

2. I don't remember exactly how much money I have in the bank, but I know it's

   _____ $500. I might have more. I'll have to call the bank to check.

3. I'm going to take a nap so that I can _____ late to watch that TV

   special.

4. Take your umbrella. The weather report said that rain is _____ later

   this afternoon.

5. The service in that restaurant was terrible. I'm going to write a letter of

   _____ to the manager.

6. There are certain _____ of behavior and thinking that are related to depression. When doctors check patients for depression, they always ask the same questions to see if the answers are similar to those of other depressed people.

7. If you want to lose weight, you must _____ the amount of food that you eat.

8. They are concerned about their son's complete _____ of interest in his studies. He doesn't seem to be interested in any subject.

9. You have too many _____. You need to make sure you attend all of the rest of the classes, or you will have to repeat the course.

10. My town has a serious _____ problem. Students are leaving high school early and can't find jobs.

11. He works for the government. He is the _____ who is responsible for public safety.

Expanding Vocabulary

Word Families: Recognizing the Different Forms of a Word

It is important to recognize the different forms of a word. Sometimes the difference in spelling is very small, so you have to look carefully. Sometimes, there is no difference in spelling at all. In that case, you will need to check the grammar of the sentence to see if the word is being used differently.

A. Look at the target words in the box. Then, in the summary of the reading below, circle the words that are related to these target words, but are different parts of speech. Do <u>not</u> circle the word if it is the same part of speech as in the word box.

| absence (noun) | concern (noun) | dropout (noun) | official (noun) |
| complaint (noun) | depressed (adj) | experiment (noun) | reduced (verb) |

Writing Tip: When writing a summary, you must put the ideas in your own words. One way to do this is to change the grammar of the sentence and use different forms of the words, for example *complain* (verb) instead of *complaint* (noun).

It's 7:20 a.m., and teenagers are standing in line on the sidewalk in front of the local coffee shop. They complain that school starts too early in the morning, so they have to drink coffee to stay awake in class. They also complain of being depressed. Some students are absent because they can't wake up, and students who are absent a lot are more likely to drop out of school. This concerns many parents and school officials, so some schools are experimenting with a change in school start times. They hope that if teens can sleep a little later in the morning, they will be able to pay better attention in class. They also hope that the later start times will result in a reduction in the number of students who miss class. And some teens are reporting that their depression has disappeared since they started getting more sleep. If the experiment works, the schools will probably make the change official.

B. Complete the chart with the words you circled in exercise A.

NOUNS	VERBS	ADJECTIVES
	complain	

Word Grammar: Participial Adjectives

Some adjectives are formed by adding *-ing* or *-ed* to the end of a verb. These adjectives are called **participial adjectives**. Look at the examples.

Verb: depress	Participial Adjective (*-ing* form): depressing	Participial Adjective (*-ed* form): depressed
Expresses an action	Describes a person or thing that **causes** a feeling or reaction	Describes a person who **experiences** a feeling or reaction
Example: *The story* **depresses** *John.*	Example: *It is a* **depressing** *story.*	Example: *John felt* **depressed** *after reading the story.*

A. Complete the sentences with the *-ing* or *-ed* form of the **boldfaced** verbs.

1. Your theory **fascinates** me. I think it is _____.

2. Science **fascinates** my daughter. She is _____ by everything related to science.

3. That teacher likes to **challenge** her students. The homework she gives is usually _____.

4. I like my teachers to **challenge** me. I learn more when I feel

   _____.

5. If you **threaten** a wild animal, it might attack you. When wild animals feel

   _____, they can be very dangerous.

6. It is against the law to **threaten** someone with words or actions. I am going to report his _____ behavior to the police.

7. Your behavior at home **concerns** me, but your behavior at school is even more

   _____.

8. My low grades **concern** me. My parents are _____ too. They are afraid that I won't be able to get into a good university.

B. Working with a partner, answer the questions. Make sure you use the correct form of the **boldfaced** words.

1. What is the most **fascinating** movie that you have ever seen? Explain why you felt so **fascinated** by it.
2. If a friend feels **depressed**, what can you do to make him or her feel better?
3. What is the most **challenging** thing that you have ever done?
4. Do you like easy classes, or do you prefer to feel **challenged**? Why?
5. What are some of the things people do when they feel **threatened**?
6. What are you most **concerned** about these days?

CRITICAL THINKING

A. Discussion

Share your ideas in a small group. As you talk, try to use the vocabulary below. Each time someone uses a target word or phrase, put a check (✓) next to it.

☐	absence/absent	☐	expert
☐	at least	☐	lack
☐	complaint/complain	☐	likely
☐	concern/concerned/concerning	☐	official
☐	depressed/depressing/depression	☐	reduce/reduction
☐	dropout/drop out	☐	stay up

1. Look back at paragraph 1 of the reading. How does the writer start the reading? Why does she start it this way? For example, why doesn't she start with statistical information on sleeping rates? What effect does this type of introduction have on you? Do you like this style? Why or why not?

2. The article gives two main reasons for poor sleep patterns in teenagers: biology and habit (or behavior). What types of information does the writer use to explain the different reasons? Research results? Statistics? Interviews? Which of these two reasons—biology or habit—does the writer emphasize more? Use specific information from the reading to support your answer.

3. What are the ways that some parents and schools are trying to address teenagers' sleep problems, according to the reading? Can you think of another way to address this problem? Work as a group to come up with another possible solution.

4. Paragraph 8 on page 46 begins with a question, but the writer never answers it directly. What can you infer the answer to be? What evidence in the paragraph supports your inference?

> **Critical Thinking Tip:** Writers sometimes make statements without explaining why they are true. Learn to question such statements. Write "But why?" in the margin next to the statement. Then try to think of a reason yourself.

5. In the last paragraph of the reading, the writer says "Big changes in school start times may not be possible in some areas." However, the writer never explains why this may not be possible. What reasons can you think of? Consider not only the teenagers' point of view, but also the points of view of all of the other people affected by school starting and ending times, for example younger students, parents, teachers, and school staff such as bus drivers.

6. Talk about other problems that specifically affect teenagers. Talk about the possible causes of the problems, and come up with some solutions.

B. Writing

Complete one or both of these writing topics. When you write, use at least five of the target words from the chapter. Underline the target words in your paper.

> **Writing Tip:** To become a better writer, read actively, and read a lot. As you read, pay attention to how good writers organize their ideas and use vocabulary effectively.

1. Imagine that you are the parent of a teenage girl in the Edina school system, and you do not agree with the change in the school start times. Write a letter about your concerns to an official at your daughter's high school.

2. Choose a problem that affects teenagers, and write an essay explaining the problems, the causes, and some possible solutions. Be sure to support your major points with details. Use the reading "Sleepy Teens" as an example of how to organize your essay.

CHAPTER 5

Growing Up Gifted

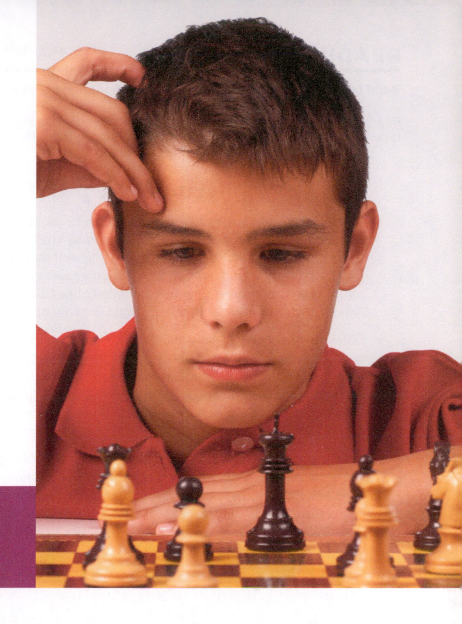

LEARNING OUTCOME

❯ Learn about a child prodigy

GETTING READY TO READ

Talk with a partner.

1. Do you have a special skill or talent (for example in sports, music, painting, mathematics, science)? What is it? At what age did you become aware that you had this talent?

2. If you could choose to be talented in one thing, what would you choose? Why?

3. A *child prodigy* is someone who shows remarkable talent in a particular subject at a very young age. Put a check (✓) next to the phrases that you believe would describe most child prodigies. Compare your answers, and discuss any differences. Child prodigies . . .

☐ know a lot about many different things   ☐ have a large vocabulary

☐ want to be perfect   ☐ love school

☐ are happy   ☐ are original thinkers

☐ are self-confident   ☐ become very successful adults

READING

Read the definitions beside the reading. Then read "Growing Up Gifted." If you see a new word, circle it, but don't stop reading. You can learn the new word later.

Growing Up Gifted

1 At the age of 18, Canadian teen chess[1] player Pascal Charbonneau had all the qualities of a child prodigy. He was smart, knew a lot about a variety of subjects, had **achieved** a lot at a young age, and was confident in his abilities. But Charbonneau did not like to be called a prodigy. "Winning a **championship** at this age is considered special, but I don't like thinking of myself as someone who is very different from other people," he said at the time.

2 Like many eighteen-year-olds, Charbonneau was trying to decide where to go to college. School had always been easy for him, as it is for most **gifted** students. Many gifted students choose to finish school early to avoid getting bored, but Charbonneau decided to cruise through[2] his classes so he could **concentrate on** chess and some of his other interests, such as sports and French **literature**.

3 In general, gifted students **tend to** have an insatiable appetite[3] for information. They are also **perfectionists**. In addition, most are independent and **sensitive** to **injustice**. Other characteristics include specific ability in one area along with the ability to concentrate on it for a long time, excellent reading ability, a large vocabulary, originality, rapid mastery[4] of new skills, and an ability to see connections between ideas.

4 Having these characteristics can be challenging, even depressing, said 18-year-old Charbonneau. He was **critical** of even his best performances. "I'm rarely ever happy with what I do."

5 Charbonneau knew that the **pressure** on him would soon begin to grow, as every young chess player tried to become the next champion. That pressure has destroyed a lot of talented young people. For example, many young musical prodigies have walked away from their careers after discovering they will not become the star[5] of their dreams, says Francois Gagne. Gagne is an expert on gifted children who worked at the University of Quebec at Montreal, Canada for many years, researching the topic. "When you are a prodigy, your goal is to become an international master musician," he said. "If you cannot become someone at the very top,[6] you are not interested in becoming a musician in an orchestra."[7]

6 World-famous violinist Itzhak Perlman has seen many talented young musicians simply **burn out**. "Rarely do you see people **survive**, and that's the goal, to survive your gift," he once told the *New York Times*.

7 Charbonneau did survive his gift. He became a Grandmaster of chess in 2006, and has represented Canada and the United States in a number of major team events over the years. He studied mathematics and finance[8] at the University

[1] *chess* = a game for two players who move their playing pieces across a special board to try to get their opponent's King

[2] *cruise through* = do something well with very little effort

[3] *have an insatiable appetite* = want more and more of something

[4] *mastery* = complete understanding or great skill

[5] *a star* = a famous and successful performer in entertainment

[6] *at the very top* = successful and famous

[7] *an orchestra* = a large group of musicians playing many kinds of instruments

of Maryland in the United States, graduating in 2006. He then went on to work as a financial analyst[9] in New York City.

8   Between 2 and 5 percent of young people are gifted, two to three years beyond their **peers**. But extremely gifted prodigies—the Beethovens and Mozarts—are much less common, perhaps one in a million, said Gagne. Here are some facts about several well-known child prodigies:

- Probably the most famous child prodigy of all, Wolfgang Amadeus Mozart (1756–1791) began writing music before he was five. By age six, he had written a remarkable amount of music and performed throughout Europe.

- Some of Ludwig van Beethoven's (1770–1827) music was **published** when he was only twelve. **Despite** losing his hearing as an adult, he continued to write music until his death.

- It is often said that the great scientist Albert Einstein (1879–1955) failed at school. In fact, he did well and could be described as a prodigy. Einstein was always a high achiever, although his best work was done when he was in his twenties.

[8] *finance* = the control of money that is earned and spent, especially for a company or government

[9] *an analyst* = someone whose job it is to examine or think about something carefully and make recommendations about it

Quick Comprehension Check

A. Read these sentences **about the reading**. Circle T (true), F (false), or ? (can't determine the answer from the reading). If you circle T or F, write the number of the paragraph with the answer on the line.

1. Pascal Charbonneau enjoyed the attention he got for being a child prodigy.   T   F   ?   _____

2. Gifted students often finish school earlier than other students.   T   F   ?   _____

3. Child prodigies in very different areas, such as music or chess, share certain basic characteristics.   T   F   ?   _____

4. Many musical prodigies become famous musicians.   T   F   ?   _____

5. Most child prodigies are not very successful later in life.   T   F   ?   _____

B. Work with your class. Share your answers from part A. Go back to the reading to find the reason why a sentence is true or false. Correct the false sentences.

EXPLORING VOCABULARY

Thinking about the Target Vocabulary

Guessing Strategy: Positive or Negative Meaning

You learned in Chapter 2 that one way to guess the meaning of an adjective is to determine whether it has a positive or negative meaning. In fact, the same strategy can be used with any part of speech—adjective, noun, verb, or adverb. Look at the example.

> *He's smart, has **achieved** a lot at a young age, and is confident in his abilities.*
>
> Because the words *smart* and *confident* have positive meanings, you should be able to guess that the verb *achieve* has a positive meaning too.

A. Find these target words in the reading. Do they have a positive or a negative meaning? Write P (positive) or N (negative).

_____ 1. burn out

_____ 2. championship

_____ 3. gifted

_____ 4. critical

_____ 5. survive

B. Look at the target words. Which ones are new to you? Circle them here and in the reading. The numbers in parentheses help you find the words in the paragraphs.

Target Words

achieved (1)	perfectionists (3)	burn out (6)
championship (1)	sensitive (3)	survive (6)
gifted (2)	injustice (3)	peers (7)
concentrate on (2)	critical (4)	published (7)
literature (2)	pressure (5)	despite (7)
tend to (3)		

C. Read "Growing Up Gifted" again. Look at the context of the new words. Can you guess their meanings?

D. Complete the word form chart. Fill in the shaded areas of the chart with the target words from the reading. Write the base form of the verbs and the singular form of the nouns.

NOUNS	VERBS	ADJECTIVES	OTHER
	achieve		

Understanding the Target Vocabulary

These sentences are **about the reading**. Complete them with the words in the box. Circle the words in the sentences that help you understand the meanings of the target words.

burn out	despite	peers	published
championships	gifted	perfectionists	sensitive
concentrate on	injustice	pressure	survive
critical	literature		

Vocabulary Tip: Most of the target words in this book are among the most common words in English. The glossed words are less common, but might be useful to learn, depending on your interests.

1. _____ children have special talents, and usually learn things at an earlier age than their _____ .

2. Gifted children can usually _____ one subject for a long period of time, without getting bored.

3. Gifted children are often interested in many different subjects. For example, Pascal Charbonneau has won many chess _____ , but he also likes to read French _____ and play sports.

4. Another characteristic of gifted children is that they understand other people; they are _____ to the feelings of others.

5. Gifted children do not like it when other people are treated unfairly. They do not like to see _____ .

6. Prodigies are rarely satisfied with their performance. They are _____ of themselves, even when they perform brilliantly.

7. Prodigies don't like to make even a very small mistake. They are _____ .

8. The lives of musical prodigies are not easy. Everyone expects them to perform brilliantly all of the time. Some prodigies cannot deal with the constant _____ and decide to quit performing.

9. Because of the pressure on them, many gifted young musicians get so tired that they stop performing. They _____ .

10. Beethoven was one of the most famous musical prodigies. He wrote and

_____ music at a very young age.

11. _____ their talent, many prodigies never become famous. That is

because it is very difficult to compete and _____ at the top level in

any field.

DEVELOPING READING SKILLS

Understanding Major Points

Identifying Major Points

A reading of more than one paragraph usually has one main idea supported by several major points (also called main points). After the introduction of the main idea (usually in the first paragraph of the reading), each new paragraph usually develops a different major point.

When you finish a paragraph, think about why the writer chose to start a new paragraph. Ask yourself:

- How is the topic of the new paragraph different from the topic of the previous one?

And/or

- What is the purpose of the new paragraph?

Asking these questions will help you identify the major points. The differences in the details that support each major point should help you answer the questions. For example, in paragraph two of "Growing Up Gifted," the details are all about the *school life* of gifted students, while the details in paragraph 3 are about the *characteristics* of gifted students.

It is helpful to write the major points in the margin of the reading. This will help you find information more easily when you look for it again. It is also a way to remember what the writer said, outline the ideas, and even study for tests. If you are unable to identify the major point, write a '?' in the margin so that you will remember to ask about it later.

Identify the major points of the reading on page 56. Circle the letter that best completes each sentence.

1. The purpose of paragraph 2 is to explain

   a. how gifted teenagers deal with school.
   b. the interests that Charbonneau had at school.

2. The purpose of paragraph 3 is to explain

   a. the characteristics that many gifted students share.
   b. why gifted students like to learn about a lot of different things.

3. The purpose of paragraph 5 is to explain

    a. the goals of musical prodigies.

    b. the pressure that gifted young people face.

4. The purpose of paragraph 8 and the bullet points after it is to explain

    a. the work of several well-known prodigies.

    b. the difference between being gifted and being a very gifted prodigy.

Reading Tip: Writers sometimes include bulleted lists in a reading. *Bullet points* are often used to call attention to important or interesting information, or to highlight details or examples.

Understanding Inference

Making Reasonable Inferences

An **inference** is more than just a guess. You should always have a good reason for making an inference. You should also be careful that your inference does not go too far beyond what is written in the text. Look at the sentence.

Einstein was always a high achiever, although his best work was done when he was in his twenties.

It would *not* be correct to infer from this sentence that the work that Einstein did in his 30s and 40s was bad. That inference goes too far beyond what is written.

Read these sentences from "Growing Up Gifted." Then, read the two sentences that follow. Put a check (✓) next to the sentence that is a reasonable inference. The numbers in parentheses are the paragraphs where you can find the sentences.

1. Having these characteristics can be challenging, even depressing, said Charbonneau. He is critical of even his best performances. "I'm rarely ever happy with what I do." (4)

    ☐ a. Child prodigies are more unhappy with their best performances than they are with their poor performances.

    ☐ b. Child prodigies are often unhappy because they have trouble accepting anything less than perfection.

2. Charbonneau knows that the pressure on him will soon begin to grow, as every young chess player tries to become the next champion. (5)

    ☐ a. Charbonneau was the winner of the last chess championship.

    ☐ b. Charbonneau will probably be the next chess champion.

3. World-famous violinist Itzhak Perlman has seen many talented young musicians simply burn out. "Rarely do you see people survive, and that's the goal, to survive your gift," he once told the *New York Times*. (6)

    ☐ a. Many gifted young musicians do not have successful careers, despite having remarkable talent.

    ☐ b. Many young musicians do not live long enough to achieve their goals.

BUILDING ON THE VOCABULARY

Using the Target Vocabulary in New Contexts

Complete the sentences with the target words in the box. Be careful. There are two extra words.

achieved	critical	literature	published
burn out	despite	peer	sensitive
championship	gifted	perfectionist	tend to
concentrate on	injustice	pressure	

1. I'm concerned that you are working too hard. I know you enjoy your job now, but if you aren't careful, you'll _____ by the time you're thirty!

2. She's a gifted mystery writer. She's already written at least three books. Her first book was _____ ten years ago.

3. Be careful how you talk to him. He's very _____. Yesterday, he was in tears because of something a classmate said to him.

4. I hate it when teachers treat their male and female students differently. It's not fair. The _____ really makes me angry.

5. _____ the complete lack of proof that he was involved in the crime, he was arrested and put in jail.

6. In English _____, William Shakespeare stands out as one of the most brilliant writers.

7. I'm a _____. I am never satisfied unless I do something exactly right.

8. Stop playing around on the computer and _____ your homework! It's almost time for bed.

9. After 100 performances in just three months, she got very sick and had to go in the hospital. The doctors said that the _____ of performing live seven nights a week was too much for her.

10. My daughter has been placed in a program for _____ children. Her teachers think that the challenge of interacting with other talented children will be good for her.

11. He's very sensitive. He doesn't like it when his teachers are even just a little

_____ of his work.

12. He is a remarkable tennis player. He is only 13, but he has already _____

more than many players twice his age.

13. Teenagers _____ get less sleep than they need.

Expanding Vocabulary

Word Families: Related Words

Sometimes within the same word family, there is more than one word for the same part of speech. Usually, the two words have related, but different, meanings. Look at these sentences.

You shouldn't **criticize** him. He is doing the best he can.

Would you please read my essay and **critique** it?

The verbs _criticize_ and _critique_ are in the same word family. They have related, but different, meanings. _Criticize_ means "to judge someone or something severely." _Critique_ means "to evaluate the positive and negative aspects of someone or something."

Study the chart. Then, complete the sentences with words from the chart. If there are two words listed for the same part of speech, check the meanings in the dictionary. Be careful: you will not use all the words.

NOUN (person)	NOUN (thing)	VERB	ADJECTIVE
	achievement	achieve	
	concentration	concentrate	
critic	criticism, critique	criticize, critique	critical
publisher	publication	publish, publicize	public
	tendency	tend	
	pressure	pressure, pressurize	
perfectionist	perfection	perfect	perfect
champion	championship	champion	

1. He received an award for remarkable _____ in the arts.

2. Just like her mother, she has a _____ to get depressed.

3. A book _____ will often ask writers to go out on book tours to

_____ their new books. Book tours help increase sales.

4. Because air pressure outside of an airplane is much lower than at sea level, it is necessary to _____ the air inside the plane so that the passengers get enough oxygen.

5. I'm tired of all the complaints and _____ . I'm just trying to do the best job I can.

6. Thank you for your _____ of my performance in the competition. It was very helpful to me.

7. I did badly on the test because my _____ was poor.

8. Please don't _____ him. You know how sensitive he is.

9. She beat all of her competitors. She is the new _____ .

10. He's a good soccer player, but he wants to be better. He wants to _____ his skills.

11. The film _____ didn't like the movie at all, but I loved it.

12. It doesn't matter how hard you try. You will never achieve _____ .

Word Grammar: Gerunds after Prepositions

Prepositions can be followed by nouns or pronouns. Since **gerunds** (base form of verb + -ing) act as nouns, they can follow prepositions, too. Look at the sentence from the reading.

*"If you cannot become someone at the very top, you are not interested **in becoming** a musician in an orchestra."*

A. Complete the sentences with the -ing form of the verbs below.

achieve	burn out	criticize	pressure	publish

1. Great news! There are two companies interested in _____ your new book. You're going to have a career as a writer!

2. He's decided to take a long vacation. He's been working so hard lately that he's afraid of _____ .

3. Instead of _____ everyone else's work, why don't you concentrate on improving your own?

4. I don't believe in _____ children to do things that they aren't

   ready for. If we push them too much when they are young, they'll burn out.

5. Despite _____ more than anyone else in his class, he was not

   selected to participate in the end-of-year performance.

B. Complete the sentences with information about yourself. Use a gerund after the preposition.

1. I like to be left alone when I'm concentrating on _____

   _____.

2. I don't believe in _____.

3. Instead of _____, I _____.

4. Despite _____, I _____.

CRITICAL THINKING

A. Discussion

Share your ideas in a small group. As you talk, try to use the vocabulary below. Each time someone uses a target word, put a check (✓) next to it.

☐ achieve/achievement	☐ peer
☐ burn out	☐ perfectionist/perfect/perfection
☐ champion/championship	☐ pressure
☐ concentrate on	☐ sensitive
☐ critic/critical/criticize/criticism	☐ survive
☐ gifted	☐ tend to
☐ injustice/just/unjust	

1. In paragraph 1, the writer says ". . . Charbonneau does not like to be called a prodigy." In paragraph 4, he says that Charbonneau finds it depressing to be gifted. Does that surprise you? Why do you think Charbonneau feels this way? Use both information from the reading and your own ideas to answer the question.

2. The reading says that one of the characteristics of gifted children is a tendency to be sensitive to injustice. However, the reading does not explain why. Why do you think gifted children might be more sensitive to injustice than other people? Use both information from the reading and your own ideas to answer the question.

3. Sometimes, school officials take the best students out of regular classes and put them in classes with other gifted children. Considering what you learned about Charbonneau from the reading, do you think he would like to be in this type of

Critical Thinking Tip: You will not agree with everything that you read. However, it is important to carefully consider new information. If the information is reliable and it challenges something that you believe to be true, maybe you should reconsider your opinion.

special class? Why or why not? Support your opinion with information from the reading.

4. Make a list of the advantages and disadvantages of putting gifted students in different classes from their less talented peers. Consider how this might affect not only the gifted students but also the other students.

5. When you were a child, did your parents ever pressure you to develop a talent or skill, or to achieve something difficult? If so, explain what happened. Was it a positive or a negative experience? If you have children, will you pressure them in the same way? Why or why not?

B. Writing

Complete one or both of these writing topics. When you write, use at least five of the target words from the chapter. Underline the target words in your paper.

> **Writing Tip:**
> When you write an opinion essay, make sure that you support your opinion with details such as facts, statistics, and examples.

1. Write an essay in support of or against separating gifted and other students in different classes.

2. Choose a famous person who was a child prodigy. Do some research about the person. Then, write an essay about him or her. Remember to write the essay in your own words, and follow your teacher's instructions on how to identify the sources you used for your research. Your essay should include the following information:

- Date and place of birth
- Age that the prodigy's talent was discovered
- How the prodigy's talent was discovered
- Major achievements
- Current situation (for someone who is still living)
- Any other interesting information that you discover

CHAPTER 6

School Bullies

LEARNING OUTCOME

❯ Learn about bullying

GETTING READY TO READ

Talk in a small group.

1. A **bully** is someone who uses his or her strength or power to frighten or hurt someone who is weaker. A **victim** is someone who has been attacked or treated very badly. Were there any bullies in your school? What did they look like? Who were their victims? What did they do to their victims?

2. Put a **B** next to the words that you think describe most bullies, and a **V** next to the words that you think describe most victims. If you think a word describes both bullies and victims, write both **B** and **V**. Write **N** if you think a word describes neither bullies nor victims. Compare your answers.

_____ popular   _____ weak

_____ male   _____ intelligent

_____ confident   _____ given a lot of freedom by parents

_____ depressed   _____ poor

Read to Find Out: What are the different types of bullying?

Read the definitions below the reading. Then read "School Bullies." If you see a new word, circle it, but don't stop reading. You can learn the new word later.

School Bullies

1   A middle school student is regularly threatened and beaten by his classmates. A 15-year-old girl drops out of school after she receives hundreds of text messages telling her that she is stupid. These are just two examples of an ugly side of school life: bullying.

2   Dr. Dan Olweus, an expert in bullying from Norway, studies **aggression** in schools. On his website, bullying is defined as "aggressive behavior that is **intentional** and that involves an imbalance in power. Most often, it is repeated over time." Notice that the definition includes the word aggressive, rather than **violent**. That is because not all bullying is **physical**; often, it is emotional. In a recent report on bullying in the United Kingdom, 44% of students from 13 to 20 years old reported that they had been bullied at least once a week. In studies **conducted** in the United States, 25% of students reported that they had been bullied.

3   Who are the bullies? They can be male or female, and they are often popular among their peers; they do not have low **self-esteem** or **anxiety**. Instead, they have a strong need for power and domination.[1] According to Dr. Olweus, "Too little love and care in childhood and too much freedom are conditions that strongly contribute to the development of bullies." Bullying is not affected by a family's **economic** situation; bullies come from both rich and poor **backgrounds**.

4   And the **victims**? **Based on** his research, Dr. Olweus claims that "the typical victim tends to be more anxious and less secure than his classmates and usually has a negative **attitude** toward violence." In **surveys**, parents of male victims report that their sons are often cautious[2] and sensitive at an early age. In addition, often they are not physically strong; this makes it easier for bullies to **pick on** them.

5   There are several types of bullying. First, there is physical bullying. Physical bullying involves violence. There is direct contact between the victim and the bully, such as hitting, kicking, and scratching. Both girls and boys can be victims and aggressors, but physical bullying more often involves boys.

6   Second, there is verbal[3] bullying. Verbal bullying involves face-to-face **insults**. The bully often says he is "just joking," but his goal is **humiliation**. Both girls and boys are involved in verbal bullying, but some research shows that it is more **harmful** to girls.

7   Third, there is social bullying. Social bullies do not interact with their victims face-to-face. Instead, they talk about them behind their backs and do not include them in social activities. Girls are often the victims. This is probably

[1] *domination* = the act of controlling someone or something

[2] *cautious* = careful to avoid danger or risks

[3] *verbal* = related to words, or using words

because, according to research, girls are more sensitive to their social position. If we **examine** the **data**, we see that social bullying and physical bullying are equally harmful to the victim's emotional health.

8   Finally, there is cyber bullying, which is the newest form of bullying. It involves the use of social and electronic media such as text messages, instant messaging, and gaming websites. Cyber bullying is indirect, and the bullies are often anonymous.[4] Because cyber bullying is new, there is not much data on its long-term effects.

[4] *anonymous =* not known by name

9   There are several differences between cyber bullying and traditional bullying. First, cyber bullying is usually anonymous. Second, it is not limited to a particular place, such as school. This means that the victim has no safe place; the cyber bully can always find him or her. Third, the messages that the cyber bully sends are almost impossible to remove from the Internet. Fourth, the number of people who can see those messages is unlimited. Fifth, victims are unlikely to ask for help.

10 There is a lot of interest in cyber bullying. Studies show that the effects of cyber bullying are similar to other forms of bullying. Victims tend to have low self-esteem and higher rates of depression and anxiety than those who have not experienced bullying. Interestingly, cyber bullying does not appear to have created a new type of victim. Victims of cyber bullies share the same characteristics as victims of more traditional bullying. On the other hand, some studies show that cyber bullying has created more bullies. This is probably because cyber bullying is indirect and anonymous; it is easier to hurt someone who you do not see, and who does not see you.

Quick Comprehension Check

A. Read these sentences **about the reading**. Circle T (true), F (false), or ? (can't determine the answer from the reading). If you circle T or F, write the number of the paragraph with the answer on the line.

1. Bullies do not tend to have a lot of friends.   T   F   ?   _____

2. Bullies tend to have more freedom than other kids.   T   F   ?   _____

3. Bullies often have a lack of self-confidence.   T   F   ?   _____

4. Victims of bullying usually dislike fighting and tend to be weak.   T   F   ?   _____

5. Many victims did not get enough love when they were children.   T   F   ?   _____

6. Girls are rarely the victims of physical bullying.   T   F   ?   _____

7. More girls than boys are involved in verbal bullying.   T   F   ?   _____

8. Social bullying is indirect.   T   F   ?   _____

9. Cyber bullying is the most dangerous type of bullying.   T   F   ?   _____

B. Work with your class. Share your answers from part A. Go back to the reading to find the reason why a sentence is true or false. Correct the false sentences.

EXPLORING VOCABULARY

Thinking about the Target Vocabulary

Guessing Strategy: Semicolons

Semicolons (;) are a form of punctuation. The information that follows the semicolon is an explanation of the first sentence. If you are unfamiliar with a word before or after the semicolon, pay close attention to the information on the other side of the semicolon. It can often help you guess the meaning of the unfamiliar word. Look at the example:

> Bullying is not affected by a family's **economic** situation; bullies come from both rich and poor **backgrounds**.

The information on the right side of the semicolon tells us that bullies can be rich or poor. This indicates that the target word **economic** is related to money. The information on the left side of the semicolon talks about the family's situation. This indicates that the target word **background** is related to a type of family situation.

A. Read the sentences, and circle the best answer.

1. That is because not all bullying is **physical**; often, it is emotional.
   A **physical** interaction with someone involves

   a. talking
   b. touching

2. In addition, often victims are not physically strong; this makes it easier for bullies to **pick on** them.
   When you **pick on** someone, you

   a. choose them to help you.
   b. do something bad to them.

3. Victims of bullies tend to be **anxious**; they get nervous very easily.
   Someone who is **anxious**

   a. finds it difficult to relax.
   b. finds it easy to be a victim.

B. Look at the target words. Which ones are new to you? Circle them here and in the reading. The numbers in parentheses help you find the words in the paragraphs.

Target Words

bullies (title)	physical (2)	victims (4)	insults (6)
aggression (2)	conducted (2)	based on (4)	humiliation (6)
anxiety (3)	self-esteem (3)	attitude (4)	harmful (6)
intentional (2)	economic (3)	surveys (4)	examine (7)
violent (2)	backgrounds (3)	pick on (4)	data (7)

C. Read "School Bullies" again. Look at the contexts of the new words. Can you guess their meanings?

D. Complete the word form chart. Fill in the shaded areas of the chart with the target words from the reading. Write the base form of the verbs and the singular form of the nouns.

NOUNS	VERBS	ADJECTIVES
bully		

Understanding the Target Vocabulary

These sentences are **about the reading**. Complete them with the words in the box. Circle the words in the sentences that help you understand the meanings of the target words.

aggression	data	insult	self-esteem
attitude	economic	intentional	survey
based on	examines	physical	violent
conducted	humiliation	pick on	

1. Dr. Olweus is an expert on bullying. His conclusions about bullying are

   _____ many years of experience.

2. Dr. Olweus has _____ a lot of research on the topic. He collects

   _____ from many different countries and _____ it; he

   looks at the information carefully to find patterns.

3. Forty-four percent of students in the United Kingdom who answered a

   _____ on bullying reported that they had been victims.

4. Bullies are just as likely to come from rich families as from poor families. Bullying is not related to the bully's _____ background.

5. Bullying always involves _____ of some kind, but it is not always _____. It can also be emotional.

6. Another characteristic of bullying is that it must be _____; that is, the bully knows what he is doing, and wants to do it.

7. Bullies often _____ children who are not very strong.

8. Using an _____, such as calling someone a bad name, is one type of verbal bullying.

9. The purpose of calling someone bad names is _____; the victim feels ashamed.

10. Bullies are often very confident. They have high _____.

11. The bully's _____ toward his victim is threatening; he considers his victim weak and wants his victim to feel scared.

12. Typically, victims are not at all _____; that is why they don't usually fight back when they are attacked by a bully.

DEVELOPING READING SKILLS

Understanding Main Ideas and Major Points

Answer the questions.

1. What is "School Bullies" about? Write one or two sentences that give the main idea.

_____

_____

2. Which types of bullying involve direct, face-to-face interaction between the bully and the victim? Which types of bullying do not involve face-to-face interactions?

_____

_____

Semicolons and Relationships between Ideas

As you learned in the Guessing Strategy of this chapter, the information that follows a semicolon is an explanation of the sentence before the semicolon. There are different types of explanations. One type of explanation involves cause and effect. Sometimes, the sentence on one side of the semicolon expresses a reason or cause, and the other sentence gives the effect or result.

Result   Reason

They are often popular among their peers; they do not have low self-esteem or anxiety.

In this example, the sentence after the semicolon explains *why* bullies are often popular: because they do not have low self-esteem or anxiety. In other words, they are confident, and confident people are often more popular than those without confidence.

Read the sentences from the reading and answer the questions.

1. Often they are not physically strong; this makes it easier for bullies to pick on them.

   Why is it easy for bullies to pick on victims?

   _____

   _____

   _____

2. This means that the victim has no safe place; the cyber bully can always find him or her.

   Why does a victim of cyber bullying never feel safe?

   _____

   _____

   _____

3. This is probably because cyber bullying is indirect and anonymous; it is easier to hurt someone who you do not see, and who does not see you.

   Cyber bullying is indirect and anonymous. Why has this led to an increasing number of bullies?

   _____

   _____

   _____

BUILDING ON THE VOCABULARY

Using the Target Vocabulary in New Contexts

A. Complete the sentences with the target words in the box. Be careful. There are two extra words.

aggression	based on	economic	self-esteem
anxiety	bullies	examine	survey
attitude	conduct	harmful	victims
background	data	humiliation	

1. My daughter really doesn't like to read. Her _____ toward her literature class is terrible. She complains about it all the time.

2. When we finish the experiment, we will _____ the results and then write up a report.

3. My husband lost his job _____ just one customer complaint. I think that is very unjust.

4. Despite the town's serious _____ problems, the people voted to buy new computers for the schools.

5. I can't concentrate on my work because I have so much _____ about my math test.

6. We don't have enough _____ on the causes of depression. We need to conduct more research.

7. The school is trying to find out why there are so many absences among students in the third grade. They have asked the parents of all third graders to complete a _____.

8. People with a strong educational _____ often have a higher social position than people with less education.

9. My son never thinks he does anything right. His teachers say that he doesn't have much _____.

10. To test their theories, scientists often _____ experiments.

11. Many animals react with _____; they will attack when they feel threatened.

12. Looking at a computer screen all day can be _____ to your eyes.

13. One of the jobs of the police is to help _____ of crime.

Expanding Vocabulary

Word Families: Using a Dictionary

A dictionary usually includes all forms of a word in the same word family. When you look in the dictionary for one member of the word family, look above and below the dictionary entry. Depending on spelling, entries for related words should be close by. In some dictionaries, all forms of a word will be listed at the end of the dictionary entry.

B. Complete the shaded parts of the chart with the correct forms of the words. Check the answers in your dictionary. There may be more than one word for some word forms.

NOUNS	VERBS	ADJECTIVES
aggression		
anxiety		
		economic
humiliation		
victim		
		violent

> **Vocabulary Tip:** Learn to recognize "words inside of words." For example, look at the word *anxious*. What word from this chapter is it similar to?

C. Work with a partner and complete the words with the correct form from the chart. Then answer the questions.

1. What should parents do if they have an **aggress**_____ child?

2. What kinds of things make you feel **anxi**_____?

3. If you had to **econom**_____, what things would you stop spending money on?

4. Whom should you survey if you want to find out about how well the

   econom_____ is doing?

5. How do bullies choose a person to **victi**_____?

6. Do women and men react differently when they are **humiliat**_____?

7. Why do some teenagers become **violen**_____?

Word Grammar: Collocations with Verb + Noun

Certain nouns are used with certain verbs. Look at the sentence.

*Dr. Olweus **conducted a survey** on school bullies.*

The noun *survey* is often used with the verb *conduct*. Other nouns that are often used with *conduct* are *research* and *experiment*. When *conduct* is used with these nouns, it means "do," and it follows this pattern:

conduct	a survey / research / an experiment	on	(something)

D. Work with a partner and answer the questions. Make sure you use the correct form of the **boldfaced** words.

1. Do you think that it's morally wrong for scientists to **conduct experiments on** laboratory animals? Why or why not?

2. If you could **conduct a survey on** the lives of gifted children, what questions would you ask?

3. What are some of the things that doctors and scientists are **conducting research on** today?

CRITICAL THINKING

A. Discussion

Share your ideas in a small group. As you talk, try to use the vocabulary below. Each time someone uses a target word, put a check (✓) next to it.

☐ aggression/aggressive/aggressor
☐ attitude
☐ background
☐ based on
☐ bully
☐ harmful
☐ humiliation/humiliate/humiliated/humiliating
☐ pick on
☐ self-esteem
☐ victim/victimize
☐ violence/violent

1. Was any of the information about the characteristics, personalities, or backgrounds of bullies in paragraphs 2, 3, 4, and 10 new or surprising to you? Which information?

2. In paragraph 3, Dr. Olweus is quoted as saying, "Too little love and care in childhood and too much freedom are conditions that strongly contribute to the development of bullies." How do you think these particular conditions make it more likely that someone will become a bully?

3. In paragraphs 6 and 7, the writer talks about girls as victims of bullying. What kinds of bullying does the writer describe? How does this bullying affect girls?

Critical Thinking Tip: When you read, think about what you already know in the reading and what is new to you. Highlight the new information.

What explanations does the writer give for this behavior and its consequences? Do you agree? Does this fit with your own personal experience and knowledge of the topic?

Critical Thinking Tip: Before forming an opinion on a topic, learn about it from several different sources. Your personal experience is just one source. Learn more about a topic by discussing it with people whose backgrounds and experience are different from yours.

4. In paragraph 9, when describing cyber bullying the writer says, "This means that the victim has no safe place; the cyber bully can always find him or her." What does the writer mean?

5. Imagine that you are a parent. Based on what you have learned about bullies and victims from the reading and this discussion, how will you prevent your child from becoming a victim or a bully?

B. Writing

Complete one or both of these writing topics. When you write, use at least five of the target words from the chapter. Underline the target words in your paper.

1. Design a survey to find out about the challenges faced by teenagers in the country where you are living. Your survey should include at least five questions, and at least five target words from this chapter. When you have finished writing your survey, have your teacher check it. Then, conduct the survey on the other members of your class, or peers from other classes. Finally, write a report on your group survey project. Your report should include:

   - What you were trying to find out
   - Who participated
   - How many people participated
   - The results
   - Interesting patterns in the results
   - What you think about the results

2. Write a story about a school bully. It can be a true story, or you can use your imagination. Try to make the story "come alive" for your reader by using specific descriptive vocabulary rather than general words. For example, when explaining how someone felt, you can say "She felt humiliated," rather than "She felt bad."

   Tell the story from the point of view of one or more of the following people:

   - The bully
   - The bully's friend
   - The bully's parents
   - The victim
   - The victim's friend
   - The victim's parents
   - A teacher

Writing Tip: When writing a story, think carefully about point of view. The same events will sound very different depending on who tells the story.

Checkpoint

LEARNING OUTCOME

❯ Review and expand on the content of Unit 2

LOOK BACK

A. Think About This

Think again about the topics you checked in the *Think About This* exercise on page 43. Which topics did you actually read about in the unit? Check (✓) them.

- ☐ diseases that affect both the young and the old
- ☐ young people with remarkable talent
- ☐ how children's personalities change as they become teenagers
- ☐ how much easier it is to be a teenager today than in the past
- ☐ challenges that young people face in school

Do you want to add any other "challenges of youth" you discovered in Unit 2?

_____

B. Remember the Readings

What do you want to remember most from the readings in Unit 2? For each chapter, write one sentence about the reading.

Chapter 4: Sleepy Teens

_____

Chapter 5: Growing Up Gifted

_____

Chapter 6: School Bullies

_____

Read the text. Do not use a dictionary.

The Teenage Brain

1   After conducting much research, scientists now have definite proof of what parents have known for centuries: Teenagers are different from everyone else. And the differences go much deeper than simple behavior. In fact, the brains of teenagers are very different from those of children or adults.

2   Until recently, scientists believed that the human brain was fully developed by the age of three. According to this theory, the teen behaviors that most concern parents—risk-taking, a lack of sensitivity to how their actions affect both themselves and others, increased aggression, reduced concentration, a negative attitude—were thought to be due to bad parenting or changes in body chemistry. However, new technology has allowed researchers to examine the healthy brain at work, and what they have discovered might surprise you. Not only does the brain continue to grow past the age of three, but the brain of a teenager is larger than that of an adult.

3   As teen brains are flooded with chemicals during adolescence,[1] the brain grows. However, at the same time, the cells of the brain that are used more compete with those that are used less. Only the cells[2] and the connections between the cells that are used the most will survive the competition. Those that are used less begin to die off until the brain reaches what will be its adult size.

4   The way that teens spend their time influences which connections remain, and which disappear. Based on this knowledge, experts advise parents to be sensitive to how their teenagers spend their time. What teens do today will affect their brains for the rest of their lives.

[1] *adolescence* = the period of time, from about 13 to 17 years of age, when a young person is developing into an adult

[2] *a cell* = the smallest part of an animal or plant that can exist on its own

Quick Comprehension Check

A. Read these sentences **about the reading**. Circle T (true), F (false), or ? (can't determine the answer from the reading). If you circle T or F, write the number of the paragraph with the answer on the line.

1. Scientists now know that the human brain continues to develop for years after we are born.   T   F   ?   _____

2. The brain of a three-year-old is larger than the brain of a teenager.   T   F   ?   _____

3. People with big brains are smarter than people with smaller brains.   T   F   ?   _____

4. If a teenager uses a particular part of the brain too much, the brain cells in that area will die off.   T   F   ?   _____

5. Teen behavior has an important effect on the physical development of the brain.   T   F   ?   _____

B. Go back to the reading to find the reason why a sentence is true or false. Correct the false sentences.

Guessing Meaning from Context

Answer this question.

What is the meaning of *flooded with* in the first line of paragraph 3?

_____

Understanding Main Ideas

Answer this question.

What is the main idea of the reading?

_____

Understanding Inference

Read these sentences. Then, check (✓) the sentences you can infer from the text. The numbers in parentheses are the paragraphs that the sentences come from.

1. Scientists now have definite proof of what parents have known for centuries: Teenagers are different from everyone else. (1)

   ☐ a. Until recently, scientists did not know exactly why teenagers behave the way that they do.

   ☐ b. A long time ago, parents proved that teenagers are different from everyone else.

2. Until recently, scientists believed that the human brain was fully developed by the age of three. (2)

   ☐ a. There is new scientific information to suggest that the human brain continues to grow past the age of three.

   ☐ b. Scientists used to believe that humans are more intelligent at the age of three than at any other time in their lives.

3. Based on this knowledge, experts advise parents to be sensitive to how their teenagers spend their time. What teens do today will affect their brains for the rest of their lives. (4)

   ☐ a. Experts think that if parents are more sensitive to what teenagers need, teenagers will behave better, and their brains will be healthier.

   ☐ b. Experts think that parents should help their teenagers to develop healthy ways of spending their time so that their brains will be healthier.

EXPANDING VOCABULARY

Read the following sentences, and write definitions of the **boldfaced** words.

1. She is an excellent student, but she is never satisfied with her grades. She is an **overachiever**.

   Overachievers are people who *put a lot of pressure on themselves to perform*

   well, and are very unhappy if they don't achieve everything they want to.

2. He's very clever, but he is lazy. He could be successful if he tried a little harder. He is an **underachiever**.

   Underachievers are people who _____

   _____.

3. Artists try to communicate their ideas and feelings through their art. **Self-expression** is very important to them.

   Self-expression is the act of _____

   _____.

A. Read these sentences, and pay attention to whether the **boldfaced** phrasal verb takes an object or doesn't take an object. Write *O* (object) or *NO* (no object).

   1. _____ He went to college, but he **dropped out** after just one year.

   2. _____ Stop **picking on** your little brother.

   3. _____ How late did you **stay up** last night?

B. Write answers to these questions. Use the **boldfaced** phrasal verbs in your answers.

1. What are some of the reasons that teenagers **drop out** of high school?

    _____

2. Has anyone ever **picked on** you? Who?

    _____

3. How late do you usually **stay up**?

    _____

Word Families: The Suffix -ize

The suffix -ize shows that a word is a verb. Here are some verbs that end in -ize. (The words in parentheses are target words that are in the same word family.)

criticize (critical)	pressurize (pressure)	victimize (victim)
economize (economic)	publicize (publish)	

Complete these sentences with the verbs.

1. Don't let that bully _____ you! Protect yourself!

2. My husband lost his job, so we really have to _____.

3. I don't like to _____ my problems. I prefer to keep them private.

4. You shouldn't _____ your teacher. She is only trying to help you.

5. Before engineers figured out how to _____ the inside of airplanes,

   flying at very high altitudes was not possible.

PLAYING WITH WORDS

There are 12 target words from Unit 2 in this puzzle. The words go across (→) and down (↓). Find the words and circle them. Then use them to complete the sentences below.

```
R  E  B  A  C  K  G  R  O  U  N  D  S  A
D  M  P  O  R  D  E  S  P  I  T  E  M  A
Q  W  E  T  L  I  O  L  J  P  O  N  R  B
U  C  R  E  P  A  T  T  E  R  N  D  O  S
G  I  F  K  Z  H  V  C  D  K  S  Q  T  E
J  F  E  A  G  G  R  E  S  S  I  O  N  N
G  H  C  O  T  S  B  F  R  P  J  R  I  C
I  V  T  F  S  U  R  V  I  V  E  B  Y  E
F  L  I  F  C  E  L  T  R  O  P  L  E  S
T  W  O  I  M  D  I  N  V  H  A  A  D  N
E  G  N  C  C  U  K  Y  L  Z  F  C  A  U
D  B  I  I  N  L  E  W  X  P  J  K  T  W
A  X  S  A  O  Y  L  T  A  G  L  I  A  O
F  M  T  L  X  S  Y  A  M  B  A  L  L  Y
```

1. He was a high-school dropout. He does not have a strong educational _____.

2. The researcher's _____ prove that his theory is correct.

3. Children whose parents are depressed are more _____ to become depressed themselves.

4. Some people think that the rise in physical _____ in the schools is due to the violence that children see on television.

5. Why do you have so many _____? Have you been sick?

6. She's a _____. She always wants to do everything exactly right. She hates making mistakes.

7. He did poorly on the test due to his _____ of knowledge.

8. If you don't study, you will never _____ at that university.

9. I would like to find curtains that match the _____ on the sofa.

10. He is a government _____, so he cannot be too critical of the government.

11. They went to the beach _____ the bad weather.

12. She has won several piano competitions. She is very _____.

BUILDING DICTIONARY SKILLS

Finding the Correct Meaning

Many words have more than one meaning. Look at the dictionary entries below. Read each sentence and write the number of the meaning.

---

sur·vive /səˈvaɪv/ v [I,T] **1** to continue to live after an accident, illness, etc.: *Only one person survived the crash.* **2** to continue to live normally or exist in spite of difficulties: *Few small businesses survived the recession.* | *How do you manage to* **survive on** *such a low salary?* | *It's been a tough few months, but* **I'll survive**. **3** to continue to exist after a long time: *Only a few Greek Plays have survived.*

---

1. a. _____ Only three people **survived** the airplane crash.

   b. _____ There is a lot of competition in the food business these days. It isn't easy for new restaurants to **survive**.

---

pres·sure¹ /ˈprɛʃə/ n **1** [U] an attempt to make someone do something by using influence, arguments, threats, etc.: *Kay's family is* **putting pressure** *on her to get married.* | *The company is* **under pressure** *to reduce costs.* | *The president faces* **pressure from** *militants in his own party.* **2** [C,U] the conditions of your work, family, or way of living that makes you anxious, and cause problems: *I've been* **under** *a lot of* **pressure** *at work lately.* | *There is a lot of* **pressure on** *children these days.* | *The* **pressures of** *modern life* **3** [C,U] the force that a gas or liquid has when it is pushed and held inside a container: *The air pressure in the tires might be low.* **4** [U] the force produced by pressing on someone or something: *The* **pressure of** *his hand on her shoulder.*

---

2. a. _____ She's having a hard time. The **pressure** of work, school, and family is too much for her.

   b. _____ There is a lot of **pressure** on him to accept the job.

   c. _____ Did you check the tire **pressure**? Do we need to add air?

---

back·ground /ˈbækɡraʊnd/ n **1** [C] someone's education, family, and experience: *kids from very different* **ethnic/religious/cultural backgrounds** | *Steve* **has a background in** *computer engineering.* | *The position would suit someone* **with a background in** *real estate.* **2** [C usually singular] the area that is behind the main things that you are looking at, especially in a picture or photograph: *Palm trees swayed* **in the background**. **3 in the background** someone who keeps or stays in the background, tries not to be noticed: *The president's wife preferred to stay* **in the background**. **4** [singular] sounds that are in the background are not the main ones that you can hear: *I could hear cars honking* **in the background**.

---

3. a. _____ We didn't give her the job because she doesn't have the educational **background** we are looking for.

   b. _____ When I was talking to my friend on the phone, I could hear her son crying in the **background**.

   c. _____ What's that in the **background**? Is it a person, or a tree?

THE SCIENCE OF WHO WE ARE

THINK ABOUT THIS

Look at the picture and read the title of the unit. How much do you know about the following topics? Rank your answers.

1 = I know a lot　2 = I know some things　3 = I know a little　4 = I don't know anything

_____ 1. DNA

_____ 2. the discoveries of Gregor Mendel

_____ 3. genetic engineering and gene therapy

_____ 4. genetic testing

_____ 5. genetic diseases

CHAPTER 7

The Science of Genetics

Gregor Mendel

LEARNING OUTCOME

❯ Learn basic information about the science of genetics

GETTING READY TO READ

Complete the chart with the names of family members who are similar to you in appearance or personality. Then share your answers in a small group.

HOW I AM SIMILAR TO PEOPLE IN MY FAMILY	
Characteristic	**Family member's name and relationship to me**
Face (for example, eyes, nose, mouth, shape)	
Body size and shape (for example, height and weight)	
Character (for example, shy, funny)	
Other?	

READING

Read the definitions beside the reading. Then read "The Science of Genetics." If you see a new word, circle it, but don't stop reading. You can learn the new word later.

The Science of Genetics

1 Who are we? Where did we come from? How are we related to each other and to other living things? The written record of the search for the answers to these questions goes back at least 2,500 years. At that time, Pythagoras, the famous Greek mathematician,[1] believed that children got all of their physical **traits** from their fathers. Later, Aristotle, the Greek philosopher,[2] **realized** that children **inherit** characteristics from both of their parents. However, he incorrectly believed that a child was the direct product of the mixing of the mother's and father's blood.

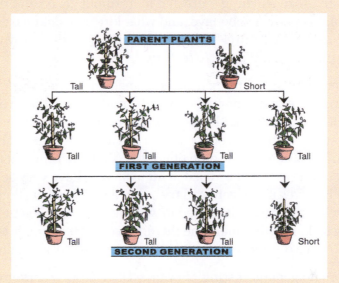

Gregor Mendel's pea plant experiment

2 Modern genetics (the science that helps us to understand how and why we get traits from our parents) was not born until the nineteenth century. The father of modern genetics was Gregor Mendel, an Austrian scientist. Through eight years of experiments on pea[3] plants, Mendel proved that characteristics from the "mother" plant and characteristics from the "father" plant are not mixed together when the two plants cross-pollinate[4] and produce the next **generation** of plants. Rather, the characteristics that are dominant (stronger) will **come out** in the first generation. The characteristics that are recessive (weaker) will only appear in the second generation.

3 For example, if you take a very short pea plant and cross-pollinate it with a very tall pea plant, you might expect the new pea plant to be of average height. But in fact, the first generation of plants will all be very tall, because that characteristic is dominant. Short plants will not appear until the second generation, because that characteristic is recessive.

4 The theories that Mendel developed using plants were later applied to all living things, including human beings. Future research that would explain how parents pass traits on[5] to their children through their **genes** grew out of Mendel's work.

[1] *a mathematician* = someone who studies or teaches mathematics

[2] *a philosopher* = someone who teaches about life and what it means, and how we should live

[3] *a pea* = a small round green seed that is cooked and eaten as a vegetable

[4] *cross-pollinate* = transfer pollen (a powder produced by plants) from one plant to another

[5] *pass traits on* = give someone or something a particular trait

5   What is a gene? Explained very simply, a gene is a set of **instructions** that you get from your parents before you are born. Your genes are similar to an instruction book for a computer. When you open the book, you see a list of all of the parts of the computer. Then, you see instructions telling you how to make the computer work. Your genes, like the instruction book, contain a complete list of all of the parts that make a human being. They also contain instructions on how to put the parts together to make one special **individual**—you.

6   Today, scientists are learning more and more about genes and their effect on what we look like, how we behave, and what kinds of sicknesses we have or are likely to get in the future. They are using this information in two areas: *genetic engineering* and *genetic testing*.

7   Through genetic engineering, scientists change how genes work. They sometimes **replace** one gene in a **cell** with another gene that works better in some way. Because all living things (not only humans) have genes, scientists use genetic engineering to produce plants and animals that are healthy, grow rapidly, or are useful to us in some other way. Gene therapy is a type of genetic engineering that is sometimes used in humans who have very serious health problems. It involves using genes to try to **cure** an **illness** in someone who is already sick, or to **prevent** someone with the genes for a genetic **disease** from getting sick. At this time, gene therapy is experimental. It is only used on patients who have diseases that cannot be treated or cured in any other way.

8   When doctors do genetic testing, they take DNA[6] from a person (or other living thing) and examine it carefully. One important use of genetic testing in humans is to discover if someone has or might get a genetic illness. Then the doctors might put him or her in a scientific study and use gene therapy to treat or prevent the disease. Genetic testing can also be used to **determine** the **gender** of a fetus,[7] although doctors often use other, simpler techniques to get this information.

9   If experimental gene therapy is successful, some day genetic testing and engineering might be used to allow parents to choose **desirable** traits or **get rid of** undesirable ones before their child is even born.

[6] *DNA* = deoxyribonucleic acid, an acid that carries genetic information in a cell

[7] *fetus* = a young human or animal before birth

Quick Comprehension Check

A. Read these sentences **about the reading**. Circle T (true), F (false), or ? (can't determine the answer from the reading). If you circle T or F, write the number of the paragraph with the answer on the line.

1. Around 2,500 years ago, most people already knew that we get characteristics from both our mother and father.   T   F   ? _____

2. The study of how and why certain characteristics are passed from one generation to the next is called genetics.   T   F   ? _____

3. People look different from one another because they have different genes.   T   F   ? _____

4. Genes do not have an effect on behavior.   T   F   ? _____

Reading Tip: The way that you read depends on your purpose. When you are reading for a class, highlight new information or anything that is difficult to remember. That will make it easier to find when you need to review it.

5. Genetic engineering is used on plants and animals. T F ? ____

6. In some cases, doctors use genetic engineering to find out if someone is sick. T F ? ____

7. Today, parents can use genetic engineering to change a child's sex before the child is born. T F ? ____

8. Some people do not think that genetic engineering should be used on humans. T F ? ____

B. Work with your class. Share your answers from part A. Go back to the reading to find the reason why a sentence is true or false. Correct the false sentences.

EXPLORING VOCABULARY

Thinking about the Target Vocabulary

Guessing Strategy: In-text Definitions

When writers use technical terms or introduce people important in a particular field, you might not need to guess the term's meaning or find out who the person is. Often, the terms are defined in the text itself, and the people are identified by the information that follows their names. The definitions and information are either in parentheses or between commas directly after the terms or names. Look at the examples.

*Rather, the characteristics that are **dominant** (**stronger**) will come out in the first generation. The characteristics that are **recessive** (**weaker**) will only appear in the second generation.*

*At that time, **Pythagoras, the famous Greek mathematician**, believed that children got all of their physical traits from their fathers.*

Pay attention to words or phrases in parentheses and between commas. They often contain definitions or important information.

A. Read the sentences and answer the questions. Use the in-text definitions to help you.

1. Later Aristotle, the Greek philosopher, realized that children inherit characteristics from both of their parents.

   Who was **Aristotle**? _____

2. Modern genetics, the science that helps us to understand how and why we get traits from our parents, was not born until the nineteenth century.

   What is **modern genetics**? _____

   _____

3. Many scientists are doing research in gene therapy (using the genes of a human cell to treat serious disease).

   What is **gene therapy**? _____

   _____

B. Look at the target words. Which ones are new to you? Circle them here and in the reading. The numbers in parentheses help you find the words in the paragraphs.

Target Words

traits (1)	genes (4)	cure (7)	gender (8)
realized (1)	instructions (5)	illness (7)	desirable (9)
inherit (1)	individual (5)	prevent (7)	get rid of (9)
generation (2)	replace (7)	disease (7)	
come out (2)	cell (7)	determine (8)	

C. Read "The Science of Genetics" again. Look at the context of the new words. Can you guess their meanings?

D. Complete the word form chart. Fill in the shaded areas of the chart with the target words from the reading. Write the base form of the verbs and the singular form of the nouns.

NOUNS	VERBS	ADJECTIVES
trait		

Understanding the Target Vocabulary

A. These sentences are **about the reading**. Complete them with the words in the box. Circle the words in the sentences that help you understand the meanings of the target words.

cell	determine	illnesses	replace
come out	gender	individual	traits
cure	generation	realize	
desirable	genes		

1. A long time ago, people didn't know why children tended to look like their

   parents. They didn't _____ that characteristics are passed from

   one _____ to the next.

2. Today, we know that our _____ contain all of the information that is necessary to make a human being. They contain a list of details on how to "build" a human being.

3. One _____ is different from another because each person has his or her own genes.

4. The science of genetics (the study of how characteristics are passed from one generation to another) has shown that some _____ will appear in the first generation. Other weaker ones will not _____ until the following generation.

5. Through gene therapy, doctors are trying to help people with genetic _____ get better. They are trying to _____ them.

6. In one experimental technique, scientists remove a gene that is not working correctly from a _____ (the smallest part of a person or other living thing). Then, they _____ it with a healthy gene.

7. It is possible for scientists to use genetic testing before birth to find out a child's _____, that is, whether the child is male or female.

8. Genetic testing can also be used to _____ whether a child is likely to develop a genetic illness.

9. In the future, parents might be able to make sure that their children are born with _____ traits, such as intelligence or beauty.

B. Read the sentences and circle the words that help you understand the meanings of the bold face target words. Then circle the correct answers.

1. We get many **traits** from our parents. Eye color and height are two examples. *Traits* are

   a. gifts. b. characteristics. c. interests.

2. If a boy has a genetic **disease**, it means that his genes are not working correctly, so he has health problems. *Disease* means

   a. sickness. b. trouble. c. fever.

3. In the future, doctors hope they can **prevent** some types of sicknesses through gene therapy. If they are successful, people won't get these sicknesses. *Prevent* means

    a. begin doing something. b. stop something before it happens. c. fix completely.

4. In the future, scientists will try to **get rid of** genes that cause sickness. This would be the best solution because people would never worry about these sicknesses again. *Get rid of* means to cause something to

    a. become smaller. b. get better. c. disappear.

5. Children look like their parents because they **inherit** genes from them. *Inherit* means

    a. receive. b. require. c. get money.

DEVELOPING READING SKILLS

Scanning

Find the information about these topics in "The Science of Genetics." Scan the reading, and write the paragraph number (1–9).

_____ a. The birth of modern genetics

_____ b. The definition of a gene

_____ c. Possible future uses of genetic testing and engineering

__1__ d. Some past ideas about how humans get their traits

_____ e. What genetic engineering is used for

_____ f. What scientists are learning about genes

_____ g. What happens when you cross a small pea plant with a tall one

_____ h. How later scientists used Mendel's research

_____ i. What genetic testing is used for

Summarizing

Writing a Summary

When you **summarize** a text, you should include the main idea and the major points about the main idea. Your summary should include details only if they are necessary to clarify the major points. Always write a summary in your own words.

Write a sentence about each of the nine paragraph topics from the Scanning exercise above. Use information from the reading, but do not copy. Include only the most important information. Together, the nine sentences should summarize the reading.

Paragraph 1: *In the past, there were many different theories about why children look and act like their parents.*

Paragraph 2: _____

_____

Paragraph 3: _____

_____

Paragraph 4: _____

_____

Paragraph 5: _____

_____

Paragraph 6: _____

_____

Paragraph 7: _____

_____

Paragraph 8: _____

_____

Paragraph 9: _____

_____

BUILDING ON THE VOCABULARY

Using the Target Vocabulary in New Contexts

Complete the sentences with the target words in the box. Be careful. There are two extra words.

came out	determines	get rid of	instructions
cells	genders	illness	prevents
cured	generations	individual	realize
desirable	genes	inherits	trait

1. I don't know how to play that game. Please read the _____ to me.

2. Great news! He isn't going to die. The doctors _____ him!

3. That house is expensive because it is in a _____ location, in the best part of town.

4. Sometimes, parents and children don't understand each other because they come from different _____. The age difference can make it difficult for them to communicate.

5. The men in his family have been tennis champions for generations. The talent must be in their _____ and passed on from great-grandfather to grandfather, grandfather to father, and father to son.

6. Doctors now realize that anxiety is an _____, with real physical causes.

7. I'm sorry. I didn't _____ that I hurt you.

8. Each _____ in the class must participate in at least one experiment.

9. Everyone has two types of blood _____: red and white.

10. The mechanic will call you when he _____ the cause of the problem.

11. Everyone was surprised when the news of his marriage _____. They had kept it a secret. Nobody even knew he had a girlfriend.

12. Most schools in my country are co-educational. That is, they accept students of both _____.

13. Loyalty is the _____ that I value most in a friend.

14. Those shoes are so old. They look terrible! You need to _____ them and buy new ones.

Expanding Vocabulary

Word Families: Adjectives ending in *-able*

Some adjectives are formed by adding the suffix *-able* to the end of the verb. The meaning of the adjective is "capable of doing" or "able to do," the action of the verb. For example, *desirable* means "capable of being desired." Notice that if the verb ends in *-e*, the *-e* is dropped before adding the suffix.

A. Complete the word form chart. Write the correct form of the missing words. Check your answers in your dictionary.

NOUNS	VERBS	ADJECTIVES
		desirable
	prevent	
	cure	

Vocabulary Tip: Some suffixes change the form of the word but not the meaning. For example, the adjective *creative*, with the suffix *-ive*, is very similar in meaning to the verb *create*. Other suffixes, however, change the meaning of the word, often by adding information. *-able* is a suffix that adds meaning.

B. Complete the sentences with words from the chart. Be careful. You will not use all the words.

1. Sicknesses caused by insects are _____. If you protect yourself

   from insect bites, you won't get these sicknesses.

2. Don't worry. She's sick now, but she's not going to die from that disease. It is

   _____.

3. His _____ to become a scientist is so strong that he spends every

   minute studying and conducting experiments.

4. Scientists are working hard to find a _____ for that disease.

5. The _____ of forest fires is the responsibility of the Department of

   Fire Safety.

6. They own a _____ piece of land. Many people would like to buy it,

   but they won't sell.

C. Working with a partner, answer the questions. Make sure you use the correct form of the **boldfaced** words.

1. Sometimes your **desires** for the future do not match the **desires** of your family or other people that you love. Has this ever happened to you? If so, what did you do? If not, what do you think you would do?

2. Make a list of diseases that are **preventable**. Talk about how you can **prevent** them.

3. Which diseases are currently **incurable**? Which of those diseases do you think scientists will find a **cure** for in your lifetime?

Word Grammar: Collocations with Verb + Direct Object + Preposition

Some verbs are followed by a prepositional phrase. With some of these verbs, you need to include a direct object before the preposition. The correct preposition depends on the verb. Most dictionaries will give you the correct preposition and show you whether a direct object is necessary. Look at the examples.

- He **prevented** us **from** finding out the truth.
- The doctor **cured** her **of** her illness.
- She **inherited** a lot of money **from** her grandmother.
- I damaged her computer, but I **replaced** it **with** a new one.

Write answers to these questions. Use the **boldfaced** words in your answers.

1. If you have children, what will you try to **prevent** them **from** doing?

_____

_____

2. What would you do if you unexpectedly **inherited** $1,000,000 **from** a relative you had never met?

_____

_____

3. Write about a time when you broke or lost something that belonged to someone else and you had to replace it. What did you **replace** it **with**?

_____

_____

4. If you had the power to **cure** people **of** one disease, which disease would you choose? Explain why you chose that disease.

_____

_____

CRITICAL THINKING

A. Discussion

Share your ideas in a small group. As you talk, try to use the vocabulary below. Each time someone uses a target word, put a check (✓) next to it.

☐ come out	☐ get rid of
☐ desire/desirable/undesirable	☐ illness
☐ determine	☐ individual
☐ disease	☐ inherit
☐ gene/genetic	☐ prevent/preventable
☐ generation	☐ trait

1. Based on what you learned in the reading, as well as your own prior knowledge, decide which of the following news stories could be true. Be ready to explain your answers to the class. Refer to specific information from the reading wherever appropriate.

   • Most farmers in the United States use special seeds to grow food. The genes of these seeds have been changed. The plants that grow from them grow faster and are larger than the plants grown from regular seeds. The plants also get fewer diseases.

- Scientists are now able to take a few cells from a human heart and grow a new heart from them. This new heart can replace the heart of someone with heart disease.

- Scientists are now experimenting with growing organs inside of pigs. These organs are genetically similar to human organs. In the future, doctors hope to be able to replace the diseased organs of humans with the organs grown inside pigs.

- Scientists have discovered the gene for intelligence. Parents can now use genetic testing before their baby is born to find out whether their child is going to be intelligent or not.

- Genetically engineered skin can be grown in a lab. It is commonly used to treat burn victims.

2. Choose one of the true news stories above and talk about it in your group. Make a list of the pros and cons of this use of genetic engineering. Think carefully about the various reasons that people might be in favor of or opposed to it. Consider religious beliefs, ideas about morality, safety and health concerns, or another standard that you and your group come up with. After considering the pros and cons, give your opinion, if you feel you have enough information to do so. Explain the reasons for your opinion.

> **Critical Thinking Tip:** You might be asked for your opinion on something that you know very little about. It is acceptable to say that you have no opinion because you don't know much about the topic.

B. Writing

Complete one or both of these writing topics. When you write, use at least five of the target words from the chapter. Underline the target words in your paper.

1. Genetic testing now makes it possible for people to find out if they have a higher than average chance of getting certain genetic diseases. Write a short essay discussing the advantages and disadvantages of knowing this information, but do not take a position. Rather, just present the two sides. You can start with the following sentence: *There are both advantages and disadvantages to knowing if you have a high risk for getting a genetic disease.*

2. Write a letter to the editor giving your opinion about one of the topics raised in this unit.

> **Writing Tip:** Writing about something is often a good way to teach yourself about a topic and discover how you feel about it. Writing about the pros and cons of a topic without taking a position is a good way to deepen your understanding.

CHAPTER 8

Designing the Future

GETTING READY TO READ

Answer the questions. Then compare your answers with a partner.

1. Look at the list of adjectives. If you had a **son** and could choose only three characteristics, which would you choose and why? Put a check (✓) next to three or add your own.

   ☐ strong   ☐ thin   ☐ handsome   ☐ honest

   ☐ intelligent   ☐ funny   ☐ kind   ☐ successful

   ☐ other _____

2. Now check the three adjectives that you would choose if you had a **daughter**.

   ☐ strong   ☐ thin   ☐ beautiful   ☐ honest

   ☐ intelligent   ☐ funny   ☐ kind   ☐ successful

   ☐ other _____

READING

Read the definitions beside the reading. Then read "Designing the Future." If you see a new word, circle it, but don't stop reading. You can learn the new word later.

Designing the Future

1   A young couple has decided that it is time to have a baby. So, what is the first thing they do? They go shopping! But not for clothes or furniture. That will come later. Before anything else, they must decide whether they want a girl or a boy. Next, it is time to consider their future child's intelligence. Do they want a gifted child, or would a child with an average level of intelligence be **acceptable**? And what about personality? Do they care if their child is shy? Is kindness important to them? Finally, it is time to consider physical traits. What eye color would they prefer? What about height and weight? Do they want an **athletic** child, so that he or she can play tennis with Mom? There are so many **features** to choose from!

2   **Actually**, the situation described above does not happen today. But a recently developed technique in genetic engineering has **led** many scientists **to** believe that changing a human embryo's[1] DNA, and thus its traits, is scientifically possible. If this sounds more like science fiction[2] than science, think again. The technique is called CRISPR.[3] According to experts, using CRISPR to cut out and replace a piece of human DNA would be remarkably easy. Jennifer Doudna, a respected **biologist** and the co-developer of the technique, recently said "Any scientist with molecular biology skills and knowledge of how to work with [embryos] is going to be able to do this."

3   Already, genetic testing can be used to **identify** gender very early in the embryo's development. The genes that mark for[4] a number of genetic diseases can also be identified. Some scientists are **convinced** that they will soon find the genes for a wide variety of traits—physical **appearance**, artistic talent, a tendency toward depression—just about anything you can imagine. And if scientists know the gene or genes that control a specific trait, it is at least theoretically possible that CRISPR could be used to replace an undesirable trait with a more desirable one.

4   But just because scientists *can* do it, does it mean they *will* do it? Guoping Feng, a biologist at the Massachusetts Institute of Technology (MIT), thinks so. In the future, he hopes to use CRISPR to replace human genes that cause disease with healthy ones. He believes it will take about 10 to 20 years for the technology to be safe enough to use in humans. "It's hard to predict the future," Feng said, "but correcting disease **risks** is definitely a possibility and should be supported. I think it will be a reality."

5   Not everyone shares Feng's positive attitude, however. Doudna, the scientist who co-developed CRISPR, organized a meeting to **restrict** the use of the technique on human embryos. At the end of the meeting, Doudna and a group

[1] *an embryo* = an animal or human that has not yet been born, and has just begun to develop

[2] *science fiction* = a type of writing that describes imaginary future developments in science and their effect on life, for example traveling in time

[3] *CRISPR* = an acronym, or abbreviation, for "clustered regularly interspaced palindromic repeats"

[4] *mark for* = signal or show the presence of (something)

of experts in genetics, ethics,[5] and law called for scientists to agree not to use CRISPR to produce children with genetic changes. However, the group supports basic research using CRISPR, including experiments on embryos.

6 What do non-experts think about all of this? It is difficult to know, but a recent survey conducted in the United States found that 46% of adults approved of using genetic engineering to reduce the risk of serious diseases. However, 83% said that changes to make a baby more intelligent would not be acceptable. Of course, this is only one survey from one country. Perhaps it is more instructive to remember that **historically**, whenever the once unimaginable has become possible—cars, airplanes, and the Internet, for example—it soon becomes common. If the technology exists, how can we prevent "trait shopping" by parents who want a "perfect" baby?

7 Scientists do not agree on the morality of producing children with genetic changes, or the exact day when it will happen. But most do agree that day is **approaching**. This **brings up** very difficult social and moral questions. What are the long-term[6] health risks of introducing genetic changes that will be passed on to future generations? Will too many parents choose to have children of the same gender, leading to a **shortage** of boys or girls? What will happen to children whose parents cannot afford to give them the **advantages** enjoyed by their genetically "designed" peers? How will society treat "imperfect" children? **In short**, will changing human genes change **humanity** itself?

[5] *ethics =* moral rules or principles of behavior for deciding what is right and wrong

[6] *long-term =* continuing for a long period of time into the future

Quick Comprehension Check

A. Read these sentences **about the reading**. Circle T (true), F (false), or ? (can't determine the answer from the reading). If you circle T or F, write the number of the paragraph with the answer on the line.

1. Parents can now choose what their future children will look like. T F ? ____

2. CRISPR is a technique used to create DNA. T F ? ____

3. CRISPR is not difficult for scientists to use. T F ? ____

4. Scientists have found the genes for many inherited traits, and in the future expect to find even more. T F ? ____

5. One of the developers of CRISPR wants to limit how it is used on humans. T F ? ____

6. Even if genetic engineering makes it possible for parents to "design" their children, most parents won't use the technology. T F ? ____

7. Scientists think it is immoral to change human genes. T F ? ____

8. The use of genetic engineering to produce children with changed genes is likely to happen in the future. T F ? ____

Reading Tip: When you read something about the future, pay attention to what is true now, and what may be possible in the future. Look for words such as *possible, probably,* and the auxiliary verbs *will, be going to, may, might, could,* and *would.*

B. Work with your class. Share your answers from part A. Go back to the reading to find the reason why a sentence is true or false. Correct the false sentences.

EXPLORING VOCABULARY

Thinking about the Target Vocabulary

Guessing Strategy: Dashes

Understanding punctuation can help you understand the meaning of unfamiliar words. The **dash** (—) is a type of punctuation. Writers use dashes to focus the reader's attention on important information. Often, writers put examples between two dashes. Look at the example.

*Some scientists are convinced that they will soon find the genes for a wide variety of traits— physical **appearance**, artistic talent, a tendency toward depression—just about anything you can imagine.*

In this case, the word before the dash is *traits*. The words after the dash are specific examples. Although you may not understand the exact meaning of all the words in the examples, you can guess the general meaning from the context. For example, you can guess from the context that the target word *appearance* is an example of a trait.

A. Read the sentences with the dashes. Then complete the following sentence(s) about the **boldfaced** target word.

1. Changing human genes brings up serious social issues—health risks in future generations, a possible **shortage** of boys or girls, the negative effects on "imperfect" children—so many people worry about using it.

   A possible **shortage** of boys or girls is an example of _____. The definition of **shortage** might be _____.

2. In the future, a child's **appearance**—height, weight, eye and hair color—might be determined before birth.

   Some examples of **appearance** are _____. The definition of **appearance** might be _____.

3. **Advantages** that rich parents might be able give their children—above-average intelligence, physical beauty, no danger of genetic diseases—will not be available to those who cannot afford them.

   Some examples of **advantages** are _____. The definition of **advantage** might be _____.

4. Some scientists believe that the **risks** of using CRISPR on human beings—possible damage to the genes, health problems, genetic changes in future generations—make it immoral to use the technique.

   Some examples of **risks** are _____. The definition of **risk** might be _____.

B. Look up the definitions of the target words in exercise A in your dictionary. Are they similar to your definitions?

C. Look at the target words. Which ones are new to you? Circle them here and in the reading. The numbers in parentheses help you find the words in the paragraphs.

Target Words

acceptable (1)	led to (2)	restrict (5)	shortage (7)
athletic (1)	identify (3)	historically (6)	advantages (7)
features (1)	convinced (3)	approaching (7)	in short (7)
actually (2)	appearance (3)	brings up (7)	humanity (7)
biologist (2)	risks (4)		

D. Complete the word form chart. Fill in the shaded areas of the chart with the target words from the reading. Write the base form of the verbs and the singular form of the nouns.

NOUNS	VERBS	ADJECTIVES	OTHER
		acceptable	

Understanding the Target Vocabulary

These sentences are **about the reading**. Complete them with the words in the box. Circle the words in the sentences that help you understand the meanings of the target words.

acceptable	biologist	historically	lead to
actually	brings up	humanity	restrict
approaching	convinced	identified	
athletic	features		

1. _____ , people with genetic diseases often chose not to have children. They did not want to pass their genes on to the next generation. In the future, that could change.

2. Scientists have already _____ the genes for a number of genetic diseases.

3. According to _____ Guoping Feng, the day is _____ when it will be possible to get rid of genetic diseases. Other scientists, however, think it will never happen.

4. It might seem incredible, but in the future, parents might _____ be able to "design" their children before they are born. This would make it possible for parents to choose the traits they want, similar to the way they choose the _____ of a new car.

5. For some parents, physical traits are important. They like to play sports, so they would like to determine their children's _____ ability.

6. People are starting to ask some very difficult questions about genetic engineering. Genetic engineering _____ some complex questions.

7. Some people worry that genetic engineering could have a negative effect on all of _____. In fact, they think it might change what it means to be human.

8. Other people think that there is nothing wrong with using genetic engineering on humans. They think that this use of technology is _____.

9. The biologist Guoping Feng is _____ that using CRISPR on human embryos is a good thing. Other scientists are not so sure. They want to _____ the use of CRISPR to curing disease.

10. A serious concern is that genetic engineering will _____ social problems. For example, what will happen if only the rich can afford to design their children?

DEVELOPING READING SKILLS

Making Inferences

Read these sentences from "Designing the Future." Then, read the two sentences that follow. Put a check (✓) next to the sentence that is a reasonable inference. The numbers in parentheses are the paragraphs where you can find the sentences.

1. Do they want an athletic child, so that he or she can play tennis with Mom? (1)
   - [ ] a. Mom is a tennis player.
   - [ ] b. Mom doesn't have anyone to play tennis with.

2. If this sounds more like science fiction than science, think again. (2)

   ☐ a. The article is based on real scientific information.

   ☐ b. You should not read science fiction.

3. Doudna, the scientist who co-developed CRISPR, organized a meeting to restrict the use of the technique on human embryos. (5)

   ☐ a. Doudna is concerned about how the technique will be used.

   ☐ b. Doudna wants other people to stop using the technique.

4. Of course this is only one survey from one country. (6)

   ☐ a. Only one country has done a survey on this issue.

   ☐ b. We need more data on this issue.

Summarizing

Complete this summary of "Designing the Future." Write as much as you can without looking back at the reading. Then, compare your summary with a classmate's. If there are any differences, decide whose summary is more accurate. Finally, go back to the reading to check your summary and to add any missing information.

> **Writing Tip:**
> Writing a summary from memory is a good way to check your understanding of a reading. It also prevents copying from the reading.

Because of a _____ engineering _____ called CRISPR, many scientists believe that in the future, parents will be able to _____.

Already, scientists use genetic testing to _____. They have also identified _____.

Some scientists are in favor of _____. Other scientists are worried about _____.

In one survey, 46% of non-experts said that _____, while 83% said that _____.

Despite the opinions of many scientists and non-experts, in the future it will probably be possible _____.

The use of genetic engineering to "design" children leads to some difficult moral questions. The most important question is, will using genetic engineering on human beings _____?

BUILDING ON THE VOCABULARY

Using the Target Vocabulary in New Contexts

Complete the sentences with the target words in the box. Be careful. There are two extra words.

acceptable	athletic	historically	lead to
advantages	biologist	humanity	restricted
appearance	bring up	identify	risks
approach	convinced	in short	shortage

1. He can't throw a ball or run fast. He isn't very _____.

2. I had a lot of homework to do, but my sister _____ me to go to the movies with her.

3. The work of Austrian scientist Gregor Mendel, the father of genetics, is important for all of _____. Even today, Mendel's discoveries continue to help people.

4. You look different. Your new haircut really changes your _____.

5. Travel to that region is _____. You can only go there if you get permission from the government.

6. Bad eating habits can _____ illness and other physical problems.

7. I'm sorry, but this paper is not _____. It is very messy and has many errors. You are going to have to write it again.

8. The police published the criminal's picture in the newspaper and posted it on websites. They hope that someone will be able to _____ him.

9. There are many _____ to having a good education. For example, people who are well-educated usually earn more money than people with less education.

10. He is attractive, intelligent, and successful. _____, he's the perfect man for you!

11. It hasn't rained in almost a year. There is a water _____.

12. Slow down as we _____ the traffic light. My house is on the corner, just after the light.

13. I don't like to ski or ride horses because I don't like to take _____ . I prefer safer sports such as tennis.

14. You should _____ your concerns in class. Your teacher will help you.

Expanding Vocabulary

Word Families: Adjectives ending in -ous

The adjective ending -ous means "full of." Therefore, the adjective *advantageous* means "full of advantages." The addition of certain suffixes, including -ous, can change the syllable stress on a word. You can look in your dictionary to find out which syllable is stressed. In most dictionaries, the symbol ' is placed at the beginning of the stressed syllable.

A. Look at the pronunciation guides for the following words. Answer the questions.

ad·van·tage /əd'væntɪdʒ/ *n* **1** [C,U] something that helps you to be better or more successful than others [≠ **disadvantage**]: *Her computer skills gave her an* **advantage over** *the other applicants.* | *He turns every situation to his* **advantage**. **2 take advantage of sth** to use a situation or thing to help you do or get something you want: *He* **took advantage of** *the* **opportunity** *given to him.* **3** [C] a good or useful quality that something has: *Good restaurants are one of the many* **advantages of** *living in a big city* **4 take advantage of sb** to treat someone unfairly or to control a particular situation in order to get what you want

ad·van·ta·geous /ˌædvæn'teɪdʒəs, -vən-/ *adj* helpful and likely to make you more successful [≠ **disadvantageous**]

> **Vocabulary Tip:** An English/English dictionary is very helpful when you learn new words. In addition to definitions, there is usually information about grammar, usage, and pronunciation.

1. a. How many syllables are in the noun **advantage**? _____

   Which syllable is stressed? _____

   b. How many syllables are in the adjective **advantageous**? _____

   Which syllable is stressed? _____

anx·i·e·ty /æŋ'zaɪəti/ *n* [U] a strong feeling of worry about something: *a lifestyle that creates stress and anxiety* | *workers'* **anxiety about** *being fired*
anx·ious /'æŋkʃəs, 'æŋʃəs/ *adj* **1** very worried about something or showing that you are worried: *June is* **anxious about** *the results of her blood test* | *an anxious look*

2. a. How many syllables are in the noun **anxiety**? _____

   Which syllable is stressed? _____

   b. How many syllables are in the adjective **anxious**? _____

   Which syllable is stressed? _____

> **mys·te·ri·ous** /mɪˈstɪriəs/ *adj*. **1** strange and difficult to explain or understand: *the mysterious disappearance of our neighbor* **2** not saying much about something because you want it to be a secret: *Oliver is being very **mysterious about** his plans.*
>
> **mys·ter·y** /ˈmɪstəri/ *n* (plural **mysteries**) **1** [C] something that is difficult to explain or understand: *The location of the stolen money **remains a mystery**.* | *It won't be easy to **solve the mystery**.* **2** [C] a story, especially about a murder, in which events are not explained until the end: *the Sherlock Holmes mystery stories* **3** [U] a quality that makes someone or something seem strange, interesting, and difficult to explain or understand: *There's an **air of mystery** about him that intrigues people.*

3. a. How many syllables are in the noun **mystery**? _____

    Which syllable is stressed? _____

   b. How many syllables are in the adjective **mysterious**? _____

    Which syllable is stressed? _____

B. Talk with a partner. Answer the questions. Use the **boldfaced** words in your answers. Make sure you stress the correct syllable.

1. When you feel **anxious**, what do you do to relax?

2. In life, which is more **advantageous**—physical beauty or intelligence? Why?

3. Which field of science is the most **mysterious** to you? Why do you feel it is a **mystery**?

Word Grammar: Adverbs

Adverbs modify verbs, adjectives, other adverbs, or entire sentences. Many adverbs are formed by adding *-ly* to the end of the adjective form of the word. Adverbs are placed close to the words they modify. Look at the examples.

Examples	Explanations
They waited anxiously for the doctor's call.	The adverb *anxiously* modifies the verb *waited*.
She is a remarkably good cook.	The adverb *remarkably* modifies the adjective *good*.
She spoke very convincingly about the issue.	The adverb *very* modifies the adverb *convincingly*.
Actually, she's not a biologist. She didn't even graduate from college.	The adverb *actually* modifies the whole sentence that follows it.

A. Fill in the shaded areas of the chart with the adverb forms of the target words from this chapter and previous ones. Check a dictionary for the correct spelling of the adverb forms.

NOUNS	ADJECTIVES	ADVERBS
actuality	actual	
anxiety	anxious	
athlete	athletic	
conviction	convincing	
history	historic	
humanity	humane	
remark	remarkable	

B. Complete the sentences with the *adverbs* from the chart. Use the adverb that *best* fits the context of the sentence. Do not use a word more than one time.

1. _____, women stayed at home and took care of the children.

   Today, however, many women work outside of the home.

2. It is not acceptable to hurt an animal on purpose. Animals should be treated

   _____.

3. He sings _____ well. He is a great performer.

4. What an athlete! She can play almost any sport well. She is _____

   gifted.

5. Most people think he's been playing the piano for years. _____, he

   just began playing three months ago.

6. The parents watched _____ as the doctor examined their sick son.

7. He spoke so _____ that everyone believed him, but in fact, he

   was lying.

CRITICAL THINKING

A. Discussion

Share your ideas in a small group. As you talk, try to use the vocabulary below. Each time someone uses a target word, put a check (✓) next to it.

☐ acceptable		☐ humanity, humane, humanely	
☐ advantage, advantageous		☐ identify	
☐ appearance		☐ lead to	
☐ athletic, athletically		☐ restrict	
☐ convince, convincingly		☐ shortage	
☐ feature			

1. When you read the first paragraph of the reading, what effect did it have on you? For example, were you surprised? Interested in what would come next? Why do you think the writer started the reading in that way?

2. In paragraph 4, what do you think the question "But just because scientists *can* do it, does it mean they *will* do it?" means? According to the reading, is there an answer to this question? If so, what is the answer?

> **Critical Thinking Tip:** When a writer asks a question, try to answer it in your head. This will keep you engaged and help you see how well you understand the reading. If you can't answer the question(s), maybe you missed something important.

3. Does it surprise you that Jennifer Doudna wants to restrict the use of a technique that she co-developed? Do you think her reaction is common in science—that is, a scientist who developed something tries to restrict its use? Explain your answers. Do you know of another example from the past when something similar happened? Tell your group about it.

4. Are the writer's conclusions about what might happen in the future positive or negative? How do you know? Use information from the text to support your answer.

5. Discuss the writer's concerns in paragraph seven. Discuss each question. Do you share these concerns? Explain your answers.

B. Writing

Complete one or both of these writing topics. When you write, use at least five of the target words from the chapter. Underline the target words in your paper.

1. Imagine that in the future you will be able to design your own child. What traits do you want your son or daughter to have? Write a letter to your future child explaining why you wanted him or her to have these traits.

2. Write an essay supporting one of the following positions. Support your position with information from the readings in chapters 7 and 8, as well as your own ideas.

Genetic engineering will do more harm than good to humanity.

Genetic engineering will do more good than harm to humanity.

CHAPTER 9

A Terrible Inheritance, A Difficult Decision

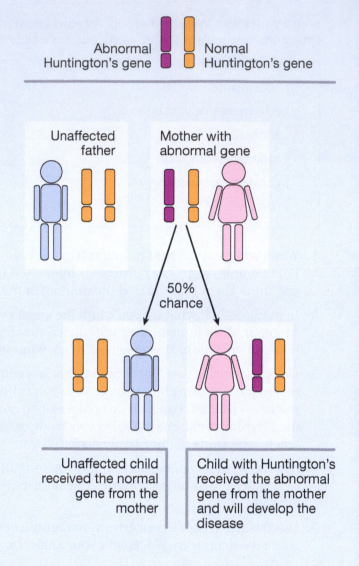

Abnormal Huntington's gene | Normal Huntington's gene

Unaffected father

Mother with abnormal gene

50% chance

Unaffected child received the normal gene from the mother

Child with Huntington's received the abnormal gene from the mother and will develop the disease

Genetic Inheritance of Huntington's Disease: The Basics

LEARNING OUTCOME

❯ Learn about a genetic disease and its effects

GETTING READY TO READ

Talk with a partner. Look at the diagram and the title of the chapter. Then answer the questions.

1. What do you think "a terrible inheritance" refers to?

2. What could the "difficult decision" be?

3. What do you think the reading will be about?

READING

Read the definitions beside the reading. Then read "A Terrible Inheritance, A Difficult Decision." If you see a new word, circle it, but don't stop reading. You can learn the new word later.

A Terrible Inheritance, A Difficult Decision

1 If you had a risk of developing a genetic disease, would you want to be tested for it? What **factors** would affect your decision? If there were no way to prevent, treat, or cure the disease, would you still want to be tested? As gene research **progresses**, these are questions that a growing number of people are facing. As many are discovering, there are no easy answers.

2 Meet Katharine Moser. Moser is an occupational therapist[1] at Terence Cardinal Cooke Health Care Center, a nursing home on the Upper East Side of Manhattan. In 2002, Moser's maternal[2] grandfather died at Cooke. He had Huntington's Disease, a **severe** genetic illness that attacks the brain. Victims of the disease usually begin to show symptoms[3] when they are 40 to 50 years old. Early symptoms can include emotional changes such as depression, and behavioral changes such as aggression. As the disease progresses, victims **suffer** from a loss of control over their movements, difficulty in thinking and talking, and severe emotional **complications**. After ten to twenty years of suffering, victims lose all ability to move and finally die.

3 There is no special **diet** that you can follow to prevent Huntington's. There is no medicine that doctors can **prescribe** to treat it, and there is no **operation** they can perform to fix it. If one parent suffers from Huntington's, his or her children have a 50 percent chance of inheriting the gene that causes the disease. And if you have the gene, you will definitely develop the illness. There is no **effective** treatment. All of its victims get worse, and then die. No one has ever **recovered** from it.

4 At the age of 23, Moser made the decision to be tested for Huntington's. Her decision was unusual. Since there is no treatment or cure, most people at risk for Huntington's do not see any **benefit** to being tested. And knowing that you will one day get the disease can be harmful to your mental health and your relationships. In fact, Moser's own mother did not agree with her daughter's decision. If her daughter had the harmful gene it would mean that she had it, too. And Moser's mother did not want to know because, as she said, "You don't want to know stuff like that. You want to enjoy life."

5 Nancy Wexler, like Katharine Moser, comes from a family with a history of Huntington's. Her mother, grandfather, and three of her uncles died of the disease. And like Moser, Wexler works closely with victims of the disease. She is a neuropsychologist[4] at Columbia University and is **in charge of** the Hereditary Disease Foundation. She is an expert in Huntington's. In fact,

[1] *an occupational therapist* = someone who helps people with physical or emotional problems do different activities

[2] *maternal* = on the mother's side of the family

[3] *a symptom* = a physical or psychological condition which shows that you have a particular illness

[4] *a neuropsychologist* = a doctor who has special training in the nervous system and how it affects someone's psychological health

she was involved in the discovery of the gene for the disease in 1993. That discovery led to the development of a genetic test for the disease. It is the same test that Moser decided to take years later.

6   Wexler, like Moser, had always **intended** to have the test when it became available. But when she was actually faced with the decision of whether or not to be tested, she realized that she did not want to know. If the test were positive for the gene, she felt that her life would be **poisoned** by the knowledge. "If you take the test, you have to be prepared to be really depressed," said Nancy. "I've been depressed. I don't like it."

7   Moser had the test in 2005. It was positive for the deadly gene. However, she says that she is not sorry that she was tested. "I'm the same person I've always been. It's been in me from the beginning." At first, it was difficult for her to be around the Huntington's patients at work. However, she now finds strength and purpose in working with them. She is also involved in raising money for research on Huntington's Disease. Mostly, she is busy living her life. "I have a lot to do. And I don't have a lot of time."

8   Sadly, Moser's mother has not spoken to her daughter since she found out the results of the test. In an interview, her mother said, "It's a horrible illness. . . . Now he [my husband] has a wife who has it. Did she think of him? Did she think of me? Who is going to marry her?"

9   Wexler has never been tested, but it seems that she has been more **fortunate** than Moser. She is now in her 60s, past the age when symptoms of the disease usually appear. As Wexler continues her research, Moser goes on with her life. She is working, playing tennis, going to church, learning to ride a unicycle,[5] spending time with her best friend, traveling . . . and hoping that the work of Wexler and others will lead to a cure soon—before it is too late for her and thousands of others.

[5] *a unicycle* = a vehicle that is like a bicycle but has only one wheel

Quick Comprehension Check

A. Read these sentences **about the reading**. Circle T (true), F (false), or ? (can't determine the answer from the reading). If you circle T or F, write the number of the paragraph with the answer on the line.

1. Fifty percent of people with Huntington's can be cured of the disease. T   F   ?   _____

2. Most people at risk for Huntington's get tested for the gene. T   F   ?   _____

3. Huntington's Disease is a genetic illness that only affects women. T   F   ?   _____

4. Nancy Wexler decided not to be tested for Huntington's. T   F   ?   _____

5. Nancy Wexler will never get Huntington's. T   F   ?   _____

6. Katharine Moser wishes that she had never been tested for Huntington's. T   F   ?   _____

7. Katharine Moser's mother has Huntington's. T F ? ____

8. Katharine Moser's life today is very different from the way it was before she had the test. T F ? ____

B. Work with your class. Share your answers from part A. Go back to the reading to find the reason why a sentence is true or false. Correct the false sentences.

EXPLORING VOCABULARY

Thinking about the Target Vocabulary

Guessing Strategy: Antonyms

Antonyms are words that have opposite meanings. Look at the example.

There is no effective treatment, and all of its victims get worse and then die. No one has ever recovered from it.

The words *get worse* and *recover* are antonyms. You already know the meaning of *get worse*, so you should be able to guess from the context that *recover* has the opposite meaning, *to get better*.

A. Read the sentences and circle the antonym of each **boldfaced** target word. Then write a definition of the **boldfaced** word.

1. Some diseases **progress** for a while and then stop. Others just keep progressing.

   Definition: _____

2. It seems that Wexler is **fortunate**; she is 60 years old and has not developed the disease. Moser, on the other hand, is unlucky. She has the disease.

   Definition: _____

3. For Moser, there are **benefits** to knowing that she has the disease, but Wexler can only see the disadvantages.

   Definition: _____

> **Vocabulary Tip:**
> Wait until you know a word well before learning its antonym. Otherwise, you may confuse the two words.

B. Look at the target words. Which ones are new to you? Circle them here and in the reading. The numbers in parentheses help you find the words in the paragraphs.

Target Words

factors (1)	complications (2)	effective (3)	intended (6)
progresses (1)	diet (3)	recovered (3)	poisoned (6)
severe (2)	prescribe (3)	benefit (4)	fortunate (9)
suffer (2)	operation (3)	in charge of (5)	

C. Read "A Terrible Inheritance, A Difficult Decision" again. Look at the context of the new words. Can you guess their meanings?

D. Complete the word form chart. Fill in the shaded areas of the chart with the target words from the reading. Write the base form of the verbs and the singular form of the nouns.

NOUNS	VERBS	ADJECTIVES	OTHER
factor			

Understanding the Target Vocabulary

A. These sentences are **about the reading**. Complete them with the words in the box. Circle the words in the sentences that help you understand the meanings of the target words.

diet	intends	progresses	suffered
effective	operation	recovered	
fortunate	prescribe	severe	

1. Huntington's Disease _____ over a period of ten to twenty years until the person with the disease finally dies.

2. No one has ever _____ from Huntington's. There is no cure or treatment.

3. The effects of the disease are _____. They make it impossible to live a normal life. For example, most people lose control of their arms or legs.

4. Because Huntington's is caused by a gene, doctors cannot perform an _____ to cut it out of your body.

5. Doctors cannot _____ a drug to prevent it.

6. You can't slow down the disease by eating a special _____.

7. Katharine Moser's grandfather and Nancy Wexler's mother _____

    and eventually died from Huntington's.

8. Wexler was involved in developing a very _____ test for

    Huntington's disease. In fact, the test is 100 percent reliable.

9. Wexler is now past the age when most people begin to show symptoms, so

    she probably will not get Huntington's. She is more _____ than

    Moser, who tested positive for the disease.

10. Despite the bad news, Moser has a positive attitude. She _____ to

    use the time that she has left to enjoy life, and to help others with the disease.

B. Read the paragraph and match the **boldfaced** words with their definitions.

Imagine that you have a 50 percent chance of getting a terrible genetic illness twenty years from today. Will you be tested for the disease? What **factors** will affect your decision? If there is no way to prevent, treat, or cure the disease, will you still want to be tested for the gene? Is there any **benefit** in knowing that you will get the disease? Will that knowledge **poison** your life? Or will it help you to plan for and feel more **in charge of** your own future?

Word	Definition
_____ 1. factor	a. influence someone's thoughts or emotions in a bad way, or make them feel very unhappy
_____ 2. benefit	b. something that gives you advantages or improves your life in some way
_____ 3. poison	c. controlling or responsible for a group of people or an activity
_____ 4. in charge of	d. one of several things that influence or cause a situation

DEVELOPING READING SKILLS

Interpreting a Diagram

Understanding Diagrams

Readings about scientific or technical topics often include both text and **diagrams**. The diagrams usually illustrate a specific part of the text to make it easier to understand. Understanding the connection between a written text and a diagram is an important reading skill.

Read "A Terrible Inheritance, a Difficult Decision" again. Then look at the diagram of Katharine Moser's family tree. Based on the reading and what you see in the diagram, circle and label the figures that represent the people from Katharine's family who are mentioned in the reading. Write K (Katharine), KG (Katharine's grandfather), and KM (Katharine's mother).

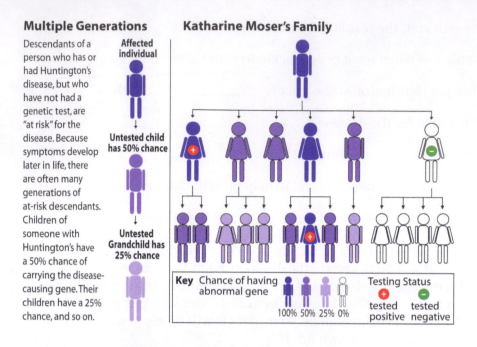

BUILDING ON THE VOCABULARY

Using the Target Vocabulary in New Contexts

Complete the sentences with the target words in the box. Be careful. There are two extra words.

complications	factor	poison	recovered
diet	in charge of	prescribed	severe
effective	operation	progressed	

1. You are eating too much. It isn't healthy. You need to change your

   _____ .

2. Even when you have just a simple operation, something can go wrong. There is

   always the danger of _____ .

3. He has _____ very quickly in his career. He has been at the company

   for only one year, but he's already in charge of three departments and 100

   employees.

4. She saw mice in her apartment, so she is going to get something to

_____ them or get rid of them in some other way.

5. There is going to be a _____ snowstorm tonight. I think we should

stay home.

6. He's a very _____ teacher. His students learn a lot from him.

7. Her job is very important. She is _____ 1,000 workers.

8. He hurt his leg very badly skiing. He needs to have an _____ to fix it.

9. One _____ to consider when buying a car is the cost.

Expanding Vocabulary

Word Families

A. Read these sentences, and write the target words that are in the same word families as the **boldfaced** words.

1. The patient's **recovery** was faster than his doctors had expected.

Target word: _recover_

2. She had a bad cough, so her doctor wrote her a **prescription** for cough medicine.

Target word: _____

3. I'm sorry. It was never my **intention** to hurt you.

Target word: _____

4. In this book, there is a **progression** of activities from easy to difficult.

Target word: _____

5. Eating the right kinds of food is **beneficial** to your health.

Target word: _____

B. Match the **boldfaced** words from part A to their definitions.

_____ 1. recovery
_____ 2. prescription
_____ 3. intention
_____ 4. progression
_____ 5. beneficial

a. a change or development from one situation or state to another

b. the act of getting better after an illness

c. something that you plan to do

d. good for you

e. a piece of paper from your doctor that allows you to get the medicine you need

Word Grammar: Collocations—Specialized Vocabulary

Medicine, like any other professional field, has specialized vocabulary that includes many collocations. Look at the **boldfaced** collocations in the examples.

- She **suffers from** high blood pressure.
- She is in the hospital, **recovering from** a serious illness.
- He has very high cholesterol, so he has to **follow a strict diet**.
- The doctor who **performed the operation** made a serious mistake.

A. Rewrite the following sentences with the correct collocations. Write one word in each space.

1. My father has skin cancer.

   My father _____ _____ skin cancer.

2. After his illness, he got better in a week.

   He _____ _____ his illness in a week.

3. Dr. Smith will be in charge of the operation.

   Dr. Smith will _____ _____ _____.

4. His doctor told him to be very careful about what he eats.

   His doctor advised him to _____ _____

   _____ _____.

> **Writing Tip:**
> Using the correct collocations when you write will make your writing sound much more fluent and natural.

B. Write answers to these questions. Use the **boldfaced** collocations in your answers.

1. If you were **suffering from an incurable illness**, would you want your doctor to tell you, or would you rather not know?

   _____

   _____

2. Why do children usually **recover from an illness** more quickly than elderly people?

   _____

   _____

3. Have you ever watched a doctor **perform an operation on television**? If so, describe it. If not, would you like to? Why or why not?

   _____

   _____

4. People who suffer from certain diseases have to **follow a strict diet**. Name a couple of these diseases. Make a list of the foods that are restricted for each one.

_____

_____

CRITICAL THINKING

A. Discussion

Share your ideas in a small group. As you talk, try to use the vocabulary below. Each time someone uses a target word, put a check (✓) next to it.

☐ beneficial	☐ effective	☐ fortunate	☐ progress	☐ severe
☐ complication	☐ factor	☐ prescribe	☐ recover	☐ suffer from

1. In paragraphs 4 and 8, you learn about Moser's difficult decision and her mother's reaction to it. What was the decision she made? How did her mother react? Using information in the reading and your own experience, explain why you think Katharine told her mother about the results of the test. Why do you think her mother reacted the way she did?

2. What can you infer about the differences between Moser's and Wexler's characters and personalities? What are the similarities? Refer to specific parts of the reading to support your answers. Then discuss whose character is more similar to your own.

3. Paragraph 4 in the text says, "Since there is no treatment or cure, most people at risk for Huntington's do not see any benefit to being tested." Can you think of any benefits to being tested? What would the benefits be? Use information from the reading and your own ideas to support your answer.

4. Imagine a day when doctors and scientists will be able to prevent or cure all diseases. Will this be a completely positive thing? Can you imagine any problems that this might lead to?

> **Critical Thinking Tip:** When you read about other people, try to imagine yourself in a similar situation. This will help you get more involved in the reading, and understand and remember the information.

> **Reading Tip:** If you are reading a text that compares and contrasts two different ideas or people, you can annotate the text by writing an *S* next to similarities and a *D* next to differences.

B. Writing

Choose Discussion question 3 or 4 and write an opinion essay based on the question. When you write, use at least five of the target words from the chapter. Underline the target words in your paper. Use information from the readings in the unit, as well as your own ideas, to support your opinion.

LEARNING OUTCOME

❯ Review and expand on the content of Unit 3

LOOK BACK

A. Think About This

Think again about the answers you gave in the *Think About This* exercise on page 85. How much do you know now? Have you learned new things in this unit? Write a number next to each topic.

1. I know a lot   2. I know some things   3. I know a little   4. I don't know anything

_____ 1. DNA

_____ 2. the discoveries of Gregor Mendel

_____ 3. genetic engineering and gene therapy

_____ 4. genetic testing

_____ 5. genetic diseases

B. Remember the Readings

What do you want to remember most from the readings in Unit 3? For each chapter, write one sentence about the reading.

Chapter 7: The Science of Genetics _____

_____

Chapter 8: Designing the Future _____

_____

Chapter 9: A Terrible Inheritance, A Difficult Decision _____

_____

Read the text. Do not use a dictionary.

GM Food

1   Historically, it took individual farmers generations of experimentation to develop the strongest, healthiest, and fastest-growing variety of a crop. Today, however, due to rapid progress in gene research, farmers can buy seeds whose genes have been carefully changed in a laboratory. The crops that grow from these genetically engineered seeds grow faster and are stronger and less likely to suffer from disease than traditional crops. In short, they have all the traits that farmers used to spend generations developing. The food that is produced from these crops is called genetically modified (GM).

2   In the United States, it is difficult to find food that does not contain at least some GM products. Actually, it is not always possible to even determine whether you are buying GM food in the U.S. That is because food labels in the United States do not always identify products that have been genetically modified. In Western Europe, however, things are different. Most food is labeled. Walk into almost any supermarket in France, Great Britain, or Italy, and you will see labels on the food that read "GM free." By reading the labels, customers can identify those products that have not been genetically modified.

3   Why the difference? Although scientists say that GM food is harmless, many Europeans do not believe it. They express concern about the possible negative effects of growing and eating GM food. They worry about the effect it might have on the health of individuals and the environment. Finally, many Europeans are especially sensitive to this issue because of the importance of food to their culture.

4   In the United States, however, scientists and farmers who produce GM food argue that it is not only harmless but actually beneficial to humanity. They claim that by growing GM crops, farmers can produce much more food in a shorter period of time. In that way, GM products can help prevent hunger in parts of the world suffering from food shortages.

Quick Comprehension Check

A. Read these sentences **about the reading**. Circle T (true), F (false), or ? (can't determine the answer from the reading). If you circle T or F, write the number of the paragraph with the answer on the line.

1. In the past, farmers had no way to develop healthier, faster-growing plants.   T   F   ?   _____

2. Today, most farmers in the United States benefit from the progress that scientists have made in the field of genetic engineering.   T   F   ?   _____

3. By reading food labels, customers in the United States can decide for themselves whether or not to buy food that contains GM products.　T　F　?　____

4. Many western Europeans are worried that GM food could make them sick.　T　F　?　____

5. It is difficult to find GM food in Europe today.　T　F　?　____

B. Go back to the reading to find the reason why a sentence is true or false. Correct the false sentences.

Guessing Meaning from Context

Answer these questions.

1. Look at the word *crops* in paragraph 1. Write some examples of crops.

_____

2. What is the meaning of the word *modified* in paragraph 1?

_____

3. Look at the word *labels* in paragraph 2. What information is often written on these kinds of labels?

_____

Understanding Major Points

Answer these questions. Use your own words. Do not copy from the text.

1. What is the definition of genetically modified food?

_____

2. What are some of the benefits of genetically modified food?

_____

3. What are some of the possible problems with genetically modified food?

_____

Expanding Vocabulary

Word Grammar: Transitive and Intransitive Verbs

Some verbs must have a noun immediately after them. This noun is called a **direct object**. Verbs that need a direct object are called **transitive verbs**. The verb "love" is a transitive verb.

		verb	direct object
Transitive:	*I*	*love*	*ice cream.*

Other verbs do not have a direct object. These verbs are called **intransitive verbs**. The verb "listen" is an intransitive verb: *He is listening to the radio,* or *He is listening.* We can't say *He is listening radio.*

		verb	**object of the preposition**
Intransitive:	He	*is listening*	*to the radio.*
		verb	**0 object**
	He	*is listening.*	

A. Look at the **boldfaced** verbs in these sentences. Circle T (transitive verb), or I (intransitive verb).

1. Their research **is progressing** rapidly.   T   I
2. To **prevent** heart disease, you should eat a healthy diet.   T   I
3. I don't like to see anyone **suffer**.   T   I
4. When his grandmother died, he **inherited** her house.   T   I

B. On a piece of paper, write your own sentences with the verbs from part A.

Word Families: Prefixes

Look at these sentences.

Fortunately, your disease is not severe.

Unfortunately, it is incurable.

A **prefix** is a word part added to the beginning of a word. It changes the word's meaning. The prefixes *un-* and *in-* both mean *not*. Other common prefixes include *dis-*, which also means *not*, and *mis-*, which means *wrong* or *bad*.

Complete these sentences with your own ideas. There is more than one correct way to complete each sentence.

1. If your father gives you **unrestricted** use of his car, you can *use it any time*

   you want .

2. If your parents **disinherit** you, you won't _____

   _____ .

3. If you suffer a **misfortune**, your friends might _____

   _____ .

4. If your way of doing something is **ineffective**, you should _____

   _____ .

5. If your boss tells you that your work is **unacceptable**, you should _____

   _____ .

6. If someone insults you and then tells you it was **unintentional**, you should _____

_____ .

PLAYING WITH WORDS

You can play the game **Concentration** alone, but it is more fun if you play with one, two, or three other students.

- **Step 1:** Choose 10 words from the unit that you are having trouble learning. Take 20 blank index cards, and make 10 cards with just the words written on them, and 10 cards with the definitions of the 10 words written on them.

- **Step 2:** Next, mix the cards up well, and lay them facedown on a large desk or table, four cards across and five cards down.

- **Step 3:** Now, turn over any two cards, and try to remember what is written on them and where they are. If they form a match—a word or phrase on one card, a matching definition on the other—pick them up from the board and keep them, and take another turn. However, leave the other cards exactly where they were. If the two cards you turn over do not match, turn them both back over. Now it's the next person's turn. Play until all of the cards have been matched up. The winner is the person who has the most cards.

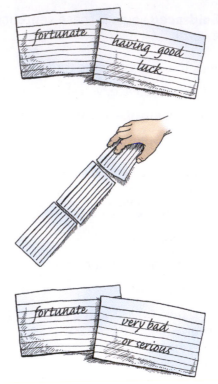

BUILDING DICTIONARY SKILLS

Finding Collocations

Your dictionary is an excellent resource for learning collocations. Look carefully at the entire dictionary entry, including the example sentences, for patterns of words that occur together.

A. These dictionary entries come from the *Longman Dictionary of American English*. Look carefully at each one, and then complete the sentences below. Write one word in each space.

> **in·struc·tion** /ɪnˈstrʌkʃən/ *n* **1 instructions** [plural] information or advice that tells you how to do something, how to use a piece of equipment or machine, etc. [= **directions**]: *Follow the instructions at the top of the paper.* | *Did you read the instructions first?* | *He gave us instructions on/about how to fix the toilet.* | *Inside you'll find instructions for setting up your computer.* | *He gave instructions to keep the ball on the ground, not to kick it high.* **2** [U] teaching in a particular skill or subject: *She's never had any formal instruction* [= lessons or classes] *in music.* — **instructional** *adj*

1. _____ the instructions on the label.

2. I fixed the light. The electrician _____ me instructions over the phone.

> **pre·scribe** /prɪˈskraɪb/ *v* [T] **1** to say what medicine or treatment a sick person should have: *Doctors commonly **prescribe** steroids **for** children with asthma.* **2** *formal* to state officially what should be done in a particular situation: *a punishment prescribed by the law*
>
> **pre·scrip·tion** /prɪˈskrɪpʃən/ *n* **1** [C] a piece of paper on which a doctor writes what medicine a sick person should have, or the medicine itself: *a **prescription for** painkillers* **2 by prescription** a drug that you get by prescription can only be obtained with a written order from the doctor [≠ **over the counter**]

3. My dentist _____ pain medicine _____ me.

4. My dentist wrote me a _____ _____ pain medicine.

> **di·et¹** /ˈdaɪət/ *n* **1** [C,U] the type of food that you eat each day: *Many kids don't get enough fruit in their diet.* | *The animals live on a **diet of** fruit and insects.* **2** [C] a plan to eat only particular kinds or amounts of food, especially because you want to get thinner or because you have a health problem: *a low-fat diet* | *No dessert for me –I'm **on a diet**.*
>
> **diet²** *v* [I] to eat less or eat only particular foods in order to lose weight: *Jill's always dieting.*

5. I can't have any ice cream. I am _____ _____

_____ .

B. On a piece of paper, write your own sentences about yourself and your life with the words from part A.

Vocabulary Self-Test 1

Circle the letter of the word or phrase that best completes each sentence.

1. That performer _____ received $10,000 for just one performance.
   a. rapidly   b. reportedly   c. morally   d. historically

2. The scientist conducted some _____ to find out how much sleep most teens need.
   a. experiments   b. equipment   c. championships   d. patterns

3. I'm tired because I _____ too late last night.
   a. stayed up   b. grew out of   c. stood out   d. burned out

4. The cat _____ her on the face.
   a. scratched   b. survived   c. cured   d. prevented

5. Poems are often written in _____.
   a. spin   b. insult   c. humiliation   d. rhyme

6. That team has won several _____.
   a. complaints   b. championships   c. cells   d. features

7. Leave your little brother alone. Don't _____ him.
   a. pick on   b. bring up   c. drop out   d. call for

8. To be successful, it is important to have high _____.
   a. mystery   b. self-esteem   c. concern   d. violence

9. When your grandmother dies, you are going to _____ this house.
   a. progress   b. contribute   c. reduce   d. inherit

10. The government spends very little money on education. Almost 60 percent of the people in the country are _____.
    a. live   b. athletic   c. illiterate   d. anxious

11. Don't work so hard. You'll _____.

    a. stay up   b. burn out   c. in charge of   d. pick on

12. This is a _____ area. You cannot enter.

    a. talented   b. remarkable   c. moral   d. restricted

13. He is not doing well in school because he has a bad _____.

    a. appearance   b. individual   c. attitude   d. official

14. Stay in school. If you _____, you will never get a good job.

    a. recover   b. identify   c. prevent   d. drop out

15. He is _____ from a very serious disease.

    a. examining   b. reducing   c. conducting   d. suffering

16. She is very _____. She is good at most sports.

    a. economic   b. athletic   c. intentional   d. characteristic

17. He went to the pharmacy to get the medicine that his doctor _____.

    a. suffered   b. examined   c. announced   d. prescribed

18. She is on a very restricted _____. She can only eat vegetables.

    a. appearance   b. background   c. diet   d. proof

19. They _____ to kill him if he didn't give them all of his money.

    a. poisoned   b. insulted   c. threatened   d. survived

20. _____, women have made less money than men.

    a. In charge of   b. Based on   c. Historically   d. Physically

21. She is in the hospital, recovering from a serious _____.

    a. cure   b. humanity   c. operation   d. victim

22. I'm your friend. I will always _____ you.

    a. stand by   b. pick on   c. grow out of   d. get rid of

23. I believe in freedom and _____ for all people.

    a. justice   b. humiliation   c. background   d. mystery

24. Because of its beauty, that painting _____.

    a. burns out   b. stands out   c. brings up   d. calls for

25. He won the competition _____ his illness.

    a. due to   b. based on   c. despite   d. at least

26. We gave her the job because of her strong _____ in international business.

    a. pattern   b. instruction   c. background   d. challenge

27. Please stop making so much noise. I need to _____.

    a. concentrate   b. determine   c. identify   d. prescribe

28. Fortunately, the patient _____ from the illness.

    a. suffered   b. contributed   c. intended   d. recovered

29. She is the most _____ woman I know. She wins every competition that she enters!

    a. beneficial   b. fortunate   c. advantageous   d. depressed

30. His work is _____, but not brilliant.

    a. acceptable   b. severe   c. heavenly   d. evil

31. There are many _____ to getting a university education.

    a. complaints   b. concerns   c. traits   d. advantages

32. I'm so sorry I woke you up. I didn't _____ it was so early.

    a. identify   b. realize   c. intend   d. examine

33. Teenagers are usually very concerned about the opinions of their _____.

    a. experts   b. personalities   c. peers   d. perfectionists

34. He is an _____ man. He set fire to a large building. Fortunately, however, everyone survived.

    a. evil   b. original   c. expert   d. intentional

35. I wasn't _____ in the project. He did it by himself.

    a. fascinated   b. involved   c. related   d. threatened

36. You don't need to bring any _____. We have everything we need to do the job.

    a. technique   b. theory   c. equipment   d. challenge

See the Answer Key on page 265.

GETTING EMOTIONAL

THINK ABOUT THIS

How comfortable are you at expressing the following emotions? Rank your answers.

1 = very comfortable
2 = comfortable

3 = not very comfortable
4 = very uncomfortable

- anger
- excitement
- fear
- frustration
- joy
- sadness

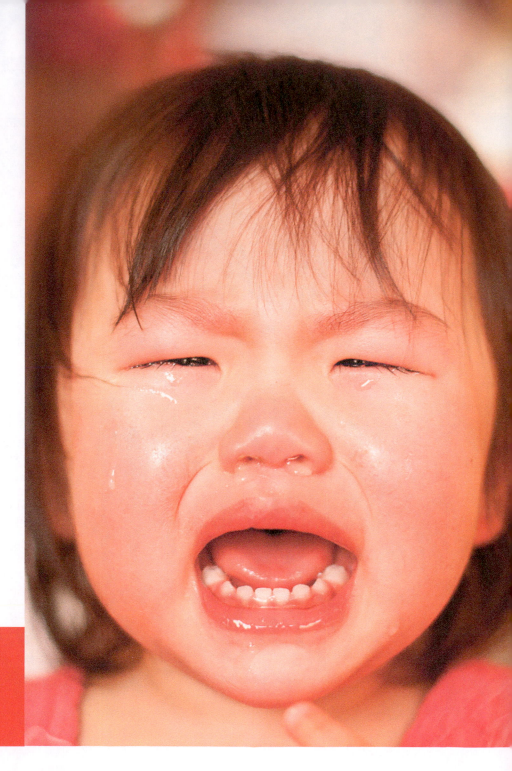

CHAPTER 10

Can You Translate an Emotion?

LEARNING OUTCOME

❯ Learn about the relationship between culture and the expression of emotion

GETTING READY TO READ

Talk with a partner.

1. In general, is it easy or difficult for you to express your emotions? Are you more, less, or equally as emotional as other people in your family? Which emotions do you find difficult to express?

2. Who is the most emotional person you know? Describe him or her. In your opinion, is the fact that he or she is so emotional positive or negative? Why?

Read to Find Out: Are human emotions universal?

Read the definitions beside the reading. Then read "Can You Translate an Emotion?" If you see a new word, circle it, but don't stop reading. You can learn the new word later.

Can You Translate an Emotion?

1   In the Northwest of Canada, there is a group of people called the Utkuhikhalingmiut ("Utku"). According to anthropologist[1] Jean L. Briggs, author of the book *Never in Anger*, the Utku have no real word in their language for anger. And even more remarkable, adults rarely seem to get angry. The word that they use to describe the angry behavior of foreigners **translates** not as anger, but rather as "childishness."[2]

2   Similarly, the Ifaluk people of Micronesia seem to rarely get angry. However, **in contrast** to the Utku, they talk about anger all the time and have many words to describe it. They consider anger to be evil—a demon,[3] in fact—and fear it.

3   The expression of **grief** and gratitude[4] is central to the Kaululi culture of Papua New Guinea. In contrast, people from the United States generally spend very little time talking about grief or gratitude. Research on American males shows that they are **particularly** uncomfortable expressing these emotions.

4   What is going on here? Aren't we all human beings? Don't we all feel the same basic emotions? This is a topic that philosophers,[5] scientists, religious leaders, and anthropologists, among others, have been arguing about for centuries. Most researchers today believe that a limited number of emotions are **universal**. However, there is not complete agreement on which emotions humans **indeed** share. Fear and anger are almost always included; **guilt**, joy, **shame**, **disgust**, and surprise are also considered by many to be universal. But then how can we explain the Utku and the Ifaluk?

5   Dr. Robert C. Solomon, professor of philosophy at the University of Texas at Austin, has argued that emotions are, at least in part, culture-specific. In one essay, he says that even among people from the same culture, it is difficult to get agreement on what an emotion is. For example, most anthropologists would not consider love to be an emotion, but if it is not an emotion, then what is it?

6   Another challenge is how to determine that two people are indeed feeling the same emotion. You can **observe** people's behavior, and ask them to describe their emotions, but it is impossible to directly observe what they are feeling. This becomes even more complex when you are trying to compare emotions across cultures.

7   We tend to **associate** certain behaviors with specific emotions, but of course our associations are based on what those behaviors mean in our own culture. For example, imagine you are a teacher in the United States with a student from another country. Your student has failed the class. You learn that his

[1] *an anthropologist* = a person who studies people, their societies, beliefs, etc.

[2] *childishness* = behavior that is typical of a child

[3] *a demon* = an evil spirit

[4] *gratitude* = the feeling of wanting to express thanks for something kind that someone has done

[5] *a philosopher* = a person who studies or teaches about the world, life, death, etc.

behavior has changed. Suddenly, he is avoiding his friends and spending all of his time alone. If you are from the United States, you will probably describe his emotional state as depressed. Why? In U.S. culture, there is a belief that people who suddenly change their behavior and avoid other people are often depressed. However, if you have some knowledge of the student's culture, you might **recognize** his behavior as an expression of deep shame at disgracing[6] his family.

⁶ *disgrace* = do something so bad that people lose respect for you

8   Of course, this example is very simple—it does not mean that people from your student's culture do not ever experience depression, or that people from the United States do not feel shame. However, can someone from a culture that does not place the same value on family **honor** really understand this deep feeling of disgrace? In other words, is shame really the same emotion in all cultures?

9   Another reason to believe that not all emotions are universal is the fact that different languages characterize emotions in different ways. For instance, in the ancient Indian languages of Sanskrit and Bengali, emotions are described as being either *sattva* (lightness), *rajas* (movement), or *tamas* (heaviness). Interestingly, two of the examples of *sattva*—**cheerfulness** and nobility[7]— are not generally considered to be emotions in English. Is this just a language difference? Or does it **reveal** that people across cultures do not share a similar emotional experience?

⁷ *nobility* = the quality of being morally good or generous in a way that should be admired

10   The mystery of whether emotions are universal or culturally specific is one that most likely will never be solved. That probably contributes to our fascination with the subject.

Quick Comprehension Check

A. Read these sentences **about the reading**. Circle T (true), F (false), or ? (can't determine the answer from the reading). If you circle T or F, write the number of the paragraph with the answer on the line.

1. All languages have words for the most basic human emotions.   T   F   ?   _____

2. In the Utku culture, people who express anger are considered childish.   T   F   ?   _____

3. The basic human emotions are universal, not culture-specific.   T   F   ?   _____

4. Because we cannot know exactly what other people are feeling, we observe their behavior and then try to guess what they are feeling.   T   F   ?   _____

5. The shame that an American feels is different from the shame that a person coming from another country feels.   T   F   ?   _____

6. Different languages describe emotions in different ways.   T   F   ?   _____

7. The word *sattva* means cheerfulness.   T   F   ?   _____

> **Reading Tip:** If the title of a reading is a question, try to answer the question before you read. Then as you read, check your answer against the information in the reading.

B. Work with your class. Share your answers from part A. Go back to the reading to find the reason why a sentence is true or false. Correct the false sentences.

EXPLORING VOCABULARY

Thinking about the Target Vocabulary

Guessing Strategy: Words with similar meaning

You learned in the Guessing Strategy for Chapter 4 that to avoid repeating words, writers often use synonyms. They also use words that have similar meaning, but are different word forms. Look at the example.

Many researchers today believe that a limited number of emotions are **universal**. *However, there is not complete agreement on which emotions* **humans** *indeed* **share.**

Based on the context, you can guess that the words *universal* and *humans share* have a similar meaning, even though *universal* is an adjective and *humans share* is a noun + a verb.

A. Read the sentences, and write the word or words that are similar in meaning to the **boldfaced** target word.

1. His emotions are not hidden from anybody. He **reveals** whatever he is feeling.

   Reveals is similar in meaning to _____.

2. We **associate** certain behaviors and specific emotions. For example, we often make the connection between crying and sadness, although crying can sometimes be an expression of happiness.

   Associate is similar in meaning to _____.

3. Your **guilt** is obvious. It is clear from the expression on your face that you know that you did something wrong.

   Guilt is similar in meaning to _____.

B. Look at the target words. Which ones are new to you? Circle them here and in the reading. The numbers in parentheses help you find the words in the paragraphs.

Target Words

translates (1)	universal (4)	disgust (4)	honor (8)
in contrast (2)	indeed (4)	observe (6)	cheerfulness (9)
grief (3)	guilt (4)	associate (7)	reveal (9)
particularly (3)	shame (4)	recognize (7)	

C. Read "Can You Translate an Emotion?" again. Look at the context of the new words. Can you guess their meanings?

D. Complete the word form chart. Fill in the shaded areas of the chart with the target words from the reading. Write the base form of the verbs and the singular form of the nouns.

NOUNS	VERBS	ADJECTIVES	OTHER
	translate		

Understanding the Target Vocabulary

These sentences are **about the reading**. Complete them with the words in the box. Circle the words in the sentences that help you understand the meanings of the target words.

associate	in contrast	particularly	shame
disgust	indeed	recognize	translate
grief	observe	reveal	universal
honor			

1. Are human emotions culturally specific, or are they _____?

2. Answering the question is _____ difficult. Why is it so difficult? Perhaps because we cannot "see" an emotion. We cannot _____ someone's feelings directly.

3. How do we know what others are feeling? We usually look at their behavior, and then _____ it with an emotion. In other words, we believe that actions _____, or show, a person's true feelings.

4. However, the same behavior in one culture might mean something different in another. Therefore, it is not always easy to _____ which emotions individuals from another country are expressing through their behavior.

5. For example, Americans think that people who suddenly change their behavior and avoid other people are depressed. _____, in another culture, this behavior might be associated with _____ and guilt.

6. Because people in some cultures believe that the reputation and

_____ of a family are very important, a student who brings shame to

his family by getting poor grades might avoid other people.

7. Another problem is that it is not always easy to _____ the words of

emotion from one language to another. _____, in the Utku culture in

Northwest Canada, there appears to be no word at all for anger.

8. Americans appear to have trouble expressing _____. For some

reason, it is difficult for them to show their deep sadness at the loss of someone or

something important to them.

9. _____ is usually considered universal. Scientists believe that it is a

useful emotion, because it stops us from eating things that could harm our health,

such as rotten meat or poisonous plants.

DEVELOPING READING SKILLS

Paraphrasing

How to Paraphrase

When you **paraphrase** a sentence, you use different words and different sentence structure, while keeping the same meaning as the original sentence. In order to paraphrase, you must make sure you really understand the writer's idea. Look at the paraphrase of this sentence from the reading.

Original sentence: Grief and gratitude are central to the Kaululi culture of Papua New Guinea.

Paraphrase: For the Kaululi people who live in Papua New Guinea, grief and gratitude are very important emotions.

You do not have to change *all* of the words when you paraphrase. In the example above, *grief* and *gratitude* are central to the meaning of the sentence and they do not have exact synonyms. That is why you should not change them.

However, you should change the sentence structure whenever possible. Notice the differences in sentence structure between the original and paraphrased sentences above.

One sentence in each set paraphrases the sentence from the reading. Circle the correct answer.

Vocabulary Tip: The more specific a word is, the less likely it is that there is an appropriate synonym to replace it. In this case, you might want to keep the word from the original text.

1. Many researchers today believe that a limited number of emotions are universal.

   a. A lot of experts agree that people of all cultures experience at least a few of the same emotions.
   b. People who study human emotions think that all human beings share the same emotions.

2. However, there is not complete agreement on which emotions humans indeed share.

   a. But the emotions noted by different groups of experts are completely different.
   b. But not all experts agree on which feelings are really universal.

3. This becomes even more complex when you are trying to compare emotions across cultures.

   a. It is particularly difficult to describe the emotions of two people who come from different cultures.
   b. It is not easy to compare people who come from different parts of the world.

Applying Information

Applying What You Understand to New Situations

When you are reading about a new idea, especially one that is difficult for you, there are many ways to check your understanding. One way is to paraphrase the new ideas. Another way is to apply what you have understood to a new situation. For example, in this reading you learn about two cultures that do not have any words for anger, and the ways people in those cultures think and behave. To check your understanding, you can think about a situation that is not described in the reading, and try to imagine how people from each culture would behave.

Answer the questions in your own words. There is more than one correct way to answer each question.

1. Based on what the reading says about the Utku and anger, how do you think the Utku might react when they see a foreign visitor get angry?

   _____

   _____

2. Now think about the Ifaluk. How might the Ifaluk react when they see a foreign visitor get angry? How would their reactions likely differ from those of the Utku?

   _____

   _____

BUILDING ON THE VOCABULARY

Using the Target Vocabulary in New Contexts

Complete the sentences with the target words in the box. Be careful. There are two extra words or phrases.

associate	honor	particularly	translate
cheerfulness	in contrast	recognize	universal
disgust	indeed	reveal	
guilt	observe		

1. It is an _____ to be seated next to the president. I feel really special.

2. I'd rather not go to that movie. I'm not _____ interested in war films.

3. If you eat something that makes you sick, you may always _____ that food with your illness. You will probably never want to eat it again!

4. Please wear a red coat so that I will _____ you in the crowd.

5. This letter is too complex for me to _____. My Spanish is not that good.

6. There are many feelings that may vary among cultures, but the need for love is probably _____.

7. The doctor is almost certain that the patient has recovered, but he still wants to _____ her for twenty-four hours.

8. *In fact* and _____ have the same meaning.

9. They will know who won the competition on Sunday, but they won't _____ the winner's name until Monday.

10. Tom felt terrible about the car accident. His _____ over hurting a child really bothered him, so he wrote an apology letter to the parents.

11. That drug can be harmful. This drug, _____, is harmless.

Expanding Vocabulary

Word Families: Emotions

Words for emotions often come in three forms: *a noun form* that names the emotion; *an adjective form* that describes the way someone feels; and *an adjective form* that describes who or what causes the feeling. For example:

Noun (names the emotion): shame
Adjective (describes the way someone feels): ashamed
Adjective (describes who or what caused the feeling): shameful

> His **shame** at what he had done bothered him for the rest of his life.
> You really hurt her. You should be **ashamed** of yourself!
> The way you treated her was **shameful**.

Study the chart. Then, complete the sentences with the correct word forms. Be careful. You will not use all the words.

NOUN (NAMES THE EMOTION)	ADJECTIVE (DESCRIBES THE WAY SOMEONE FEELS)	ADJECTIVE (DESCRIBES WHO OR WHAT CAUSED THE FEELING)
shame	ashamed	shameful
cheerfulness	cheerful	cheerful / cheery
disgust	disgusted	disgusting
guilt	guilty	guilty
fascination	fascinated	fascinating

1. This soup smells _____. I can't eat it!

2. After he stole the money, he felt so _____ that he decided to give

   it back.

3. Her shame kept her quiet her entire life. She never revealed her _____

   secret to anyone.

4. It's difficult to feel depressed around her because she's always so

   _____.

5. She has traveled all over the world and has some _____ stories to tell.

6. After I found a hair in my food, I was so _____ that I couldn't eat.

Word Grammar: Verb Patterns

Transitive verbs always have a direct object. Often, the direct object is a noun or pronoun. Look at the sentence using the transitive verb **recognize**.

pronoun   pronoun

She didn't **recognize** <u>me</u>, *but I* **recognized** <u>her</u>.

However, in some cases, the direct object is not a noun or pronoun. Look at the transitive verb **observe**.

The doctor **observed** <u>*that the patient was able to move his left leg*</u>.

In the example above, *observe* is followed by a full **clause**: *that* + subject + verb.

Different verbs have different patterns. In order to use a verb correctly, you need to learn the pattern(s) for that particular verb. If you are not sure, look in your dictionary.

A. Read the sentences with *recognize* and *observe*. Check (✓) the sentences that are correct. Put an X next to those that are incorrect.

_____ 1. When the police showed the victim several photographs, she recognized her attacker immediately.

_____ 2. The police observed him to behave in a strange way.

_____ 3. The researchers observed that all of the mice in the experiment had the same reaction to the chemical.

_____ 4. He tried to hide, but someone recognized to him.

> **Writing Tip:**
> When you learn a new verb, you also need to learn its pattern. Always pay close attention to what follows a verb.

B. Answer these questions in complete sentences. Use the **boldfaced** verbs. Make sure you use the correct patterns.

1. Choose a culture that you are familiar with. What differences have you **observed** between that culture and your own?

_____

_____

2. What would you do if you **recognized** your favorite actor on the street?

_____

_____

CRITICAL THINKING

A. Discussion

Share your ideas in a small group. As you talk, try to use the vocabulary below. Each time someone uses a target word, put a check (✓) next to it.

- ☐ disgust/disgusted/disgusting
- ☐ grief
- ☐ guilt/guilty
- ☐ honor
- ☐ in contrast
- ☐ indeed
- ☐ observe
- ☐ particularly
- ☐ reveal
- ☐ shame/ashamed/shameful

1. Discuss the meaning of the title of the reading, "Can You Translate an Emotion?" We usually talk about translating language, not emotions. What do you think the writer means?

2. The writer says that the Utuk have no word for anger. Are there any words in your language that cannot be translated into English? Describe what they mean.

3. In what ways are the Utuk and the Ifaluk similar? In what ways are they different? What might their attitudes toward anger reveal about their cultures?

4. In paragraph 3 of the reading, the writer states that ". . . people from the United States generally spend very little time talking about grief or gratitude." Based on what you know or have observed of American culture, does this surprise you? Why or why not? What do you think this might reveal about American culture? Consider the following information about American culture when you answer the questions:

   - The American Dream: If you work hard, you can achieve anything you want.

   - Americans place a great value on independence and self-reliance.

   - American culture is very youth-oriented. As people get older, they generally do not like to reveal their age. A lot of time and money is spent on trying to look and feel "younger."

   - U.S. culture in general is more focused on the future than on the past.

5. Are there any emotions that people in your culture do not talk about very much? What are they? What might that reveal about your culture?

6. The following questions are suggested but never answered in the reading. Based on what you learned in the reading, the discussion you have just had, and your own personal experience and knowledge about other languages and cultures, answer the questions. Although these are opinion questions, make sure you explain the reason(s) for your opinion.

   - Do people from some cultures experience certain emotions more strongly than people from other cultures? Why or why not?

   - Are human emotions universal? Or are they culture-specific?

> **Critical Thinking Tip:**
> Sometimes writers use questions to get readers to think about their own experiences and relate them to the reading. The writer does not answer the questions because the answers differ based on each reader's experience.

7. Some people think that it is healthy to express emotions openly. Other people believe that it is best to control their emotions and not reveal them to others. What are the advantages and disadvantages of each approach? What is your approach? Is it individual to you, or is it influenced by your culture? Explain.

B. Writing

Write an essay based on discussion questions 5, 6, or 7. When you write, use at least five of the target words from the chapter.

CHAPTER 11

Catching an Emotion

GETTING READY TO READ

Talk with a partner.

1. Can you usually guess how people are feeling by looking at their faces?

2. Some diseases can be passed from one person to another. Do you believe that feelings can be passed from one person to another? Explain your answer. Give examples.

READING

Read to Find Out: How can you "catch" someone else's emotions?

Read the definitions beside the reading. Then read "Catching an Emotion." If you see a new word, circle it, but don't stop reading. You can learn the new word later.

Catching an Emotion

1 You wake up one day with a fever and a bad cough. Should you go to work? In the past, many employers would likely have said yes. Going to work even when you were sick showed your commitment to your job, and was considered a **virtue**. Missing work for any reason was **frowned upon**. Nowadays, however, employers would probably agree that the **proper** decision in this case would be to stay at home. After all, it is better for one sick employee to miss a day or two than to pass the illness on to everyone in the office. But now imagine this situation. You wake up in a bad **mood**. Should you be concerned about passing your mood on to your co-workers?

2 According to psychologist[1] and writer Daniel Goleman, the answer is yes. In his recent book, *Social Intelligence: The New Science of Relationships*, Goleman explains that our brains are social tools; that is, the human brain was designed for social interaction. Research shows that the human brain contains cells called *mirror neurons*.[2] According to Goleman, these neurons allow us to sense "both the move another person is about to make and their feelings, and instantaneously[3] prepare us to **imitate** that movement and feel with them." Goleman goes on to say that "mirror neurons link brain-to-brain . . . if you put a person in a meeting who is either purposely upbeat[4] or downbeat,[5] it changes the whole group's collective mood for better or worse."

3 One example of passing one's emotions on to others is through laughter. One person starts laughing **out loud**, and even though we have no idea what the person is laughing at, we begin to laugh as well. When people are alone, on the other hand, they rarely laugh out loud, even when they read or hear a very **humorous** joke. This suggests that laughter is meant to be shared.

4 When someone laughs out loud, it is easy to recognize his or her emotional state. But most emotions are not expressed in such an obvious way. How are we able to recognize them? Brain research has shown that our ability to sense others' emotions is in our genes. We may not be **conscious** of it, but we are particularly good at reading others' **facial expressions**. Even the most **reserved** people reveal some emotion on their faces. For example, a movement as small as a raised eyebrow can communicate a world of information.

5 Psychologist Paul Ekman is considered the world's leading expert on facial expressions. He has spent years identifying the **muscle** movements that **make up** the thousands of facial expressions that we use to communicate our emotions. Interestingly, Ekman's research has revealed that our facial expressions are not only a mirror of what we are feeling. Sometimes, just making a facial expression can cause us to experience a particular emotion.

[1] *a psychologist* = someone who is trained in the way that people's minds work and the way that this affects their behavior

[2] *a neuron* = a type of cell that makes up the nervous system and sends messages in the brain about feelings, sights, smells, etc.

[3] *instantaneously* = immediately

[4] *upbeat* = happy and confident that good things will happen

[5] *downbeat* = not hopeful that the future will be good

For example, if you are in a bad mood, but put on an **artificial** smile, you will start to feel better faster. In other words, sometimes the facial expression actually starts the emotional process, rather than the other way around. So if you **greet** someone with a cheerful expression on your face, both of you will be more likely to feel cheerful.

6   Now let's return to our worker who wakes up in a bad mood. What should he do? The decision might depend on the workplace. If the atmosphere is generally positive, he should get up and go to work; it is more likely that he will "catch" the positive mood of others than that he will pass on his negative mood. And if he smiles despite his bad mood, he will have an even greater chance of recovery.

7   On the other hand, if the workplace atmosphere is negative, it might mean that he's already "caught" the negative feelings of his co-workers. In that case, it might be a good idea for him to start looking for another job. And now that he understands how emotions are passed from one person to another, he should be more **choosy** about where he works. He should look for a healthy workplace where he is unlikely to "catch" negative feelings from his co-workers. At the same time, he should be more conscious of the effect that his own emotional state has on his co-workers. As Goleman says, "Mirror neurons make us far more neurally connected than we ever knew; this creates a pathway for emotional contagion.[6] If you really care about people, it gives a new spin to the term social responsibility: what emotional states are you creating in the people you're with?"

[6] *contagion* = a sickness, feeling or attitude that spreads quickly from person to person

Quick Comprehension Check

A. Read these sentences **about the reading**. Circle T (true), F (false), or ? (can't determine the answer from the reading). If you circle T or F, write the number of the paragraph with the answer on the line.

1. Mirror neurons help us to recognize other people's feelings. T F ? ____

2. When people are alone, they don't laugh as much as they do when they are with other people. T F ? ____

3. Reserved people are particularly good at understanding how other people are feeling. T F ? ____

4. We know how to read facial expressions because our parents teach us how to do it. T F ? ____

5. We have very little control over our facial expressions. T F ? ____

6. Our facial expressions can affect our emotions. T F ? ____

7. If you wake up in a bad mood, you should probably not go to work. T F ? ____

8. People should consider changing their jobs if their co-workers are often in a bad mood. T F ? ____

B. Work with your class. Share your answers from part A. Go back to the reading to find the reason why a sentence is true or false. Correct the false sentences.

EXPLORING VOCABULARY

Thinking about the Target Vocabulary

Guessing Strategy: Recognizing Word Families

When you encounter an unfamiliar word, look at it carefully. Does it look like another word you already know? If so, it might be in the same word family, but a different form. Look at the example from the reading.

We are especially good at reading others' facial expressions.

Facial is the adjective form of the noun *face*. **Expression** is the noun form of the verb express. A **facial expression** is a look on a person's face that shows what that person is thinking or feeling.

A. Read the sentences and answer questions a and b. Then discuss question c with a partner.

1. In some cultures, expressing emotions is accepted. In other cultures, expressing emotion is **frowned upon**.

   a. Does the verb *frowned* look like a noun you already know? What word is that? _____

   b. What does that word mean? _____

   c. Think about that word and read the sentence again. Can you guess what **frowned upon** means?

2. When people are alone, they rarely laugh out loud, even when they read or hear a very **humorous** joke.

   a. What noun is similar to the adjective **humorous**? _____

   b. What does that word mean? _____

   c. Think about that word and read the sentence again. Can you guess what **humorous** means?

3. People should be **choosy** about where they work. They should not work at a place with a negative atmosphere.

   a. What verb is similar to the adjective **choosy**? _____

   b. What does that word mean? _____

   c. Think about that word and read the sentence again. Can you guess what **choosy** means?

B. Check your answers in a dictionary.

C. Look at the target words. Which ones are new to you? Circle them here and in the reading. The numbers in parentheses help you find the words in the paragraphs.

Target Words

virtue (1)	imitate (2)	facial expressions (4)	artificial (5)
frowned upon (1)	out loud (3)	reserved (4)	greet (5)
proper (1)	humorous (3)	muscle (5)	choosy (7)
mood (1)	conscious (4)	make up (5)	

D. Read "Catching an Emotion" again. Look at the context of the new words. Can you guess their meanings?

E. Complete the word form chart. Fill in the shaded areas of the chart with the target words from the reading. Write the base form of the verbs and the singular form of the nouns.

NOUNS	VERBS	ADJECTIVES	OTHER
virtue			

Understanding the Target Vocabulary

These sentences are **about the reading**. Complete them with the words in the box. Circle the words in the sentences that help you understand the meanings of the target words.

artificial	facial expressions	imitate	out loud	virtue
choosy	greet	mood	proper	
conscious	humorous	muscles	reserved	

1. When humans _____ each other, they almost always look at each

   other's faces. It is the polite, _____ thing to do.

2. But there is another reason that we look at each other's faces. We want to

   know what the other person is feeling and thinking, so we observe each other's

   _____ .

3. There are hundreds of _____ in the human face. Moving just one of

   them can reveal what we are feeling.

4. If you are in a good _____ , your cheerful face will speak louder than

   any words.

5. You don't need to talk about your emotions _____ . Your face will

   speak for you.

6. In some cultures, parents teach their children to share their emotions with others. Expressing one's emotions is seen as a _____. It is considered a positive thing.

7. Even _____ people who tend to hide their emotions reveal more than they think on their faces.

8. According to psychologists, many of us do not realize the power of our own emotions. We are not _____ of how our feelings affect others.

9. When you hear something _____, you usually smile or laugh. That puts you in a good mood. Then other people _____ your facial expressions, and they begin to feel good too.

10. Sometimes you can change your bad mood by changing your facial expression. For example, if you are in a bad mood and don't feel like smiling, you can pretend to be happy by putting an _____ smile on your face. Soon, you will begin to feel happier.

11. We also pass our bad moods on to each other. That is why we should be _____ about who we spend time with. If you have a choice, spend your time with people with a positive attitude.

DEVELOPING READING SKILLS

Understanding Figurative Language

Figurative Language: What Is It?

Sometimes writers use a common word or phrase differently from the way it is normally used. They go beyond the factual (literal) meaning of the word or phrase to explain something more clearly, or to make their writing more interesting. For example, in the reading, the writer compares being in a bad mood to having a physical illness. Everyone knows that physical illnesses can often be passed on to other people. By starting with that familiar idea, the writer can then more easily explain the new idea: it is possible to pass an emotion on to someone else. When writers use language in this way, it is called **figurative language**. To understand figurative language, start by thinking about the literal (factual) meaning of the word or phrase. The literal meaning will help you understand the figurative meaning.

Reading Tip:
We usually use quotation marks (" ") to show that we are quoting someone; in other words, we are using their exact words. However, we sometimes use quotation marks to show that we are using a word or phrase in a figurative way.

Talk with a partner. All of the questions include figurative language. The number in parentheses is the paragraph where you can find the **boldfaced** figurative language. After you finish talking, write down your answers as completely as you can. Do not copy from the text. Paraphrase instead.

1. What does **catch** mean? What happens when you **catch** an illness such as the flu or a cold? What does it mean to "**catch**" an emotion? (title)

2. What is a **tool**? What does Goleman mean when he says that our brains are "social **tools**"? (2)

3. What is the purpose of a **mirror**? What does the writer mean when she says that our facial expressions **mirror** what we are feeling? (5) What is the purpose of **mirror** neurons? (2)?

4. The writer says that if someone ". . . smiles despite his bad mood, he will have an even greater chance of **recovery**." (6) What does **recovery** mean? What will the person who smiles **recover from**?

> **Writing Tip:** If the writer uses a word or phrase figuratively in a sentence, you can paraphrase the sentence by explaining the idea without the figurative language.

Understanding Reference Words

Pronouns

Pronouns (such as *he, she, it,* and *them*) are reference words. A reference word refers to a noun, noun phrase, or a clause that comes *before* or *after* it. The words *this, that, these, those, which, who,* and *whom* are also reference words.

Look back at these sentences in the reading. What do the **boldfaced** reference words mean in these sentences? Circle the answer. The numbers in parentheses help you find the words in the paragraphs.

1. "If you put a person in a meeting **who** is either purposely upbeat or downbeat, it changes the whole group's collective mood for better or worse." (2)

   Who refers to

   a. a person.
   b. a mood.
   c. a group.

2. **This** suggests that laughter is meant to be shared. (3)

   This refers to

   a. the fact that people rarely laugh out loud when they are alone.
   b. the fact that people read or hear a humorous joke and laugh.
   c. the fact that people are alone.

3. How are we able to recognize **them**? (4)

   Them refers to

   a. people who laugh out loud.
   b. most emotions.
   c. his or her emotional state.

4. We may not be conscious of **it**, but we are particularly good at reading others' facial expressions. (4)

    It refers to

    a. our ability to read facial expressions.
    b. brain research about facial expressions.
    c. how we express emotion.

Reading Tip: The pronoun *it* can refer to just one specific object, or it can refer to a sentence or a phrase.

5. Even the most reserved people reveal some emotion on **their** faces. (4)

    Their refers to

    a. others' emotions.
    b. other people.
    c. reserved people.

6. He has spent years identifying the muscle movements **that** make up the thousands of facial expressions that we use to communicate our emotions. (5)

    That refers to

    a. years.
    b. muscle movements.
    c. thousands of facial expressions.

BUILDING ON THE VOCABULARY

Using the Target Vocabulary in New Contexts

Complete the sentences with the target words in the box. Be careful. There are two extra words.

artificial	greet	mood	proper
choosy	humorous	muscle	reserved
conscious	imitate	out loud	virtue
frowned upon	make up		

1. When you travel, it is important to know which behaviors are _____

    in that culture, and which behaviors are inappropriate. That way, you will know

    how to behave politely.

2. When I learn a new language, I like to listen to what people say and then

    _____ their pronunciation.

3. Some people say that if you want to survive in this economy, you can't be

    _____ about which job you take. They think that you should feel

    fortunate to have a job.

4. I don't like food with _____ ingredients. I like to eat healthy, natural food.

5. Most people would probably agree that honesty is a _____.

6. It is faster to read silently than to read _____.

7. In some cultures, it is proper to _____ a friend with a kiss on the cheek. In other cultures, some people may use a handshake instead.

8. _____ stories can be particularly difficult to translate. That is because what is funny in one culture may not be funny in another.

9. I'm sorry I'm late. I was so involved in my work that I wasn't _____ of the time.

10. You go to the party without me. I'm not in the _____ for being around a lot of people.

11. People from England tend to be more _____ than Americans. The English tend to keep their feelings to themselves rather than expressing them openly.

12. England, Scotland, Northern Ireland, and Wales _____ the United Kingdom.

Word Families: Adjectives ending in -y

Some adjectives are formed by adding -y to the end of a noun or verb. Notice that the spelling sometimes changes when you add -y. For example, if the word ends in an -e, you need to drop the -e before adding -y. Look at the example.

*My daughter is only three years old, but she is already very **choosy**. For example, she won't let me choose her clothes. She likes to choose her own.*

Sometimes, the meaning of the adjective will be very close to the meaning of the original word; but in some cases, you will need to use the context to guess what the adjective means.

Complete the sentences with the adjectives below.

airy	juicy	moody	picky	smelly	watery

1. No one likes to invite her for dinner because she's such a _____ eater. It's impossible to remember the many types of food that she won't eat.

2. These oranges are delicious! They are so sweet and _____.

3. I don't like this coffee. It's too _____. I prefer stronger coffee.

4. This room is so bright and _____. There's so much sunlight and open

   space. And look at the beautiful view!

5. Some people do not like strong cheese. They think that it is too _____.

6. My brother is very _____. He can be cheerful one minute, and

   depressed the next.

Word Grammar: Phrasal Verbs—*Make Up*

There are several phrasal verbs that are formed with the verb **make** and the particle
up. Each one has a different meaning.

Read the definitions for *make up* and the sentences that follow. Write the letter of the
meaning next to each sentence.

a. work or study at times when you do not usually work, so that you can do all the
   work that you should have done at an earlier time
b. become friendly again with someone after you have had an argument
c. invent a story, explanation, etc.
d. combine together to form a particular system, result, etc.
e. prepare or create something by putting things together

> **Vocabulary Tip:** Words and phrases often have several meanings. Use a different word card to learn each meaning. On one side of the card, write the word or phrase and an example sentence. Write the definition on the other side.

_____ 1. I missed the exam because I was sick. Can I **make it up**?

_____ 2. That isn't a true story. He **made it up**.

_____ 3. My husband and I had a fight last week, but yesterday we **made up**.

_____ 4. I'll **make up** a list of things we need for the party, and then we can go
              shopping.

_____ 5. There are many muscle movements that **make up** our facial expressions.

CRITICAL THINKING

A. Discussion

Share your ideas in a small group. As you talk, try to use the vocabulary below. Each
time someone uses a target word or phrase, put a check (✓) next to it.

☐ conscious	☐ greet	☐ humor/humorous	☐ out loud
☐ expression	☐ facial	☐ mood/moody	☐ reserved

1. In paragraph 4, what does the writer mean when she says "For example, a movement as small as a raised eyebrow can communicate a world of information"?

2. In paragraph 7, the writer quotes Goleman as saying, "If you really care about people, it gives a new spin to the term social responsibility: what emotional states are you creating in the people you're with?" What does the pronoun *it* refer to? What does Goleman think you should do if you really care about other people?

Critical Thinking Tip: Writers often end an essay with a suggestion about what the reader should do. Sometimes writers make their suggestions directly. Often, however the reader must infer what the writer is suggesting.

3. Brain research has shown that our ability to read other people's emotions is genetic. Assuming that this is correct, why is this ability so important that it is in our genes? How does being able to read others' emotions help us survive?

4. Which of the following jobs call for the ability to read other people's emotions correctly? Rank the jobs. Explain your rankings to your group.

   1 = doesn't call for much ability to read other people's emotions correctly
   2 = calls for some ability
   3 = calls for a lot of ability

Critical Thinking Tip: If you have understood a new idea, you should be able to apply it to a new situation. If you have trouble applying the idea, then you should probably study it more carefully.

   _____ an interpreter   _____ a nurse   _____ a teacher

   _____ a salesperson   _____ a police officer   _____ a telemarketer

   _____ an athlete   _____ an actor   _____ a computer programmer

   _____ a disc jockey (DJ)   _____ a lawyer   _____ a painter (artist)

B. Writing

Complete one or both of these writing topics. When you write, use at least five of the target words from the chapter. Underline the target words in your paper.

1. Write an essay. Describe how people in your culture express emotions. Consider the following questions when writing your essay:

   • How open are people about expressing their emotions? Is expressing one's emotions considered a virtue, or is it frowned upon?

   • How do people express their emotions? On their faces? With their bodies, for example with their hands? With their words and tone of voice?

Writing Tip: To make your writing more interesting, try using figurative language.

2. Choose a profession, and write an essay explaining how the ability to read other people's emotions can contribute to one's success in that profession.

CHAPTER 12

Reading Faces

GETTING READY TO READ

Talk with a partner.

1. Look at the photographs. What emotions do you think are being expressed in the photographs?

2. Do you think it's possible to tell whether someone is lying just by looking at his or her facial expressions? Explain your answer.

READING

Read the definitions beside the reading. Then read "Reading Faces." If you see a new word, circle it, but don't stop reading. You can learn the new word later.

Reading Faces

1   Dr. Paul Ekman has been named one of the most influential psychologists of the twentieth century. He is an expert in non-verbal[1] communication, including **gestures** and facial expressions. One of his many achievements was the discovery of microexpressions. Microexpressions are facial expressions that **flash** across the face and then disappear in less than a second. Microexpressions cannot be consciously controlled, and they happen so fast that most people do not even see them. Dr. Ekman was also involved in developing a **tool** for identifying the **range** of human facial expressions, the Facial Action Coding System (FACS). While all of Dr. Ekman's work is fascinating, one area has received a lot of attention: using facial expressions to **detect** lies.

2   Many of us believe that we can tell when someone is lying. However, research shows the opposite—most of us are very bad at it. According to Ekman and other experts, only a very small percentage of the population, less than 1%, is gifted at identifying liars.

3   Researchers working with Dr. Ekman have developed three tests to determine a person's lie detection abilities: an opinion test, a crime test, and an emotion test. For each test, the researchers made short videotapes of people either lying or telling the truth. The test taker then watches the recordings to see if he can identify the liars. In the opinion test, half of the people were lying about their opinions. In the crime test, half were lying about stealing $50. In the emotion test, half were lying about their feelings.

4   To be considered gifted, or a "wizard"[2] (the term used by Ekman and other researchers), the test taker must score at least 90% on the opinion test, and at least 80% on the other two tests. After testing approximately 20,000 individuals over more than 30 years, researchers have only identified about 50 wizards.

5   And what about the other people who took the tests? Most people scored 50% or lower—almost the same result they would get if they were guessing. However, a small percentage of individuals scored 80% or higher on at least one of the tests, while doing poorly on the others. The test that they scored highly on was almost always related to their profession. For example, more police officers scored well on the crime test, while a higher percentage of therapists[3] did well on the emotion test. This is understandable. After all, experience in a profession should lead to the development of skills related to that field, shouldn't it? Surprisingly, however, most people did not even score well on the test related to their profession!

[1] *non-verbal* = without words

[2] *a wizard* = someone who is very good at something

[3] *a therapist* = someone who has been trained to give a particular form of treatment for a mental illness

6   So how do the wizards do it? According to Dr. Ekman, when people are hiding the truth, their faces "leak"[4] information; that is, their facial muscles move in ways that a wizard or someone with special training can detect. For example, anger is an emotion with a characteristic feature: a tightening[5] of the lips. However, the microexpression for anger flashes so quickly across the face that you can easily miss it. Also, people often smile when they **attempt** to hide anger. This makes it even harder to catch that brief tightening of the lips before the smile. Wizards, however, are able to identify and **interpret** these microexpressions immediately. That is how they can tell when someone is lying.

7   Imagine how useful this information could be to the police. Police officers often have only a few seconds to **calculate** the danger of a situation. Sometimes, a simple **incident**, such as stopping a speeding **vehicle**, can become violent if the police officer misreads the driver's intentions. During this type of incident, an officer's ability to recognize the difference between a real smile and one that hides **rage** is extremely valuable. It can help prevent **tragedies**, including serious **injury** and even death. Or imagine that you are falsely **accused** of a crime. Wouldn't you want to be able to call in a wizard to read the truth on your face and stand by you during the **legal** process?

8   Although less than 1% of us are natural wizards, Dr. Ekman believes that with enough **motivation** and practice, almost anyone can be trained to see and correctly interpret microexpressions. To prove his point, Ekman developed a training tape with 40 examples of facial expressions. The first time most people watch the tape, they cannot see any of the microexpressions. However, after just 30 minutes of practice and instruction, they can see all of them. And after several days of training, most people are able to not only see, but also interpret microexpressions successfully.

9   However, identifying and successfully interpreting microexpressions does not tell you *what* someone is lying about. It only tells you that the person is lying about *something*. To find out exactly what happened during a crime, for example, interpreting microexpressions is only one tool among many that can be used.

10   In 2004 Dr. Ekman retired from his position as professor of psychology at the University of California (UCSF) Medical School and started his own company, the Paul Ekman Group (PEG). PEG conducts trainings all over the world, and also develops online interactive training tools. PEG's clients have included police departments, the Central Intelligence Agency (CIA), the Federal Bureau of Investigation (FBI), health care professionals, **security** organizations, and business leaders. Interestingly, there are also many individuals who take the training to improve their personal relationships.

[4] *to leak* = When water leaks through a roof, it gets in through a small hole or crack

[5] *tightening* = the act of making something tight or stretched

Quick Comprehension Check

A. Read these sentences **about the reading**. Circle T (true), F (false), or ? (can't determine the answer from the reading). If you circle T or F, write the number of the paragraph with the answer on the line.

1. The Facial Action Coding System was developed to help determine whether someone was lying. T F ? ____

2. Most people are very bad at lying. T F ? ____

3. By taking a series of tests, you can find out how good you are at recognizing lies. T F ? ____

4. Most people just guess on the tests. T F ? ____

5. Wizards are extremely gifted at lying. T F ? ____

6. Most police officers score high on the crime test. T F ? ____

7. People who are naturally gifted at recognizing microexpressions are also good at lie detection. T F ? ____

8. Police officers who can recognize and correctly interpret microexpressions can be more effective at their jobs. T F ? ____

9. Very few people can learn how to interpret microexpressions. T F ? ____

10. Many wizards work for the police. T F ? ____

B. Work with your class. Share your answers from part A. Go back to the reading to find the reason why a sentence is true or false. Correct the false sentences.

EXPLORING VOCABULARY

Thinking about the Target Vocabulary

Guessing Strategy: Asking Questions

To guess the meaning of an unfamiliar word, focus on the words that are familiar, rather than the words that you don't know. Often, if you ask yourself one or two simple questions about the information in the context, you will be able to approximate, or get a general idea of, the meaning of the unfamiliar word.

For example: He is an expert in non-verbal communication, including **gestures** and facial expressions.

Question: "Besides facial expressions, what other ways do people communicate without words?"

Possible answer: With their hands.

This answer brings you close to the meaning of gesture: a form of communication using the hands.

A. Read the sentences and answer the questions. The answer will give you an approximation of the meaning of the **boldfaced** target word.

1. Part of a police officer's job is to stop speeding **vehicles**.

   What is something fast that a police officer would need to stop? _____

2. It can help prevent serious **injury** and even death.

   What is something that is serious but not as serious as death? _____

3. It can help prevent **tragedies**, including serious injury and even death.

   What are serious injury and death examples of? _____

B. Look at the target words. Which ones are new to you? Circle them here and in the reading. The numbers in parentheses help you find the words in the paragraphs.

Target Words

gestures (1)	attempt (6)	vehicle (7)	accused (7)
flash (1)	interpret (6)	rage (7)	legal (7)
tool (1)	calculate (7)	tragedies (7)	motivation (8)
range (1)	incident (7)	injury (7)	security (10)
detect (1)			

C. Read "Reading Faces" again. Look at the context of the new words. Can you guess their meanings?

D. Complete the word form chart. Fill in the shaded areas of the chart with the target words from the reading. Write the base form of the verbs and the singular form of the nouns.

NOUNS	VERBS	ADJECTIVES
gesture		

Understanding the Target Vocabulary

These sentences are **about the reading**. Complete them with the words in the box. Circle the words in the sentences that help you understand the meanings of the target words.

attempt	gestures	motivation	security
calculate	incidents	rage	tools
detecting	injury	range	
flash	interpret		

1. To communicate, humans use not only words but also facial expressions and

    _____ .

2. Paul Ekman is a psychologist who has spent his career identifying and learning

    how to _____ facial expressions.

3. We experience a wide _____ of emotions every day, from disgust to

    joy. We have different facial expressions for all of these various emotions.

4. We often _____ to hide our feelings by controlling our facial

    expressions. Sometimes we are successful, and sometimes we are not.

5. Microexpressions are also facial expressions, but we cannot consciously control

    them. Microexpressions _____ so rapidly across the face that most

    people don't notice them.

6. After more than 30 years of testing, Ekman and other researchers

    _____ that only about 1% of the population can see microexpressions

    without any special training.

7. This 1% of the population is very good at _____ lies. They do it

    by being able to read people's faces quickly, before they can hide what they are

    thinking.

8. Although very few people are naturally able to recognize microexpressions,

    Ekman claims that most people can be trained to do so. He has developed a set of

    training _____ that include videotapes of people's faces as they are

    experiencing a variety of emotions.

9. Police officers have a strong _____ to learn to recognize microexpressions. Why? Because understanding how someone is feeling in a dangerous situation could save lives.

10. Extreme anger, or _____, is an emotion that police officers should definitely learn to recognize.

11. The police sometimes need to deal with individuals who have emotional and psychological problems. If the police are trained in reading microexpressions, they can be more effective in protecting these people from harming themselves or causing _____ to other people.

12. In some situations, police officers who are not able to read facial expressions very well can make mistakes. For example, if a police officer cannot tell the difference between a threatening look and a worried look, he might shoot someone who was not trying to threaten him at all. These types of unfortunate _____ are more common than many people realize.

13. Private _____ companies that are responsible for keeping important business people safe often have their employees take Dr. Ekman's training.

DEVELOPING READING SKILLS

Understanding Figurative Language

Work with a partner. Each question contains both the literal and figurative meaning of the target word in bold. Discuss the questions and then write down your answers.

1. How is a flash of light similar to the way that an expression **flashes** across someone's face?

   _____

   _____

2. When a roof leaks, what does it leak? When a face **leaks**, what does it leak? What do leaky roofs and "leaky" faces have in common?

   _____

   _____

3. What does a child need to know in order to calculate the sum of two numbers, for example 2 + 2? What does a police officer need to know in order to **calculate** the danger of a situation?

_____

_____

Paraphrasing: Complex Ideas

When you paraphrase a complex sentence, your paraphrase might be longer than the original sentence. For example, it might take you two sentences to paraphrase one sentence. That is because you often need to add words to explain a complex thought.

A. One sentence in each set paraphrases the sentence from the reading. Circle the correct answer.

Reading Tip: Paraphrasing is a good way to test your understanding of a sentence. You cannot paraphrase something if you do not understand it very well.

1. Most people scored 50% or lower on the lie detection tests—almost the same result you would get if you were guessing.

   a. Most people got the same result on the lie detection test as they did when they were just guessing.
   b. When people guess on a test, they usually get at least half of the answers wrong. That is the score most people got on the lie detection tests.

2. During this type of incident, an officer's ability to recognize the difference between a real smile and one that hides rage is extremely valuable.

   a. Police officers often have to deal with situations involving angry people. Therefore, it is very important for the police to be able to tell when a smile hides angry intentions.
   b. In their interactions with the public, it is very important for the police to be able to distinguish an artificial smile from a real one. Artificial smiles can hide a wide range of emotions.

3. After several days of training, most people are able to not only see, but also interpret microexpressions successfully.

   a. People are trained for several days. At the end, they are experts in reading microexpressions.
   b. The training takes several days. People are trained to see microexpressions and then learn how to read them correctly.

B. Paraphrase these sentences from the reading. The numbers in parentheses are the paragraphs the sentences come from.

Writing Tip: Remember to change not only words, but also sentence structure when you paraphrase.

1. After testing approximately 20,000 individuals over more than 30 years, researchers have only identified about 50 wizards. (4)

_____

_____

2. Anger is an emotion with a characteristic feature: a tightening of the lips. (6)

_____

_____

3. To find out exactly what happened during a crime, for example, interpreting microexpressions is only one tool among many that can be used. (9)

_____

_____

BUILDING ON THE VOCABULARY

Using the Target Vocabulary in New Contexts

Complete the sentences with the target words in the box. Be careful. There are two extra words.

accused	flash	interpret	rage	tools
attempted	gestures	legal	range	tragedy
calculate	incident	motivation	security	vehicles
detected	injury			

1. They _____ her of stealing the jewelry. However, they never found any proof, so they had to let her go.

2. The whole family died in a home fire. It was a _____.

3. Before you decide whether to buy that business, you should get a lawyer to examine all the documents. You need good _____ advice before making that kind of decision.

4. The homeowner smelled gas, so he called the gas company. It was fortunate that he did; the workers _____ a serious gas leak in the street in front of the house.

5. Only people who live on the street are allowed to drive down it. It is closed to all other _____.

6. She hurt her leg in a skiing accident. Fortunately, the _____ was not severe.

7. When I hit my head, I saw a _____ of light before I lost

   consciousness.

8. Museums contain a lot of valuable objects that need to be protected. Therefore,

   the _____ at museums is very high.

9. I _____ to fix the sink myself, but I didn't have the proper

   _____. I ended up calling a plumber.

10. Sometimes, when we don't want to say something out loud, we use

    _____ to communicate.

11. It was very difficult to work and go to school at the same time. However, I did it

    anyway. My _____ was my desire to provide for my family.

12. After all these years of marriage, it is still not easy for me to _____

    my husband's moods. Sometimes I think he is angry when in fact he is cheerful!

    He is a bit of a mystery to me.

13. There was an _____ involving two of my daughter's classmates at

    school yesterday. I'm not sure what happened, but their parents were called in.

14. Anger is more easily controlled than _____, which is a more violent

    feeling.

Word Families: The prefix *micro-*

The prefix *micro-* means small. It is used to create many new words. For example, the word "microexpression" was created to refer to facial expressions that involve very small, almost undetectable movements of the facial muscles; microexpressions also last for a very short period of time.

Read the sentences about words with the prefix *micro-*. Then complete the sentences. When you finish, check your answers in a dictionary.

> **Vocabulary Tip:**
> Use your knowledge of prefixes to help you guess the meaning of unfamiliar words.

1. Biology is the study of life and all living organisms, both those that we can see

   with our eyes, and those that we cannot see without special instruments.

   Microbiology is the study of _____

   _____.

2. Macroeconomics is the study of the large economic forces and government and

   business decisions that affect an entire country. In contrast, **microeconomics** is the study of _____

_____.

3. A manager is someone who manages people and the work that they do. A **micromanager** is a type of manager who is usually not very popular with his employees. He is unpopular because he attempts to _____

_____.

4. Credit is money that a bank will loan to people and allow them to pay back over a period of time. In return, the banks collect interest (extra money) on the loans. People who are very poor, however, cannot usually get credit, nor can they afford to pay very much interest. Recently, some individuals and even banks in poor countries have gotten involved in **microcredit**. **Microcredit** is _____

_____.

Word Grammar: Collocations—Compound Nouns

A compound noun is a noun that was formed by joining two nouns together. Compound nouns usually start out as two separate words that are so frequently used together that they become one word. They have their own specific meaning and entry in the dictionary. *Flashlight* is an example of a compound noun.

Some compound nouns are written as one word. Others can be written as two words, but they are still thought of as one word. For example, *flashflood* can also be written as *flash flood*.

A. Match the compound nouns with their definitions.

Word	Definition
_____ 1. flashback	a. a small light that you can carry in your hand
_____ 2. flashcard	b. a very large amount of water caused by heavy rain over a short period of time that covers an area that is usually dry
_____ 3. flashflood	c. a place, event or time when trouble or violence might easily develop suddenly and be difficult to control
_____ 4. flashlight	d. a scene in a movie, play, book, etc. that shows something that happened before that point in the story
_____ 5. flashpoint	e. a small card with a word or picture on it, usually for studying

B. Complete the sentences with the words from exercise A.

1. During a _____, the director reveals that the main character was insulted and humiliated as a child.

2. Please don't drive tonight. The weather is supposed to be terrible. I heard a _____ warning on the radio.

3. Every time I learn a new word, I make a _____.

4. I always keep a _____ by my bed in case we lose electricity.

5. Stay away from that park. It's too risky to play there. It's a _____ for violence in the neighborhood.

CRITICAL THINKING

A. Discussion

Share your ideas in a small group. As you talk, try to use the vocabulary below. Each time someone uses a target word, put a check (✓) next to it.

☐ accuse	☐ gesture	☐ legal
☐ attempt	☐ incident	☐ motivation
☐ calculate	☐ injury	☐ rage
☐ detect	☐ interpret	☐ tragedy

1. Look back at paragraph 5 of the reading. Why does the writer use an exclamation point (!) at the end of the last sentence of the paragraph? What strong emotion is the writer trying to communicate? Why does the writer experience this emotion? Did you share the writer's emotion when you were reading? Why or why not?

2. In paragraph 7, the writer states that the ability to read microexpressions could help police officers prevent tragedies. How do you think this is possible? Give a specific example of a tragedy involving the police that could be prevented in this way. You can talk about the incident mentioned in the paragraph, or you can make up a different situation.

3. In paragraph 9, the writer says "To find out exactly what happened during a crime, for example, interpreting microexpressions is only one tool among many that can be used." How can microexpressions be used as tools in solving crimes? Why should the police use other tools as well? Can you infer what those other tools might be?

4. In paragraph 10, the writer states that individuals sometimes take Dr. Erkman's training in order to improve their personal relationships. What

Reading Tip: Writers sometimes reveal their attitudes through punctuation. For example, an *exclamation point* (!) is often used to show strong emotion.

Critical Thinking Tip: If the writer uses a particular incident to illustrate a main point, try making up a different incident to illustrate the same main point. This can lead you to a deeper understanding of the reading.

could an individual learn from this type of training that might help his or her relationships with friends, relatives, and co-workers?

5. In your opinion, what are some possible advantages of being a "wizard" as described in paragraph 4? What are some disadvantages? Support your ideas with information from the reading.

6. Would you like to be a "wizard"? Why or why not? Refer to your discussion of question 5 in your answer.

B. Writing

Complete one or both of these writing topics. When you write, use at least five of the target words from the chapter. Underline the target words in your paper.

1. Write an essay based on discussion question 4.

2. Write an essay explaining why you would or would not like to be a "wizard."

Checkpoint

LEARNING OUTCOME

❯ Review and expand on the content of Unit 4

LOOK BACK

A. Think About This

Look at the list of emotions from the *Think About This* exercise on page 129. Which of those emotions were mentioned in the readings in the unit? Check (✓) them.

☐ anger   ☐ frustration

☐ excitement   ☐ joy

☐ fear   ☐ sadness

B. Remember the Readings

What do you want to remember most from the readings in Unit 4? For each chapter, write one sentence about the reading.

Chapter 10: Can You Translate an Emotion?

_____

Chapter 11: Catching an Emotion

_____

Chapter 12: Reading Faces

_____

Read the text. Do not use a dictionary.

Chronic Blushing

1   People with expressive faces are probably not surprised when others sometimes "read their minds." However, even very reserved people can usually control most of their facial expressions if they make a conscious attempt to hide their feelings. But imagine what your life would be like if anyone observing you could easily detect exactly what you were thinking and feeling. What if your every emotion—guilt, shame, shock, rage, disgust, fear, humiliation—was written on your face, for the whole world to witness? For people who suffer from a condition known as chronic blushing, this unfortunate situation is an everyday reality.

2   Of course, it is normal for our faces to become hot and get red when we are embarrassed. However, for people who suffer from chronic blushing, this normal physical reaction to stress is so constant and severe that it can damage their personal and professional lives. Consider, for example, a young television news announcer just starting out in her career. She has always blushed easily, but suddenly, she notices that whenever she reports on a tragic or even humorous incident, her face, neck, and ears all turn a deep red. At first she deals with the problem by putting heavy makeup on her face before going on television. Unfortunately, the makeup gives her an artificial appearance, and she begins to lose popularity with television viewers.

3   The story of the television news announcer is just one of many that reveal the negative effects that chronic blushing can have on one's life. So, what can someone who suffers from this condition do? For minor cases, makeup works quite well. For serious cases, there is an operation that can get rid of blushing. However, it is a major operation, and most doctors will perform it only after the patient has first attempted other solutions.

Quick Comprehension Check

A. Read these sentences **about the reading**. Circle T (true), F (false), or ? (can't determine the answer from the reading). If you circle T or F, write the number of the paragraph with the answer on the line.

1. Most people are able to hide their feelings pretty well.   T F ? _____

2. Blushing is very common.   T F ? _____

3. People who blush too much can sometimes have personal and professional problems.   T F ? _____

4. Chronic blushers are much more emotional than other people.   T F ? _____

5. According to the writer, people who suffer from chronic blushing should have an operation to correct the problem.   T F ? _____

B. Go back to the reading to find the reason why a sentence is true or false. Correct the false sentences.

Guessing Meaning from Context

Answer these questions.

1. How would you define *chronic blushing*?

   _____

   _____

2. What is the meaning of *makeup* in paragraph 2?

   _____

   _____

3. What does *minor* mean in paragraph 3?

   _____

   _____

Applying Information

Answer the questions.

1. What are three jobs in which chronic blushing might be a serious problem? For each job, explain how chronic blushing might be a serious disadvantage.

   _____

   _____

2. Imagine a case in which a doctor refused to perform an operation to "cure" someone's blushing problem. Describe the case using specific details.

   _____

   _____

Paraphrasing

Paraphrase these sentences from the text.

1. People with expressive faces are probably not surprised when others sometimes "read their minds."

   _____

   _____

2. Of course, it is normal for our faces to become hot and get red when we are embarrassed.

_____

_____

3. However, it is a major operation, and most doctors will perform it only after the patient has first attempted other solutions.

_____

_____

EXPANDING VOCABULARY

Word Grammar: Collocations

Read these sentences, and look carefully at the pattern for each verb.

a. He **accused** me **of** being dishonest.

  Pattern = **accuse** someone **of** something (or **of** doing something)

b. I always **associate** the smell of rain **with** my farm.

  Pattern = **associate** something or someone **with** something or someone else

c. Could you please **translate** this **from** English **into** Chinese?

  Pattern = **translate** something **from** something (a language) **into** something else (another language)

d. The cost of a house in this town **ranges from** $175,000 **to** $400,000.

  Pattern = something **ranges from** something (an amount or size) **to** something else (another amount or size)

e. Parents should **provide** their children **with** a good education.

  Pattern = **provide** someone **with** something

On a piece of paper, write the answers to these questions in complete sentences. Use the **boldfaced** verb and preposition combinations.

1. If a teacher **accused** you **of** something you didn't do, what would you do?

2. What smell(s) do you **associate with** your childhood?

3. Is it easy or difficult for you to **translate** something **from** your first language **into** English?

4. In your city, what is the cost of renting a one-bedroom apartment? (Use **range from . . . to** in your answer.)

5. Do you think that the government should **provide** the homeless **with** a place to live? Explain your answer.

Word Families: Spelling

Some words have both a noun and verb form, but the forms are spelled differently, for example *interpret* and *interpretation*. However, many words can be nouns or verbs, with no change in spelling, as in *damage*.

All of the words in the box can be nouns or verbs. Complete the sentences with the words. Identify whether the word is used as a noun or a verb. Circle *n.* (noun) or *v.* (verb).

damage	gesture	honor	insult	range

1. a. You should never call someone that name. It is a

   terrible _____ .   n.   v.

   b. If you _____ me again, I am going to report
   you to the teacher.   n.   v.

2. a. Why did you _____ at me? What do you want?   n.   v.

   b. I'm not familiar with the _____ that you used.   n.   v.

3. a. How did you _____ my computer?   n.   v.

   b. The _____ will be expensive to repair.   n.   v.

4. a. They had a party to _____ their employees.   n.   v.

   b. The employees were proud of the _____ .   n.   v.

5. a. The salary _____ in their department is
   quite wide.   n.   v.

   b. The salaries _____ from $35,000 to $100,000   n.   v.

PLAYING WITH WORDS

Look back at the lists of target vocabulary on pages 133, 145, and 157. In a small group, write the target words that you associate with each category in the box under that category. Be ready to explain your answers. Some words might fit under more than one category, and some words might not fit under any category.

THE LAW	THE BODY	EMOTIONS
detect, guilt	gesture	reveal, guilt

BUILDING DICTIONARY SKILLS

Finding Words

When you look up a word, you can find information about other words in the same word family in the same entry or in nearby entries. For example, look at the dictionary entry below.

---

con·scious /'kɑnʃəs/ *adj* **1** [not before noun] noticing or realizing something [= **aware**]: *I became conscious of the fact that someone was watching me.* **2** awake and able to understand what is happening [≠ **unconscious**]: *Owen was still conscious when they arrived at the hospital.* **3 conscious effort/decision/attempt etc.** a deliberate effort, decision, etc.: *Vivian had made a conscious effort to be friendly.* **4** thinking that something is very important: *fashion-conscious teenagers* | *She's very conscious of safety.* —**consciously** *adv*

con·scious·ness /'kɑnʃəsnɪs/ *n* [U] **1** the condition of being awake and understanding what is happening: *Charlie fell down the stairs and lost consciousness.* | *It was two weeks before he regained consciousness.* **2** someone's mind, thoughts, and ideas: *research into human consciousness* **3** the state of knowing that something exists or is true [= **awareness**]: *The march is intended to raise people's consciousness about women's health issues.*

Below the entry for the target word **conscious**, you find the entry for the related noun **consciousness**. You also find the adverb form **consciously**, and an adjective with the opposite meaning, **unconscious**.

Look up the words in the box in your dictionary and find other forms of each word. Fill in the blanks with the correct forms of the words. If the word is a noun, you might need to make it plural.

accuse	imitate	muscle	tragedy
associate	injury	observe	translate
calculate	interpret	provide	virtue
conscious	legal	recognize	

1. Your ___calculations___ are correct, but your answer is wrong. Check your numbers again.

2. Your _____ is not very serious, but you won't be able to use your hand for a few days.

3. He has strong, _____ legs because he rides his bicycle every day to work.

4. The doctor made a _____ mistake, and as a result his patient died.

5. Can you help me with this _____. My Spanish isn't very good.

6. After watching the animals for several hours, the researcher wrote down her _____ in a notebook. Later her assistant typed them for her.

7. He said he recognized her, but I think he was lying. When he saw her, there was no

_____ on his face.

8. You can't do that. It's _____. You will be arrested!

9. The police will never believe your _____. You have no proof!

10. If you belong to the Automobile _____ and you have a problem with

your car while you are on a trip, you can call them for help.

11. Is there a _____ in your employment contract to protect you in case

you are injured while working?

12. My professor's _____ of the poem is brilliant. Many famous critics

have discussed the same poem, but her point of view is entirely original.

13. When he fell down and hit his head, he lost _____ for several

minutes, but he seemed perfectly fine after that.

14. He is a very _____ young man. He has a strong sense of right and

wrong, and always attempts to behave morally.

15. Most people would not be able to detect that the stone in your ring is not a real

diamond. It is an excellent _____ .

MAN AND BEAST

THINK ABOUT THIS

Complete the chart. Write ✓ (animal has this quality or ability), X (animal lacks this quality or ability), or ? (not sure). Then share your answers and any additional information you have about the animals in the chart.

QUALITY OR ABILITY	WHALES	BIRDS	DOGS	WOLVES	APES (MONKEYS, CHIMPS, GORILLAS)
are intelligent					
are creative					
make music					
can read human body language					

CHAPTER 13

Is Music Universal?

LEARNING OUTCOME

> Learn about similarities between human and animal "music"

Many whales communicate with each other with "whale songs."

GETTING READY TO READ

Do you think the following statements are true or false? Write T (true) or F (false). Compare your answers with a partner. (You will learn the correct answers in the chapter reading.)

_____ 1. There is one universal definition of music.

_____ 2. A wide range of animal species not only make music but also seem to enjoy it.

_____ 3. Whale "songs" are very different from human songs.

_____ 4. Some animals can actually play simple musical instruments.

READING

Read the definitions beside the reading. Then read "Is Music Universal?" If you see a new word, circle it, but don't stop reading. You can learn the new word later.

Is Music Universal?

1   It has long been said that music is universal, but now science is proving just how deeply true that statement really is. Like most people, scientists cannot define exactly what music is, but they know it when they hear it. One group of scientists has shown that human **appreciation** of music may be shared by whales, birds, and even rats; that it is remarkably **ancient**; and that studying why animals and humans appreciate music may help us better understand how the brain works.

2   In research published in the **journal** *Science*, several scientists have shown that in very basic ways, other **species** share music appreciation, and that this appreciation may be one of humanity's oldest activities. Through such research, scientists hope they may come to understand the human mind better. Perhaps they will even learn **key** information about how to deal with **damage** to the **auditory system**.

3   Jelle Atema is a biologist and co-author of one of the *Science* papers.[1] Like several of the researchers involved in the *Science* papers, Atema is both a scientist and a musician. In addition to his work in biology, he plays the flute.[2] He has carefully made exact copies of ancient bone flutes in order to play them. He wants to determine the kinds of sounds that early humans may have made.

4   "Do musical sounds in nature reveal a profound[3] **bond** between all living things?" asks one of the papers. There is a lot of **evidence** that perhaps it does. For example, the general **structure** of whale music is remarkably similar to that of human music. Indeed, the "songs" of one type of whale follow many of the same, **precise** rules that are nearly universal in human music. The two species share a similar tonal[4] **scale**, and their songs involve the introduction and variation of a central **theme**.

5   Many species of birds sing in ways that also follow the rules of human song. They use note scales similar to those used by humans, even though an **endless** variety of such scales is possible. Among some species, songs are passed from one generation to another or are shared by a group of peers. And some birds even intentionally look for objects that can be used as instruments, and then play them. For example, one type of bird uses a **hollow** log[5] as a **drum**, beating on it with a small stick it breaks off from a tree!

6   There is also evidence that music played an important part in early human history. For example, 40,000-year-old flutes have been found in northern Europe. Referring to early humans, Atema says, "To see that they spent so much time [making instruments] means music was important to them." The ability to make music, some scientists believe, may even be older than language.

[1] *a paper* = research on a particular subject that is written up and usually published

[2] *a flute* = a musical instrument shaped like a pipe, that you play by holding it across your lips and blowing into it

[3] *profound* = having a strong influence or effect

[4] *tonal* = having a particular quality of musical sound

[5] *a log* = a thick piece of wood cut from a tree

7   Mark Jude Tramo, a neurologist,[6] says he is fascinated by the complexity of the human brain's reaction to music. "There is no 'music center' in the brain," he wrote. Almost every thinking part of the brain is involved in listening to music, and when we move to the music, many of the areas controlling movement are involved too. "Imagine how much of the brain lights up when we dance!"

8   Tramo sees the research on music as a process that will lead to a better understanding of how the brain works. By learning exactly how the brain processes and "understands" the specific features that music is made of, a more complete understanding of how the brain **makes sense of** the world around us may develop. Other scientists are conducting similar research on how the brain reacts to **visual** arts. One of their motivations is to understand how the human visual system works.

9   Tramo believes that "That understanding . . . is going to help scientists in their efforts to help **the deaf** to hear, and help the blind to see."

[6] *a neurologist = a doctor who studies and treats the nervous system and the diseases related to it*

Quick Comprehension Check

A. Read these sentences **about the reading**. Circle T (true), F (false), or ? (can't determine the answer from the reading). If you circle T or F, write the number of the paragraph where you can find the answer on the line.

1. There is one universal definition of music.   T   F   ?   _____

2. Humans learned how to play music before they learned how to speak.   T   F   ?   _____

3. A wide range of animal species not only make music but also seem to enjoy it.   T   F   ?   _____

4. Whale "songs" are very different from human songs.   T   F   ?   _____

5. Some animals can actually play simple musical instruments. T   F   ?   _____

6. There is a particular area of the brain that is used specifically for music.   T   F   ?   _____

7. This research will probably lead to a cure for deafness.   T   F   ?   _____

B. Work with your class. Share your answers from part A. Go back to the reading to find the reason why a sentence is true or false. Correct the false sentences.

C. Compare the answers to your responses in the Getting Ready to Read exercise on page 174. How many did you get correct before doing the reading?

EXPLORING VOCABULARY

Thinking about the Target Vocabulary

Guessing Strategy: Descriptive Phrases

Sometimes, a word is followed by a descriptive phrase that can help you guess its meaning. Look at the example.

The **journal** *Science, published weekly,* contains scientific research on a wide range of topics.

From the descriptive phrase "published weekly" after the word *journal,* you should be able to figure out that a *journal* is something that is published regularly, like a magazine.

A. Read the sentences and pay attention to the phrases in *italics* after the **boldfaced** target words. Then write a general definition or explanation of the target word.

1. "Do musical sounds in nature reveal a . . . bond *between all living things*?" asks one of the papers.

    A **bond** is _____.

2. The **auditory** system, *responsible for our ability to hear,* can be easily damaged.

    Auditory means _____.

3. Some even intentionally look for objects in their environment that can be used as instruments, and then play them. For example, one type of bird uses a hollow log as a **drum**, *beating on it with a small stick it breaks off from a tree!*

    Drum means _____.

4. "That understanding . . . is going to help scientists in their efforts to help **the deaf** *to hear,* and help the blind to see."

    The deaf means _____.

> **Reading Tip:**
> When you see a descriptive phrase, make sure you know what word or idea the phrase describes. Usually the descriptive phrase comes immediately before or after what it describes.

B. Look at the target words. Which ones are new to you? Circle them here and in the reading. The numbers in parentheses help you find the words in the paragraphs.

Target Words

appreciation (1)	damage (2)	precise (4)	hollow (5)
ancient (1)	auditory (2)	structure (4)	drum (5)
journal (2)	system (2)	scale (4)	makes sense of (8)
species (2)	bond (4)	theme (4)	visual (8)
key (2)	evidence (4)	endless (5)	the deaf (9)

C. Read "Is Music Universal?" again. Look at the context of the new words. Can you guess their meanings?

D. Complete the word form chart. Fill in the shaded areas of the chart with the target words from the reading. Write the base form of the verbs and the singular form of the nouns.

NOUNS		VERBS	ADJECTIVES
appreciation			

Understanding the Target Vocabulary

These sentences are **about the reading**. Circle the meaning of the **boldfaced** words. Circle the words in the sentences that help you understand the meanings of the target words.

1. Scientists have recently found **evidence** that some animals produce music very similar to human music. One example is the fact that whale songs follow many of the same musical patterns as human songs. *Evidence* is used to

   a. conduct an experiment.   b. make music.   c. prove a theory.

2. There is more and more research showing that humans are not the only ones with an **appreciation** for music; it is likely that at least some animals enjoy it as much as we do. *Appreciation* means

   a. a remarkable talent.   b. excellent hearing.   c. an understanding of the importance.

3. There is an **endless** variety of musical patterns. It is therefore surprising that human songs and whale songs are so similar. If something is *endless*, it

   a. hurts your ears because it is so loud.   b. is very large or very long.   c. is so difficult that no one can understand it.

4. An example of a similarity between whale music and human music is the **scale** that they both use. Although the number of possible musical scales is in fact endless, both whales and humans "sing" with the same notes. A musical *scale* is

a. a combination of a variety of animal sounds.

b. a musical note that is sung for a long time.

c. a series of notes in a set pattern from high to low, or vice versa.

5. Like humans, whales begin their songs with a **theme**, make some changes to it, and then come back to the original theme before ending the song. The *theme* of a piece of music is

a. the part of the song that is repeated.

b. the first note of the song.

c. the most popular song in a group of songs.

6. In fact, both whale and human music follow many of the same, very **precise** rules. If a rule is *precise*, it is

a. exact and correct in detail.

b. important in a very general way.

c. interesting and every beautiful.

7. Whales are not the only **species** that sing. Birds, of course, sing all the time. *Species* means

a. a group of similar animals that can (make babies) with each other.

b. a group of related songs.

c. special animals that are remarkably breed intelligent.

8. Some birds even make simple drums by hitting a piece of wood with a stick. Interestingly, they always choose a **hollow** piece of wood. They never choose a solid piece of wood. A *hollow* piece of wood is

a. very heavy.

b. extremely dry.

c. empty inside.

9. Flutes have been found that are 40,000 years old. One scientist has played these **ancient** instruments to hear how early human music might have sounded. *Ancient* means

a. quite beautiful.

b. scientific.

c. very old.

10. By studying how the brains of both humans and animals process music, scientists hope to learn **key** information about the way the brain works in general. *Key* information is

a. very difficult.

b. very important.

c. very new.

11. Scientists hope to use this information to help people who can't hear. They hope to learn how to repair **damage** to parts of the auditory system, such as the inner ear. *Damage* means

a. physical harm.

b. scientific information.

c. harm to people who are deaf.

12. While some scientists are working to help people who can't hear, others are working to help those who can't see. They are trying to better understand the way the human **visual** system works. Our *visual* system is in charge of

a. what and how we see.

b. what and how we hear.

c. what and how we move.

13. Scientists want to know how the brain **makes sense of** the visual and auditory information it receives. When you *make sense of* something, you

    a. improve the way it works.
    b. understand how it works.
    c. hear it and watch it.

14. Despite progress in science and technology, scientists still do not completely understand the **structure** of the human brain. If they could understand the brain's *structure*, they would understand

    a. the way it is organized.
    b. what happens when we die.
    c. how to control it.

DEVELOPING READING SKILLS

Using an Outline

Understanding the Relationship between Ideas: Using an Outline

An **outline** gives an overview of the structure and most important information in a text. By organizing the information from a reading in an outline, you benefit in two important ways:

1. You check your understanding of the reading. If you can outline a reading, you probably understand it quite well; if not, you need to read it again and, if necessary, ask for help.

2. When you review the outline, you can immediately recognize the relationships among the main ideas, major points, and supporting details. This is especially helpful if you are going to be tested on the information in the text.

When writing an outline, use single words or phrases rather than full sentences, except for the main idea, which is usually written as a sentence.

This is an outline of the information contained in paragraphs 4 and 5 of "Is Music Universal?" Fill in the missing information in the outline. The Roman numeral I is for the main idea, the letters A and B are for the major points, and the numbers 1, 2, 3, and 4 are for the supporting details.

I. _____

    A. Structure of whale and human music very similar

        1. _____

        2. _____

    B. _____

        1. _____

        2. Songs passed from generation to generation

        3. _____

        4. _____

Summarizing

Use the information from your outline to write a summary of paragraphs 4 and 5 of the reading. Do not look back at the text.

Writing Tip: To avoid copying from a reading when summarizing, make an outline using just individual words or short phrases. Then look at the outline when summarizing, not the original text.

BUILDING ON THE VOCABULARY

Using the Target Vocabulary in New Contexts

Complete the sentences with the target words in the box. Be careful. There are two extra words or phrases.

appreciation	endless	key	structure
auditory	evidence	make sense of	system
bond	hollow	precise	themes
drums	journal	scale	visual

1. He was in a car accident and suffered severe _____ damage. Now he cannot hear.

2. The _____ between mother and child is very strong. Even when they live far away from each other, they always feel a connection.

3. He went to a special school for _____ arts. He studied painting and design.

4. What is the highest note that you can sing on a C major _____.

5. That movie seemed _____ it went on and on! I was really bored.

6. This lamp looks heavy, but actually it's very light because it's _____ on the inside.

7. If you are having trouble dancing to the music, just listen for the _____. They will help you to detect the beat.

8. I can't _____ these instructions. They are so hard to interpret! Can you help me?

9. The police can't prove he robbed the bank because they don't have any _____.

10. Honor for one's parents is a _____ feature of Chinese culture.

11. Courts, lawyers, and judges are key parts of the legal _____.

12. Based on client complaints, the management is changing the company

    _____. They will have fewer supervisors and provide more security

    and better customer service.

13. I like movies that deal with serious _____. I don't really like

    comedies or romances.

14. Please check your calculations before handing in your test. The measurements

    must be _____, or you will not get any points.

Word Families: Word Roots

A *root* is a part of a word with a specific meaning. For example, the target word **visual** contains the root **vis** which means *see*. The target word **auditory** contains the root *audi*, which means *hear*.

A. Read these sentences. Match the **boldfaced** words with their definitions.

1. My night **vision** is not very good. I need to wear glasses when I drive after dark.

2. The **audience** loved his performance. Everyone in the theater stood up and clapped when he finished.

3. Do you need any **audio-visual** equipment for your presentation?

4. Do you think the professor will let me **audit** her course? I don't need a grade; I just want to attend her lectures.

5. Scientists use microscopes to look at plants and animals that are so small that they are not **visible** to the human eye.

> **Vocabulary Tip:**
> Knowing the meanings of the most common word roots can help you to guess the meaning of words that contain those roots.

Word	Definition
_____ 1. vision	a. the people watching or listening to a concert, speech, movie, etc.
_____ 2. audience	b. the ability to see
_____ 3. audio-visual	c. sit in a college class and just listen without participating in the assignments or tests
_____ 4. visible	d. involving the use of recorded pictures and sound
_____ 5. audit	e. able to be seen

B. Work with a partner. Answer the questions using the **boldfaced** words.

1. Is your night **vision** as good as your day **vision**?

2. Have you ever performed in front of a live **audience**? If not, would you like to? Why or why not?

3. Have you ever given an **audio-visual** presentation in your native language? In English? If so, describe your experience.

4. In universities in your country, is it possible to **audit** classes? What are the advantages and disadvantages of auditing a class?

5. Besides microscopes, what other ways can scientists use to study things that are not **visible** to the human eye?

Word Grammar: Collocations with *System*

There are many collocations with the word *system*. A system is a set of related or connected things that work together.

The human body, for example, has systems that consist of different parts of the body, or organs, that work together. The **auditory system** and **visual system** are two of the body's systems.

There are also national systems that consist of different departments and officials that work together. The **healthcare system**, the **legal system**, and the **political system** are three important systems.

Notice the collocations with **system**:

auditory system and **visual system** (not *hearing system* or *sight system*).

healthcare system, **legal system**, and **political system** (not *health system, law system*, or *politics system*.).

Discuss the questions with a partner. Use the words in **bold** in your answers. If you do not know a word that you need, look it up in your dictionary.

1. Which organs are involved in the **auditory system**?

2. Which organs are involved in the **visual system**?

3. Compare your country's **political system** to the **political system** of another country you are familiar with. How are the **political systems** in the two countries similar? How are they different?

4. Is your country's **healthcare system** free? If not, what happens when a poor person gets sick?

5. Under your country's **legal system**, who decides whether a person is guilty of a crime? Is there a maximum number of years that someone can spend in prison? If so, what is the maximum?

CRITICAL THINKING

A. Discussion

Share your ideas in a small group. As you talk, try to use the vocabulary below. Each time someone uses a target word or phrase, put a check (✓) next to it.

☐ appreciation/appreciate	☐ drum	☐ structure
☐ audience	☐ make sense of	☐ system
☐ auditory	☐ scale	☐ the deaf
☐ bond	☐ species	☐ theme

1. Read paragraph 1 of "Is Music Universal?" again. In that paragraph, the writer lists the major points she will discuss in the reading. What are they? What examples does she give in the reading to support these points? In your opinion, does she prove that music is universal? And if so, in what way is it universal? Explain your answers.

2. In the first paragraph of the reading, the author says "Like most people, scientists cannot define exactly what music is, but they know it when they hear it." Do you agree? Based on what you have learned from the reading, why do you think that it might be difficult to write a definition of music? As a group, try to write your own definition of music and share it with the class.

3. Underline all of the quotes in the article. Why do you think the writer used quotes for that information, rather than just paraphrasing it?

4. What was the most surprising thing that you learned from the reading? Why was it surprising to you? Has this reading affected the way that you think about music? If so, explain how. If not, explain why not.

5. In your opinion, why do humans create and listen to music? Make a list of the reasons. Then make a list of why other animals may use music. What are the similarities or differences in the way humans and other animals use music?

6. The author mentions that several of the scientists involved in the research discussed in the reading are also musicians. In Chapter 2, you read about another scientist who is a musician. Albert Einstein, the famous physicist, was also a talented violinist. In fact, many famous scientists have also been musicians. Why do you think this might be true? What traits do musicians and scientists share?

> **Critical Thinking Tip:** When you see a quotation, think about why the author chose to use a quote rather than a paraphrase. Is the speaker's idea difficult to explain any other way? Are the speaker's words interesting, funny, or unusual? Is there another reason?

B. Writing

Complete one or both of these writing topics. When you write, use at least five of the target words from the chapter. Underline the target words in your paper.

1. Do some research on whale songs or bird songs. Then, write a short (1–2 page) report on what you have learned. Do not copy from the research— paraphrase and summarize.

2. Imagine that you have traveled to a planet where music does not exist. Write a letter to a friend on earth explaining what life is like without music.

> **Writing Tip:** When you research a topic for an essay, follow closely any instructions your teacher gives you about paraphrasing, using quotations, and citing (identifying) the sources you have used in your research.

CHAPTER 14

Man's Best Friend

LEARNING OUTCOME

> Learn about research on the bond between humans and dogs

GETTING READY TO READ

In your opinion, which animal is best at communicating with people? Complete the chart. Then discuss your answers in a small group.

dogs   horses   cats   birds

other (your ideas): _____

VERY GOOD AT COMMUNICATING WITH PEOPLE	CAN COMMUNICATE WITH PEOPLE, BUT NOT VERY WELL	CANNOT COMMUNICATE WITH PEOPLE

Read to Find Out: Do dogs and their human owners feel the same way about each other?

Read the definitions beside the reading. Then read "Man's Best Friend." If you see a new word, circle it, but don't stop reading. Instead, try to understand the sentence without it. You can learn the word later.

Man's Best Friend

1 Most of us are familiar with the saying: "Dogs are man's best friend." But is the feeling **mutual**? Do dogs consider humans *their* best friends? Recent research could provide an answer.

2 The latest scientific evidence shows that dogs likely **evolved** from wolves[1] much earlier than was thought before—perhaps as many as 35,000 years ago. This gives support to the theory that humans and dogs evolved together. According to the theory, humans were involved in the evolution of dogs, and dogs were involved in the evolution of humans. This is called *coevolution*. A key piece of evidence for coevolution is the fact that humans and dogs share a surprising number of genes. And some of those genes are involved in behavior.

3 One similarity between human and dog behavior is the **frequency** and purpose of eye contact. Researchers noticed that dogs spend a lot of time looking at their owners' eyes. From a scientific point of view, this was very surprising. Why? Direct, **sustained** eye contact signals aggression in most animals, including wolves, dogs' ancestors. For dogs, in contrast, **gazing** into their owners' eyes does not lead to aggression; rather, it appears to signal a close, trusting bond with their human **companions**. But why would dogs' behavior be so different from that of other species?

4 Researchers thought that it might be related to the hormone[2] oxytocin. Oxytocin is often called the "love hormone." Why? It is **released** when people hug or gaze deeply into each other's eyes, and it produces **pleasurable** feelings. The connection between sustained eye contact and the production of oxytocin is particularly important to the **establishment** of a strong bond between human parents and their newborn[3] babies.

5 To test this idea, scientists **measured** the levels of oxytocin in dogs and their human companions before and after they gazed at one another. They found an **increase** in oxytocin in both the dogs and the humans. And the longer the dogs and humans looked at each other, the more oxytocin was produced in both.

6 Scientists then performed this same experiment with wolves that were **raised** by and lived with humans from birth. Interestingly, they found that the wolves did not gaze back at the human "parents" who had raised them, and there was no increase in oxytocin production. This difference between wolves and dogs was **striking**. For a long time, researchers believed that dog behavior **resembled** the behavior of their genetic ancestors, wolves. Is it possible that due to coevolution, dog behavior is actually closer to human behavior?

[1] *a wolf* = a wild animal that looks like a large dog and lives and hunts in groups

[2] *a hormone* = a chemical substance produced by your body that influences your body's growth, development, and condition

[3] *a newborn* = a child that has just been born

7   To answer this question, researchers turned to another area of study: the ability to read body language, including facial expressions. In an experiment at the University of Veterinary Medicine Vienna, scientists taught dogs to **distinguish** between happy and angry faces. After training, the dogs could very easily tell the difference between pictures of happy and angry people that they had never seen before. This is evidence of another similarity in human and dog ability and behavior.

8   Yet another experiment shows how similar dogs are to human children. Researchers found that dogs perform **tasks** better when their owners are in the room with them. This is similar to the way that human children behave. In the experiment, dogs played with toys under three conditions: when their owners were present and talking to them; when their owners were present but silent; and then when their owners were not present. The dogs played with their toys much more when their owners were present, **regardless of** whether the owners spoke or not. However, when their owners were not present, the dogs were much less likely to play with their toys. They did not seem to be interested in performing for strangers. The conclusion? Similar to human children, dogs are much more likely to perform tasks successfully for their human "parents" (their owners) than for strangers.

9   What can we conclude from all of this research? The fact that humans commonly refer to dogs as "man's best friend" reveals the human point of view. However, is the feeling mutual? Based on the evidence available at the moment, the answer appears to be "yes."

Quick Comprehension Check

A. Read these sentences **about the reading**. Circle T (true), F (false), or ? (can't determine the answer from the reading). If you circle T or F, write the number of the paragraph with the answer on the line.

1. There is a genetic connection between humans and dogs.   T   F   ? _____

2. Dog behavior is quite similar to wolf behavior.   T   F   ? _____

3. Among most animals, looking directly into the eyes is a sign of trust.   T   F   ? _____

4. Humans establish bonds with their babies and their dogs through eye contact.   T   F   ? _____

5. Dogs and humans share a number of behavioral traits.   T   F   ? _____

6. Dogs' behavior is actually closer to human behavior than it is to wolf behavior.   T   F   ? _____

B. Work with your class. Share your answers from part A. Go back to the reading to find the reason why a sentence is true or false. Correct the false sentences.

EXPLORING VOCABULARY

Thinking about the Target Vocabulary

Guessing Strategy: Finding Words with Similar Meanings

You learned in the Guessing Strategy for Chapter 10 that to avoid repeating words, writers use synonyms. They also use words with similar meanings but different word forms. Look at the example:

They found an **increase** in oxytocin in both the dogs and the humans. And the longer the dogs and humans looked at each other, the more oxytocin was produced in both.

Words that are similar in meaning to **increase**: more (oxytocin) was produced.

Increase is a noun; *more* is an adjective and *was produced* is a verb phrase, but the noun **increase** is similar in meaning to the idea of "produce more."

A. Write the word or words in the sentences that have a similar meaning to the target words in boldface.

1. Direct, sustained eye contact signals aggression in most animals, including wolves, dogs' ancestors. For dogs, in contrast, **gazing into** their owners' **eyes** does not lead to aggression; rather, it appears to signal a close, trusting bond with their human companions.

   Word or words that are similar in meaning to **gazing into** (someone's) **eyes**:

   _____

   > **Writing Tip:** When paraphrasing, try to replace key words with words that are similar in meaning, but not in form.

2. Oxytocin is **released** when people hug or gaze deeply into each other's eyes, and it produces pleasurable feelings.

   Word or words that are similar in meaning to **released**:

   _____

3. Scientists taught dogs to **distinguish** between happy and angry faces. After training, the dogs could very easily tell the difference between pictures of happy and angry people that they had never seen before.

   Word or words that are similar in meaning to **distinguish**:

   _____

B. Look at the target words. Which ones are new to you? Circle them here and in the reading. The numbers in parentheses help you find the words in the paragraphs.

Target Words

mutual (1)	companions (3)	increase (5)	distinguish (7)
evolved (2)	released (4)	raised (6)	tasks (8)
frequency (3)	pleasurable (4)	striking (6)	regardless of (8)
sustained (3)	establishment (4)	resembled (6)	
gazing (3)	measured (5)		

C. Read "Man's Best Friend" again. Look at the context of the new words. Can you guess their meanings?

D. Complete the word form chart. Fill in the shaded areas of the chart with the target words from the reading. Write the base form of the verbs and the singular form of the nouns.

NOUNS	VERBS	ADJECTIVES	OTHER
		mutual	

Understanding the Target Vocabulary

These sentences are **about the reading**. Complete them with the words in the box. Circle the words in the sentences that help you understand the meanings of the target words.

companions	gaze	raised	striking
establishment	measured	regardless of	sustained
evolved	mutual	releases	tasks
frequency	pleasurable	resemble	

1. There are many _____ similarities between humans and dogs.

   Some scientists now believe that these remarkable similarities are likely due to

   coevolution. If humans and dogs evolved together, it should not be a shock that they

   _____ each other in many ways.

2. It is unusual for most animals to _____ into humans' eyes, except as a

   sign of aggression.

3. However, dogs look into their owners' eyes with great _____ many

   times a day.

4. Not only do dogs often look into their owner's eyes, but they also maintain eye

   contact for a few seconds. This is actually a long time for eye contact. What does this _____ eye contact mean? Why do dogs do it, unlike wolves, the

animals that dogs _____ from?

5. Research shows that when dogs look into the eyes of their human

_____ they are usually not feeling aggressive. Rather, this type of

eye contact makes the dogs feel good. In other words, it is _____ to

them.

6. But why does it feel so good? The hormone oxytocin is responsible. In humans

and dogs, eye gazing _____ oxytocin, the "love" hormone.

7. How did scientists prove this? They _____ the levels of oxytocin in

the blood of both dogs and humans before and after they gazed into each other's

eyes.

8. It seems that oxytocin is important to the _____ of a deep bond

between dogs and humans.

9. Wolves, in contrast, never learn to gaze at humans, _____ how long

they spend living with humans.

10. Even wolves that are _____ in human families from the time of birth

do not have this behavior. This is probably because their brains do not produce

oxytocin when they look at human faces.

11. Dogs, in contrast, look at humans all the time, particularly their owners.

Experiments have shown that dogs are very skilled at activities, or

_____, such as reading facial expressions.

12. This research suggests that the love of some humans for their dogs might be

_____. In other words, dogs might be able to return a human's love.

DEVELOPING READING SKILLS

Understanding the Main Idea

Look back at the reading. Underline the sentence or sentences(s) that give the main idea. Then write the main idea in your own words.

_____

_____

Reading Tip: Look at the title, the introduction (the first and sometimes second paragraph) and/or the conclusion to find the main idea of a reading.

Using an Outline

Outlining: An Effective Reading Strategy

Creating an outline is a useful strategy for understanding a reading. Outlining while you read makes you an active reader and helps you understand and remember important information. Outlining also makes you think about the relationship between ideas in a reading. An outline can be an effective guide to identifying main ideas, major points, and supporting details.

It is not necessary to use complete sentences in an outline. Key words and phrases are usually enough. However, you should always state the main idea of the whole reading in a full sentence.

In an outline, the main ideas, major points, and supporting details are usually represented in this way:

I. Main idea of the whole reading

    A. Major points that support the main idea

        1. details that support the major points

           a. information about the details (not always necessary or provided)

Organize the information in the box into an outline. All of the information comes from the reading. Look back at the reading if necessary. Some of the outline has been completed for you.

leads to strong bond	oxytocin's role
perform tasks for parents (owners), not strangers	~~direct and sustained (gaze)~~
~~coevolution of humans and dogs~~	read facial expressions
dogs' evolution from wolves—early in human history	~~released during eye gazing~~
similarity between humans and dogs: eye contact	produces pleasurable feelings
dogs and humans—many of the same genes	~~other similarities in human and dog ability and behavior~~

I. _____

   A. <u>*Coevolution of humans and dogs*</u> _____

      1. _____

      2. _____

   B. _____

      1. <u>*Direct and sustained (gaze)*</u> _____

      2. _____

         a. <u>*Released during eye gazing*</u> _____

         b. _____

         c. _____

   C. <u>*Other similarities in human and dog ability and behavior*</u> ____

      1. _____

      2. _____

Summarizing

Choose one of the major points from the outline (A, B, or C). Write a summary of that major point. Try not to look back at the text.

BUILDING ON THE VOCABULARY

Using the Target Vocabulary in New Contexts

Complete the sentences with the target words in the box. Be careful. There are two extra words.

companions	gazing	pleasurable	resembles
distinguish	increase	raise	striking
establishment	measure	regardless of	sustained
frequency	mutual	releases	tasks

1. Sometimes two animals of different species will become close _____.

   For example, my cat follows my dog everywhere, and they sleep together every

   night.

2. Mark and Michael are identical twins. Most people cannot _____ one child from the other.

3. I don't enjoy modern music very much, because I can't make sense of it. In contrast, I find classical music quite _____ to listen to. I really enjoy it.

4. I don't care why you hit him! Physical aggression is always wrong, _____ the reason.

5. If parents _____ a child with kindness and respect, the child will probably grow up to be a kind and respectful person.

6. Small children cannot usually concentrate on one thing for very long. _____ concentration is difficult for them.

7. That musical instrument _____ a drum in every way except one: it is not hollow.

8. My boss is a perfectionist. Every day he leaves me a long list of _____ to complete, each one with precise instructions.

9. I want to put a shelf in that corner space, but it needs to be exactly the right size or it won't fit. I think I need a special tool to _____ it properly.

10. Both artists admire each other's work. Their _____ appreciation is uncommon in the competitive art world.

11. When plastic is burned, it _____ harmful chemicals into the air.

12. In many countries, there is at least one official language. In the history of the United States, however, there was never an _____ of an official language. Thus, there is no official language in the United States.

13. There has been an _____ in violent crime in the city recently. It is much more dangerous now than it was when I first moved here.

14. That painting is quite _____. It is the first thing that everyone looks at when they enter the room. I wonder what visual technique the artist used.

coauthor	co-developer	coeducational	coexist	copilot

Complete the sentences with the words in the box.

1. For years, that university accepted only men, but now it is _____.

2. Many textbook writers do not like to work alone. They prefer to work with a

   _____.

3. My mother-in-law and I do not have a perfect relationship, but we manage to

   _____.

4. When the pilot got sick, the _____ had to land the plane.

5. The scientist did not develop the technique alone. She had a _____.

CRITICAL THINKING

A. Discussion

Share your ideas in a small group. As you talk, try to use the vocabulary below. Each time someone uses a target word or phrase, put a check (✓) next to it.

☐ distinguish	☐ gaze (at)	☐ release	☐ sustained
☐ evolve/evolution/ coevolution/coevolve	☐ increase	☐ resemble	
☐ frequency	☐ measure	☐ striking	

1. In paragraph 2, the writer says "The latest scientific evidence shows that dogs likely evolved from wolves much earlier than was thought before—perhaps as many as 35,000 years ago." She then says that this scientific evidence supports the theory that dogs and humans coevolved. What is *coevolution*, and how does this evidence support the theory of coevolution? You will need to infer the answer, as it is not stated in the reading.

Critical Thinking Tip:
Being able to make good inferences is one of the most important critical thinking skills. To improve, you need to practice a lot.

2. In paragraph 4, what does *it* in the first sentence refer to? What is a key similarity between humans and dogs that, according to the latest research, makes dogs behave more like humans and less like wolves?

3. Which results in paragraph 5 were more surprising to scientists: the fact that humans produce more oxytocin when they gaze at their dogs' faces, or the fact that dogs produce more oxytocin when they gaze at human faces? Explain your opinion by referring to information from previous paragraphs of the reading.

4. Why did scientists perform the experiment involving eye contact on wolves that had been raised by humans from birth, rather than on wild wolves that had been raised by other wolves?

5. What do the results of the experiment referred to in question 4 suggest?

6. In the last sentence of paragraph 7 the writer says "This is evidence of another similarity in human and dog ability and behavior." What is the similarity that the writer is referring to?

7. What does the writer conclude regarding dogs' feelings toward humans? Support your answer with specific information from the reading. Do you agree with the writer's conclusion? Why or why not?

Writing

Complete one or both of these writing topics. When you write, use at least five of the target words from the chapter. Underline the target words in your paper.

1. Interview at least six pet owners. First, find out what kind of pet they have. Then ask them how long they've had the pet. Next, ask them about their feelings toward their pet. Finally, ask them what they think their pet's feelings are toward them, and why. Write a report based on the interviews. Identify and attempt to explain any patterns that you detect. For example, are there any differences in the way cat owners answer in comparison to dog owners? Does the amount of time they've owned the pet seem to affect their answers?

2. Do you think that the type of research reported on in the reading is important? Why or why not? Write an essay expressing your opinion about the value of this type of research.

CHAPTER 15

The Mind of the Chimpanzee

Jane Goodall with a baby chimp

LEARNING OUTCOME

> Learn about chimpanzee behavior and abilities

GETTING READY TO READ

Work in a small group. Answer the questions.

1. What skills do you think chimpanzees have? Put a check next to all that apply. Then share your answers.

   ☐ invent names for common objects   ☐ recognize people after a long separation

   ☐ understand human language   ☐ use human language

   ☐ paint pictures   ☐ divide objects into categories

2. Chimpanzees are often used in research. Why do you think this is true?

Read to Find Out: What are the abilities of chimpanzees?

Look at the definitions beside the reading. Then read "The Mind of the Chimpanzee." If you see a new word, circle it, but don't stop reading. You can learn the new word later.

The Mind of the Chimpanzee

adapted from: Goodall, Jane. "The Mind of the Chimpanzee." *Through a Window*. Boston: Houghton Mifflin, 1990.

1   In the middle of the 1960s, Beatrice and Allen Gardner started a project that, along with other similar research, taught us a lot about the chimpanzee mind. They bought an **infant** chimpanzee and began to teach her the signs[1] of ASL, the American Sign Language used by many of the deaf in Canada and the United States. The Gardners achieved remarkable success with their student, Washoe. Not only did she learn signs easily, but she quickly began to put them together in **meaningful** ways. It was clear that when she saw or used a sign, she formed a picture in her mind of the object it represented. If, for example, she was asked in sign language to get an apple, she would go and find an apple that was **out of sight** in another room.

2   When news of Washoe's achievements were first announced to the scientific community, there was a lot of **protest**. The results of the research **implied** that chimpanzees had the ability to learn a human language, and suggested that chimps might **possess intellectual** skills similar to those of humans. Although many were fascinated and excited by the Gardners' discoveries, many more **bitterly** criticized the whole project. The **controversy** led to many other language projects, and the resulting research provided additional information about the chimpanzee's mind.

3   The fact that chimpanzees have excellent memories surprised no one. So it was not particularly remarkable when Washoe gave the name-sign of Beatrice Gardner, her surrogate mother,[2] after a separation of eleven years. Actually, it was no greater an achievement than the memory of dogs who recognize their owners after separations of almost as long.

4   Chimpanzees also possess pre-mathematical skills: They can, for example, easily tell the difference between *more* and *less*. They can put things into specific categories according to a particular characteristic. Therefore, they have no difficulty in separating a **pile** of food into fruits and vegetables at one time, and at another, dividing the same pile of food into *large* and *small*, even though this calls for putting some vegetables with some fruits.

5   Chimpanzees who have been taught a human language can **combine** signs creatively in order to describe objects for which they have no sign. Washoe, for example, **puzzled** the people taking care of her by asking many times for a *rock berry*. **Eventually** they discovered that she was referring to a sweet type of nut that she had been given for the first time a short time before. Another language-trained chimp described a cucumber[3] as a *green banana*,

[1] *a sign* = a hand symbol used by the deaf to communicate

[2] *a surrogate mother* = someone who takes the place of a person or animal's biological mother

[3] *a cucumber* = a long, thin rounded vegetable with a dark green skin, usually eaten raw

and another referred to an Alka-Seltzer[4] as a *listen drink*. They can even invent signs. One chimp had to be put on a leash[5] when she went outside. One day, ready to go outside but having no sign for *leash*, she showed what she wanted by holding a bent finger to the ring on her collar.[6] This sign became part of her vocabulary.

6   Some chimpanzees love to draw, and especially paint. Those who have learned sign language sometimes give a name to their artwork, "This apple"— or sweet corn, or bird, or whatever. The fact that the paintings often look, to our eyes, remarkably different from the objects themselves either means that the chimpanzees are not very good artists or that we have a lot to learn about chimpanzee art!

7   People sometimes ask why such complex intellectual powers have evolved in the chimpanzee when their lives in **the wild** are so simple. The answer is, of course, that their lives in the wild are not so simple! They use—and need—all their mental skills during normal everyday life in their complex society. Chimpanzees always have to make choices—where to go, or with whom to travel. They need highly developed social skills—particularly males who want to become leaders. And low-ranking[7] chimpanzees must learn to hide their intentions or to do things in secret if they want to survive. Indeed, the study of chimpanzees in the wild suggests that their intellectual abilities evolved over thousands of years to help them deal with daily life.

8   It is easier to study intellectual skill in the lab where, through carefully designed tests and the proper use of rewards, chimpanzees can be encouraged to **stretch** their minds to the limit. It is more meaningful to study the subject in the wild, but much harder. It is more meaningful because we can better understand the environmental pressures that led to the evolution of intellectual skills in chimpanzee societies. It is harder because, in the wild, almost all behaviors are complicated by endless variables;[8] years of observing, recording, and **analyzing** replace planned testing; the number of research subjects can often be counted on the fingers of one hand; the only experiments are nature's own, and only time—eventually—may lead to their being repeated.

[4] *an Alka-Seltzer* = a type of medicine that is put in water and then drunk, and that makes a sound when it is put in water

[5] *a leash* = a piece of rope, leather, etc., fastened to an animal's (usually a dog's) collar in order to control it

[6] *a collar* = a band put around an animal's neck

[7] *low-ranking* = having a very low social position in a group

[8] *a variable* = something that may vary in different situations

Quick Comprehension Check

A. Read these sentences **about the reading**. Circle T (true), F (false), or ? (can't determine the answer from the reading). If you circle T or F, write the number of the paragraph with the answer on the line.

1. The Gardners got an infant chimpanzee as a pet.   T F ? ____
2. Chimpanzees cannot learn how to use language.   T F ? ____
3. The Gardners taught Washoe how to use ASL because she is deaf.   T F ? ____
4. Some people were upset because they didn't think that the Gardners were taking good care of Washoe.   T F ? ____
5. Dogs have better memories than chimpanzees.   T F ? ____

6. Chimpanzees sometimes hide what they are thinking.   T F ? _____

7. It is much easier to study a chimp in the laboratory than in the wild.   T F ? _____

B. Work with your class. Share your answers from part A. Go back to the reading to find the reason why a sentence is true or false. Correct the false sentences.

EXPLORING VOCABULARY

Thinking about the Target Vocabulary

Guessing Strategy: Sentence Structure

The use of similar structures in two sentences or phrases can provide important information that can help you understand the meaning of unfamiliar vocabulary. Look at the example.

*The results of the research **implied that chimpanzees had** the ability to learn a human language, and **suggested that chimps might possess** intellectual skills similar to those of humans.*

You can see a similarity between the phrase *implied that chimpanzees had the ability* and the phrase *suggested that chimps might possess intellectual skills.* By comparing the structure of the two phrases and the use of the connecting word *and*, you can infer that the target word *imply* is similar in meaning to *suggest*, and the target word *possess* is similar in meaning to *had*.

A. Read the sentences. Then complete the statements about the target words.

1. Jane Goodall believes in speaking out against the hunting and killing of wild chimps for food. She also supports **protesting** the inhumane treatment of chimpanzees in medical laboratories.

   Protesting is similar in meaning to _____.

2. **Analyzing** the data on chimps raised in laboratories is useful. Making sense of the data on chimps raised **in the wild** is more difficult, but more valuable.

   Analyzing is similar in meaning to _____.

   In the wild is similar in meaning to _____.

B. Look at the target words. Which ones are new to you? Circle them here and in the reading. The numbers in parentheses help you find the words in the paragraphs.

Target Words

infant (1)	implied (2)	controversy (2)	eventually (5)
meaningful (1)	possess (2)	pile (4)	the wild (7)
out of sight (1)	intellectual (2)	combine (5)	stretch (8)
protest (2)	bitterly (2)	puzzled (5)	analyzing (8)

C. Read "The Mind of the Chimpanzee" again. Look at the context of the new words. Can you guess their meanings?

D. Complete the word form chart. Fill in the shaded areas of the chart with the target words from the reading. Write the base form of the verbs and the singular form of the nouns.

NOUNS	VERBS	ADJECTIVES	OTHER
infant			

Understanding the Target Vocabulary

A. These sentences are **about the reading**. Complete them with the words in the box. Circle the words in the sentences that help you understand the meanings of the target words.

bitterly	imply	pile	protest
combined	infant	possess	puzzled
controversy	out of sight		

1. Washoe is the name of a chimpanzee who was raised by a human family. She was

   an _____ when they got her.

2. The Gardners wanted to find out if Washoe (and other chimps) might

   _____ the ability to learn and use language.

3. After they had taught Washoe sign language, the Gardners designed an experiment

   to test her understanding. They asked her to get an apple that was in another room,

   _____, where Washoe couldn't see it. Washoe left the room, and came

   back with the apple.

4. Washoe could understand language. But could she use language to communicate?

   One day, Washoe _____ the people taking care of her when she

   invented her own sign, asking for a "rock berry." At first, no one could make sense

   of Washoe's sign, but they finally understood that she had invented a new sign.

5. Washoe _____ two signs that she knew, "rock" and "berry," to make a new word.

6. Not everyone in the scientific community was happy about the news of Washoe's achievements with language. In fact, there was a lot of _____ against the work that the Gardners and others were doing.

7. Some scientists were not comfortable with the idea that chimps could learn a language. If that were true, it would suggest, or _____, that chimps might be more similar to humans than some scientists were comfortable accepting.

8. There was a lot of disagreement among scientists. It was a scientific _____. Some released statements to the press criticizing the Gardners' work.

9. Scientists on both sides disagreed strongly, at times arguing _____.

10. Fortunately, the controversy led to more research. In other experiments, chimps proved that they could perform complex tasks, such as separating one _____ of objects into a number of different categories.

B. Read this paragraph about the writer of the text, Jane Goodall. Then match the **boldfaced** words with their definitions.

Jane Goodall is a scientist who has spent her life living among and studying the behavior of the chimpanzee. She has observed chimps for longer than any other scientist, and has spent endless hours **analyzing** the behavior of chimpanzees in **the wild**. She has also worked closely with other researchers who conduct experiments using chimps. In many of these experiments, the chimps are encouraged to **stretch** their minds to the limit, in order to see exactly how far their **intellectual** abilities can take them. Jane Goodall's work has led to discoveries that are **meaningful** not only to those involved in protecting wild animals, but also to anyone with an interest in evolution.

Word	Definition
_____ 1. analyze	a. an area that is natural and not controlled or changed by people
_____ 2. the wild	b. concerning the ability to think and understand ideas and information
_____ 3. stretch	c. examine or think about something carefully in order to understand it
_____ 4. meaningful	d. make as large as possible
_____ 5. intellectual	e. serious, useful, or important

DEVELOPING READING SKILLS

Understanding Major Points, Supporting Details, and the Main Idea

A. Read the sentences. There are five major points. Which of these sentences are major points? Write MP. Which are supporting details? Write SD.

  __MP__ 1. The lives of wild chimpanzees are very complex.

  _____ 2. Chimpanzees recognize people that they haven't seen in years.

  _____ 3. Chimpanzees can learn how to communicate with humans.

  _____ 4. Chimps have been taught some of the signs of ASL.

  _____ 5. Chimps are artistically creative.

  _____ 6. Chimps have good memories.

  _____ 7. All chimps learn what their position in chimp society is.

  _____ 8. Laboratory chimps find drawing and painting pleasurable, and they give names to their "artwork."

  _____ 9. Chimps understand the meaning of *more* and *less*.

  _____ 10. Chimps have some math skills.

B. Complete the chart with the information from part A. Write the details next to the major points they support. There is one supporting detail for each major point.

MAJOR POINT	SUPPORTING DETAIL(S)
1. The lives of wild chimpanzees are very complex.	
2.	
3.	
4.	
5.	

c. What is the main idea of "The Mind of the Chimpanzee"? Write it in your own words.

_____

_____

Summarizing

Use the information from exercises A, B and C to write a summary of the reading. Paraphrase rather than copying.

BUILDING ON THE VOCABULARY

Using the Target Vocabulary in New Contexts

Complete the sentences with the target words in the box. Be careful. There are two extra words or phrases.

bitterly	implying	out of sight	puzzles
combine	infant	piles	the wild
controversy	intellectual	possess	
eventually	meaningful	protest	

1. When she was an _____, her doctors discovered damage to her auditory system. Now she's three years old and almost totally deaf.

2. You are very gifted. You _____ the talent to become a great musician, but without sustained practice, you are not likely to be successful.

3. In English, we have an expression "_____, out of mind." It means that when you do not see someone for a long time, you have a tendency to forget him or her.

4. I have several tasks for you to complete today. First, please separate the laundry into _____ by color. Wash the whites first in hot water.

5. There has been a sudden increase in the number of people who are against the war. The newspaper received over one million emails of _____ in just one week.

6. There is a _____ over the establishment of a dress code at the high

   school. About half of the parents want their children to wear school uniforms, and

   the other half don't.

7. I understand why you're angry, but regardless of the reason, you need to control

   your feelings. If you continue to complain so _____, you risk losing

   your job.

8. To make that cake, first measure the flour and sugar. Then _____

   them in a big bowl.

9. Your answer _____ me. I can't make sense out of it.

10. Are you _____ that he stole the money? If that's what you're trying to

    say, you'd better have some evidence to prove it.

11. We can wait. He'll come home _____.

12. Her _____ ability is quite striking. In 30 years of teaching, I've never

    had a more intelligent student.

Word Families: Adding Variety to Your Writing

A reading is interesting due to not only the information it includes, but also the way it is written. Using a variety of sentence structures and lengths adds interest. Using different forms of a word also adds interest. Knowing different word forms allows you to choose the form you want to add interest and variety to your writing.

Study the chart. Then look at the sentences below and complete the paraphrases with the appropriate forms of the **boldfaced** words. Be careful. You will not use all the words in the chart.

NOUNS	VERBS	ADJECTIVES
analysis	analyze	analytical
controversy		controversial
implication	imply	
possession	possess	possessive
puzzle	puzzle	puzzling, puzzled
the wild		wild

1. You didn't _____analyze_____ the problem very well.

   Your _____analysis_____ of the problem was not very good.

2. He is someone who likes to **analyze** everything.

   He is an _____ individual.

3. There was a **controversy** over the president's decision.

   The president's decision was _____ .

4. What are you **implying**?

   What is the _____ of what you just said?

5. He lost everything he **possessed** in the fire.

   The fire destroyed his _____ .

6. Some children don't like to share their **possessions** with anyone else.

   Some children are _____ of the things that belong to them.

7. His angry reaction **puzzled** me.

   I was _____ by the angry way that he reacted.

8. It is important to protect animals living in **the wild**.

   We should protect _____ animals.

Vocabulary Tip: To become more flexible in your use of vocabulary, practice this type of exercise on your own. Start with a sentence that uses one form of a word. Then rewrite the sentence using a different form of the same word.

Word Grammar: *The* + Adjective

Some adjectives become nouns when the definite article *the* is placed in front of them. Look at the examples.

> *The lives of chimpanzees in* **the wild** *are not so simple.*

> *They taught an infant chimpanzee the language used by* **the deaf**.

In these sentences, the adjectives *wild* and *deaf* are used as nouns. Nouns of this kind refer to an entire category, not just one individual. Certain adjectives describing nationalities can also be used in this way. Look at the example.

> **The French** *are famous for their talented chefs.*

Be careful. Most of the time, only nationalities that have no plural form are used in this way. For example, we do not usually say *the American* to refer to the people of the United States. Rather, we use the plural noun with no article—*Americans*.

Talk with a partner. Discuss what the people below are famous for.

• The Spanish _____

• The Swiss _____

- The Chinese _____

- The Japanese _____

- The _____ (your idea)

CRITICAL THINKING

A. Discussion

Share your ideas in a small group. As you talk, try to use the vocabulary below. Each time someone uses a target word or phrase, put a check (✓) next to it.

☐ analyze/analysis   ☐ meaningful

☐ combine/combination   ☐ pile

☐ controversy/controversial   ☐ possess/possession

☐ eventually   ☐ protest

☐ imply/implication   ☐ puzzle/puzzled/puzzling

☐ intellect/intellectual   ☐ the wild/wild

1. In paragraph 2, the writer explains that "although many were fascinated and excited by the Gardeners' discoveries, many more bitterly criticized the whole project." What were the discoveries that led to this controversy? Why were people against the project? In your opinion, does controversy have a positive or negative effect on scientific research? Find examples in the reading to support your opinion.

2. According to the reading (paragraph 2), chimpanzees seem to have intellectual skills that resemble those of humans. What examples does the reading provide to support this idea?

3. Reread paragraph 3 of "The Mind of the Chimpanzee" on page 197. Put the writer's idea into your own words by stating everything affirmatively; do not use any negatives.

Reading Tip: To check your understanding of negative statements, try paraphrasing them in the affirmative (without using any negatives).

4. In several paragraphs in "The Mind of the Chimpanzee," the differences between studying chimpanzees in a laboratory and in the wild are discussed. What are the differences and what effect do they have on research? Include information from the reading and your own ideas.

5. As scientists discover more and more similarities between humans and animals, it may become difficult to define what distinguishes human beings from other animals. Make a list of the characteristics that you believe make humans different from animals.

Critical Thinking Tip: An important critical thinking skill is the ability to take something that you have learned and apply it. Being able to apply what you have learned from a reading shows solid comprehension.

6. In paragraph 5 of the reading, the writer describes how some chimps that have been taught sign language create their own, very clever signs for everyday objects—for example, "green banana" (cucumber). Choose five everyday objects, and invent your own "signs" for them. Each sign should be made of two simple words. For example, the sign for a *pencil* could be "writing stick." When you finish, see if students in other groups can guess what your "signs" mean.

B. Writing

Complete one or both of these writing topics. When you write, use at least five of the target words from the chapter. Underline the target words in your paper.

1. Research Jane Goodall's life and work and write a one- to two-page report. Do not copy from the research; instead, paraphrase, quote, and summarize. Cite your sources according to your teacher's instructions.

2. Write an essay describing the characteristics that you believe distinguish human beings from other animals.

UNIT 5

Checkpoint

LEARNING OUTCOME

> Review and expand on the content of Unit 5

LOOK BACK

A. Think About This

Review the chart in the *Think About This* exercise on page 173. Based on what you learned in Unit 5, do you want to change your answers about any of the animals?

B. Remember the Readings

What do you want to remember most from the readings in Unit 5? For each chapter, write one sentence about the reading.

Chapter 13: Is Music Universal?

_____

Chapter 14: Man's Best Friend

_____

Chapter 15: The Mind of the Chimpanzee

_____

Read the text. Do not use a dictionary.

Little Joe

1 On September 28, 2003, a 300-pound gorilla named Little Joe escaped from a city zoo in the United States. During his escape, the eleven-year-old gorilla attacked and injured a two-year-old girl and her babysitter. Fortunately, their injuries were not serious, and Little Joe was eventually captured by police and returned to the zoo. However, those who witnessed the incident will not soon forget it. Said Mark Matthews, a firefighter who lives close to the zoo, "I saw the gorilla sitting at the bus stop. Everybody was scared, including the police."

2 Rhonda Devance also spotted the gorilla, but she couldn't make sense out of what she was seeing. "I thought it was a person. I thought it was a guy with a big black jacket and a snorkel on."

3 John Dorris, who as a long-time police officer is fairly used to strange incidents, said, "I thought I'd seen it all in eighteen years."

4 The structure where Little Joe lived at the time was thought to be escape-proof, so zoo officials were puzzled at how easy it was for him to get out. However, they were not at all puzzled by the escape attempt itself. At eleven years old, Little Joe could be compared to a human teenager who has reached physical maturity but is still intellectually and emotionally immature. It is common for apes at that age to become restless and seek more freedom. Indeed, experts familiar with Little Joe said that he was a perfectly normal, healthy ape.

5 Not surprisingly, Little Joe's brief taste of freedom led to protest from those who believe that it is inhumane to keep wild animals in zoos.

Quick Comprehension Check

A. Read these sentences **about the reading**. Circle T (true), F (false), or ? (can't determine the answer from the reading). If you circle T or F, write the number of the paragraph with the answer on the line.

1. John Dorris was surprised when he saw the escaped gorilla.   T F ? ____
2. Little Joe got on a city bus.   T F ? ____
3. Little Joe's behavior was unusual.   T F ? ____
4. Little Joe escaped from the zoo because zoo workers were not watching him closely enough.   T F ? ____
5. People who think it is morally wrong to keep animals in zoos used Little Joe's story to support their opinion.   T F ? ____

B. Go back to the reading to find the reason why a sentence is true or false. Correct the false sentences.

Guessing Meaning from Context

Find the words in the reading, and match each word to its definition.

Word

_____ 1. capture

_____ 2. spot

_____ 3. snorkel

_____ 4. escape-proof

_____ 5. maturity

_____ 6. restless

_____ 7. seek

Definition

a. attempt to find or get something

b. something that people wear on their face in order to breathe under water

c. notice or recognize something that is unusual or difficult to see

d. the time when an animal or plant is fully-grown

e. catch and keep someone or something

f. impossible to get out of

g. unable to stop moving because you are impatient, anxious, or bored

Paraphrasing

Paraphrase these sentences from the text.

1. Rhonda Devance also spotted the gorilla, but she couldn't make sense out of what she was seeing.

   _____

   _____

2. The structure where Little Joe lives was thought to be escape-proof, so zoo officials were puzzled at how easy it was for Little Joe to get out.

   _____

   _____

3. However, they were not at all puzzled by the escape attempt itself.

   _____

   _____

EXPANDING VOCABULARY

Word Grammar: Collocations with *bitter*

Look at the sentence containing the target word **bitter**.

> The announcement of the government's decision to go to war led to **bitter** protest.

The word *bitter*, meaning extremely angry or unpleasant, is part of several collocations.

Complete the sentences with the correct collocation from the box.

bitter argument	bitter cold	bitter end
bitter disappointment	bitter protest	

1. She had no hat or coat to protect her from the _____.

2. The two brothers haven't spoken to each other since they had a
   _____ over money.

3. The fact that Tom did not graduate from college was a _____
   to his parents.

4. Despite the _____ of people living in the area, the city cut
   down all the trees to make room for a new parking lot.

5. The movie seemed endless, but we stayed until the _____.

Word Families: Suffixes and Word Meaning

Some suffixes just change the *form* of a word. Other suffixes change the *meaning* of the word. Look at the sentences and the words in boldface.

   1. You do not **resemble** your sister at all. There is no **resemblance** between you.

In example 1, the suffix *-ance* changes the form of the word from a verb to a noun. However, it does not change the basic meaning of the word.

   2. I thought that movie would never **end**! It felt **endless**.

In this example, the suffix *-less* means *without*, so it changes not only the form of the word from a verb to an adjective, but also the meaning of the word: endless = without end (lasting a very long time.)

Read the sentences. Pay attention to the words in boldface. Does the word with the suffix change the meaning of the word in its base form (without a suffix), or just the form of the word (e.g., from verb to adjective)? Circle the letter of the correct answer.

1. Don't worry about that snake. He cannot **harm** you. He looks scary, but he's completely **harmless**.

   a. changes the form only
   b. changes the form and the meaning

2. They don't **regard** anything that their parents say as important. They do whatever they want, **regardless** of what their parents say.

   a. changes the form only
   b. changes the form and the meaning

3. The party **pleased** everyone that was there. It was a **pleasurable** event.

   a. changes the form only
   b. changes the form and the meaning

4. They are such close **companions** that they rarely need to explain themselves out loud. They spend a lot of their time together in **companionable** silence.

   a. changes the form only
   b. changes the form and the meaning

5. You can **measure** the difference in rainfall from one year to the next. Rainfall totals are **measurable**.

   a. changes the form only
   b. changes the form and the meaning

6. When their research was published, there was a big **controversy**. Their work is often **controversial**.

   a. changes the form only
   b. changes the form and the meaning

PLAYING WITH WORDS

Complete the puzzle with words you studied in Chapters 13–15.

ACROSS

3. a group of animals or plants of the same kind

5. a baby

6. to look at someone or something for a long time

8. a magazine for professionals in a particular field, for example science and music

9. having an empty space inside

10. the number of times that something happens within a particular period

DOWN

1. important; significant

2. to tell the difference between (two things, people, etc.)

4. a large group of similar things collected or thrown together, one on top of another

7. very old

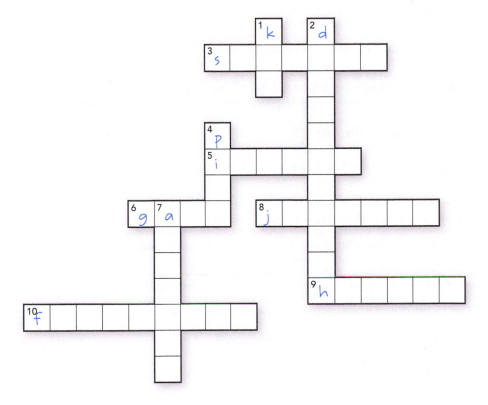

BUILDING DICTIONARY SKILLS

Finding the Correct Meaning

One Word, Several Meanings

Many words have one base form, but they have more than one meaning. Look carefully at the entries in a dictionary to find the correct meaning of a word. The word may have a different meaning in different contexts. Use the context of the reading to find the correct definition you need for the word.

Look at the dictionary entries below. Read each sentence and write the number of the meaning.

---

bit·ter /ˈbɪt̮ɚ/ *adj* **1** angry and upset because you feel something bad or unfair has happened to you: *I feel very **bitter about** what happened.* | *a bitter old man* **2** [only before noun] making you feel very unhappy and upset: *a **bitter disappointment*** | *She knew **from bitter experience** that they wouldn't agree.* **3** a bitter argument, battle, etc. is one in which people oppose or criticize each other with strong feelings of hate or anger: *a bitter legal battle over custody of the children* **4** having a strong taste, like coffee without sugar **5** extremely cold: *a bitter wind* | *We had to walk home in **the bitter cold**.* **6 to/until the bitter end** continuing until the end even though this is difficult: *We will **fight until the bitter end** to defend our land.* —**bitterness** *n* [U]

---

1. a. _____ He is **bitter** about losing his job.

   b. _____ This medicine has a **bitter** taste.

---

wild¹ /waɪld/ *adj* **1** wild animals or plants live or grow in a natural state, without being controlled by people [≠ **tame**]: *wild horses* | *wild flowers* → NATURAL¹ **2** showing strong uncontrolled emotions such as excitement, anger, or happiness: *a wild look in her eyes* | *wild laughter* | *The kids were **wild with** excitement.* **3** (*spoken*) exciting, interesting, or unusual: *Sarah's party was wild.* | *a wild haircut* **4** [only before noun] done or said without knowing all the facts or thinking carefully about them: *a wild guess* **5 be wild about sth/sb** (*informal*) to like something or someone very much: *I'm not too wild about his movies.* **6** a wild card in a game can represent any card that you want it to be **7** a wild area of land is in a completely natural state and does not have farms, towns, etc. on it

---

2. a. _____ I had a **wild** experience last night.

   b. _____ How can you make such a **wild** accusation? You have no proof!

   c. _____ I'm not **wild** about mushrooms. Please don't put any in my salad.

> **stretch¹** /stretʃ/ *v* **1** [I,T] **also stretch out** to become bigger or looser as a result of being pulled, or to make something become bigger or looser by pulling it: *My sweater has stretched all out of shape.* **2** [I,T] to reach out your arms, legs, or body to full length: *Maxie got up and stretched.* | *Klein stretched out his hand to Devlin.* • see picture on page A22 **3** [I] to spread out over a large area, or continue for a long period: *The line of people stretched around the corner.* | *The project will probably stretch into next year.* **4** [I] if cloth stretches, it changes shape when you pull or wear it, and becomes its original shape when you stop: *The shorts stretch to fit.* **5** [T] to pull something so that it is tight: *Stretch a rope between two trees.* **6 be stretched (to the limit)** to have hardly enough money, supplies, energy, time, etc. to do something: *Our resources are already stretched to the limit.* **7 stretch your legs** (*informal*) to go for a walk

3. a. _____ My new jeans are a little tight, but they will **stretch**.

   b. _____ Before you do any physical exercise, it's a good idea to **stretch**.

   c. _____ I'm going outside. I need to **stretch** my legs.

> **scale¹** /skeɪl/ *n* **1 SIZE** [singular, U] the size or level of something, when compared to what is normal: *The scale of the problem soon became clear.* | *There has been housing development on a massive scale since 1980.* | *a large/small scale research project* **2 MEASURING SYSTEM** [C usually singular] a system for measuring the force, speed, amount, etc. of something, or for comparing it with something else: *The earthquake measured 7 on the Richter scale.* | *Your performance will be judged on a scale of 1 to 10.* **3 RANGE** [C usually singular] the whole range of different types of people, things, ideas, etc. from the lowest level to the highest: *Some rural schools have 50 students while at the other end of the scale are city schools with 5,000 students.* **4 FOR WEIGHING** [C] a machine or piece of equipment for weighing people or objects: *The nurse asked me to get on the scale.* → see picture at WEIGH **5 MEASURING MARKS** [C] a set of marks with regular spaces between them on an instrument that is used for measuring: *a ruler with a metric scale* **6 MAP/DRAWING** [C,U] the relationship between the size of a map, drawing, or model and the actual size of the place or thing that it represents: *a scale of 1 inch to the mile* **7 MUSIC** [C] a series of musical notes that have a fixed order and become gradually higher or lower in PITCH **8 ON FISH** [C usually plural] one of the small flat pieces of hard skin that cover the bodies of fish, snakes, etc. → see picture on A2

4. a. _____ The doctor asked the patient to step on the **scale** so he could check her weight.

   b. _____ Before you cook the fish, you must remove the **scales**.

   c. _____ Please rate each essay on a **scale** from one to five, with one for the best one and five for the worst one.

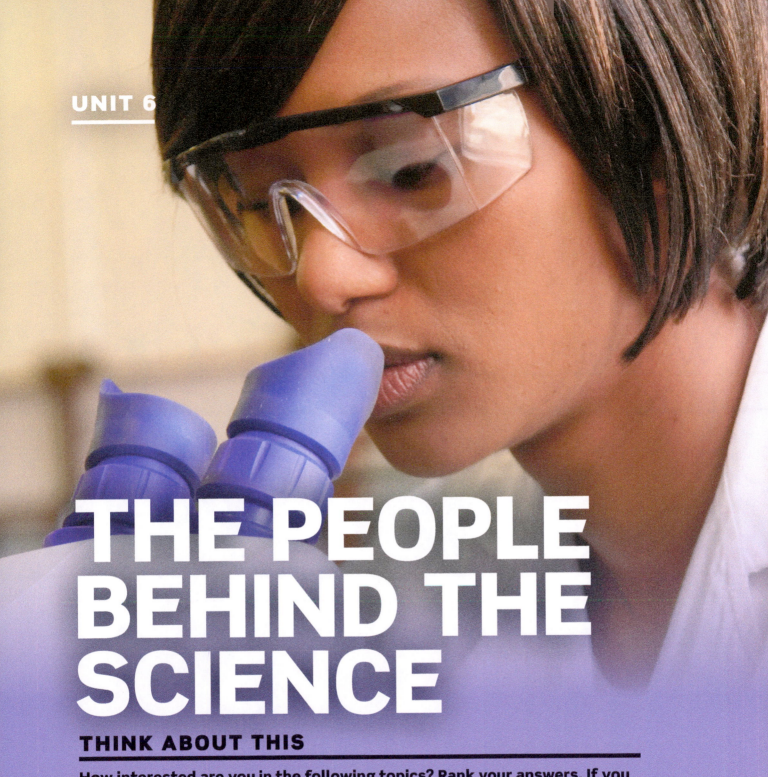

THE PEOPLE BEHIND THE SCIENCE

THINK ABOUT THIS

How interested are you in the following topics? Rank your answers. If you don't know a word, look it up in your dictionary.

1 = a lot   2 = some   3 = not at all

_____ How the first human vaccination was developed

_____ How humans are able to distinguish so many different smells

_____ How perfumes are developed

_____ How scientists become interested in their fields

_____ How workers' clothing can help them do their jobs better

_____ How a scientific theory is tested

CHAPTER 16

A Woman's Fate

GETTING READY TO READ

Talk in a small group. Discuss the questions.

1. Did your grandmother (or other older female relative) have a job outside the home? If so, what did she do?

2. Approximately what percentage of women have jobs outside the home in your country?

3. What jobs in your country are not typically done by women? By men?

READING

Read the definitions beside the reading. Then read "A Woman's Fate." If you see a new word, circle it, but don't stop reading. You can learn the new word later.

A Woman's Fate

1   The attractive, well-dressed woman holds up a pair of **gloves**. There seems to be nothing remarkable about them. But there is a story behind these gloves. It involves a war, a little girl who wanted to be a housewife, a **determined** mother, a talented student, three **prestigious** universities, and a **unique** ability to **see the big picture**.

2   Jeong-Wha Choi was born in 1946 in Seoul, Korea. The only girl in a family of four children, Choi lost her father in the Korean War. Her mother went to work as a nurse to support her family. In Korea at that time, it was unusual for a woman to work outside the home, and as a child Choi was very sensitive to her mother's absence. Although an excellent student, she **resisted** her mother's attempts to interest her in a career in medicine. She knew exactly what she wanted to do with her life, and it did not involve medical school. Choi's dream was to be a stay-at-home wife and mother. Choi's mother, however, was determined that her children attend university. Choi agreed, but with one condition—she would not study medicine; she would study home economics.

3   Choi entered prestigious Seoul National University, and did very well in her studies. Her professors encouraged her to go on to graduate school,[1] but with no intention of having a career, Choi was not interested. **Fate**, however, had different plans.

4   While Choi waited for a **suitable** husband to appear, she took a job with the government as a child welfare[2] worker. But after she had been at her job for only six months, one of her **former** professors offered her a job as an assistant in the department of Home Economics. It was an interesting opportunity, and she accepted.

5   Choi spent almost five years in the department. While she was there, she learned a lot about clothing and textiles.[3] Reading through international publications, she became fascinated by a field that did not even exist in South Korea at that time—clothing physiology. (Clothing physiology is the study of the biological **function**, or work, of clothing; specifically, how clothing can contribute to or **interfere** with the healthy functioning of the human body.)

6   Although she had always dreamed of being a wife and mother, Choi accepted the fact that perhaps it was not her fate to marry. She therefore began to look for a graduate program where she could study clothing physiology. Japan seemed to be the best choice. She taught herself as much Japanese as she could by reading textbooks and looking through Japanese fashion magazines, and in January 1973, left South Korea for Japan.

[1] *graduate school* = a college or university where you can study for a master's degree or a Ph.D.

[2] *welfare* = a government system that provides money, free medical care, food, housing, etc. for people who are unable to work

[3] *a textile* = any kind of cloth that is used for making a variety of products, for example clothing, blankets, or artwork

7   Choi expected that it would be at least a year before she would be ready to take the demanding Japanese university entrance exam. To her surprise, however, she passed after only two months of study. In March 1975, just two short years after her arrival in Japan, Choi graduated with a degree in clothing physiology from prestigious Nara Women's University. She then went on to get a Ph.D.[4] from the School of Medicine at Kobe University in Kobe, Japan.

8   As her research topic, Choi examined how Korean traditional clothing compares to Western clothing in two ways: thermal adaptability (how well the clothing allows the body to control temperature) and mobility (how well the clothing suits the wearer's movement). Choi's research **confirmed** that Korean traditional clothing, while beautiful, did not perform very well on a physiological level.

9   In September 1979, Choi returned to Seoul National University, this time as an assistant professor in the same department where she had studied and worked years before. She has since done important research on the effects of clothing on the wearer's quality of life. She and her research team conduct scientifically controlled experiments to precisely measure the ways in which clothing affects mental, physical, and occupational[5] health and **well-being**. And that's what brings us back to those gloves.

10   As a scientist, one of Choi's strengths is her ability to notice problems that others do not, and then **come up with** solutions. On a visit to the South Korean countryside, Choi noticed the green **stains** and painful cracks on the farmers' hands. After analyzing the farmers' work habits and needs, she returned to her laboratory to design a glove suitable for their work. In coming up with the final design, Choi considered a range of factors, from the rate of **sweating** to worker productivity.[6] The gloves that she and her research team invented are made of a thin, light material that "breathes," making it comfortable enough for all-day wear. The fingers of the glove are covered in a material that stops the fingers from **slipping**. At the same time, the material is thin enough for the farmers to feel what they are doing. Choi and her research group have since patented[7] their invention, and their gloves are worn today by **agricultural** workers all over South Korea. The gloves have also attracted the attention of those in other professions, including pharmacists who find that the gloves are perfectly suited to their work.

11   Eventually, Choi did marry and have two children, but she has hardly been a stay-at-home wife and mother. She has worked as a professor at Seoul National University, published many papers in her field, and has patented a number of inventions.

[4] *a Ph.D.* = a doctorate degree from a university; to get a Ph.D., a student usually needs to do research and write a thesis (similar to the length of a book) about the research

[5] *occupational* = relating to a job

[6] *worker productivity* = the rate at which workers do their jobs, and the amount of products or services they produce or provide

[7] *patent* = get an official document that says that you have the right to make or sell a new invention and that no one else is allowed to do so

Quick Comprehension Check

A. Read these sentences **about the reading**. Circle T (true), F (false), or ? (can't determine the answer from the reading). If you circle T or F, write the number of the paragraph with the answer on the line.

1. When Choi was young, her mother did not live with her family.   T F ? _____

2. Choi attended university because she needed a university degree in her chosen career.   T F ? _____

3. Choi wanted to become a doctor, but her mother did not agree.   T F ? _____

4. Choi decided to become a fashion designer.   T F ? _____

5. Choi learned Japanese so that she could study at a Japanese university.   T F ? _____

6. It took Choi a long time to learn Japanese.   T F ? _____

7. Choi became both a scientist and an inventor.   T F ? _____

8. Choi wishes that she were a stay-at-home wife and mother.   T F ? _____

B. Work with your class. Share your answers from part A. Go back to the reading to find the reason why a sentence is true or false. Correct the false sentences.

EXPLORING VOCABULARY

Thinking about the Target Vocabulary

Guessing Strategy: Signal Word *or*

In Chapter 3, you learned that the signal word *or* can help you guess the meaning of unfamiliar words. Look at the example.

> Clothing physiology is the study of the biological **function**, or work, of clothing, specifically how clothing can contribute to or **interfere** with the healthy functioning of the human body.

Function is similar in meaning to *work*. (Notice the commas.)

Interfere and *contribute to* have opposite meanings. (Notice the lack of commas.)

A. Read the sentences, and write a definition of the **boldfaced** target words.

1. At her **former**, or previous, job she worked for the government.

    Former probably means _____.

2. I couldn't decide whether to agree to his plan or **resist** it.

    Resist probably means _____.

3. We realized that we had to **come up with** a solution immediately or admit that we could not solve it.

   Come up with probably means _____.

B. Now look up the words from exercise A in a dictionary. Are your answers close to the meanings in the dictionary?

C. Look at the target words. Which ones are new to you? Circle them here and in the reading. The numbers in parentheses help you find the words in the paragraphs.

Target Words

fate (title)	resisted (2)	well-being (9)
gloves (1)	suitable (4)	come up with (10)
determined (1)	former (4)	stains (10)
prestigious (1)	function (5)	sweating (10)
unique (1)	interfere (5)	slipping (10)
see the big picture (1)	confirmed (8)	agricultural (10)

D. Read "A Woman's Fate" again. Look at the context of the new words. Can you guess their meanings?

E. Complete the word form chart. Fill in the shaded areas of the chart with the target words from the reading. Write the base form of the verbs and the singular form of the nouns.

NOUNS	VERBS	ADJECTIVES
fate		

Understanding the Target Vocabulary

A. These sentences are **about the reading**. Complete them with the words in the box. Circle the words in the sentences that help you understand the meanings of the target words.

agricultural	former	slip	sweating
coming up with	function	stains	well-being
confirm	interfere	suitable	
fate	resisted		

1. As a child, Jeong-Wha Choi decided that she would not have a career. However, life had other plans for her. It seems that being a housewife was not her

   _____ .

2. When she was a young girl, Choi _____ her mother's attempts to interest her in a career in medicine. In fact, she didn't even want to attend university.

3. A few months after Choi finished her studies at Seoul National University, one of her _____ professors at the university offered her a job.

4. When Choi started her research on traditional clothing, she was not sure whether her results would _____ or disprove the theory that Korean traditional clothing was warmer than modern clothing.

5. Because Choi was interested in analyzing problems and _____ solutions, a career in science was especially _____ for her.

6. As a scientist, Choi wanted to know if a particular type of clothing increases or decreases the wearer's health and comfort. She was interested in the clothing's effect on the physical and mental _____ of the wearer.

7. Some of Choi's projects involved South Korean _____ workers, or farmers.

8. When Choi visited agricultural workers in South Korea, she immediately noticed the green _____ that they had on their hands from cutting plants.

9. When agricultural workers are cutting plants, they need to be able to hold the plants firmly so that the plants don't _____ .

10. When Choi and her team designed gloves to help farmers in their work, they carefully considered the _____ , or work, of the gloves.

11. She wanted her gloves to be comfortable for farmers to wear even in the hot sun. Therefore, she measured the _____ rate of the farmers' hands when they were wearing the gloves.

12. She did not want the gloves to _____ with the farmers' work.

Rather, she wanted the gloves to make the farmers' tasks easier.

B. Read the first paragraph of "A Woman's Fate" again. Find the words or phrases that match the definitions below the paragraph and write them in the blanks.

The attractive, well-dressed woman holds up a pair of gloves. There seems to be nothing remarkable about them. But there is a story behind these gloves. It involves a war, a little girl who wanted to be a housewife, a determined mother, a talented student, three prestigious universities, and a unique ability to see the big picture.

Definition	**Word or Phrase**
1. Clothing worn on your hands, with separate parts to cover each finger	_____
2. Motivated to continue to do something even when it is difficult	_____
3. Admired and respected as one of the best or most important	_____
4. Unusually good and special; the only one of its kind	_____
5. Look at a situation and understand the most important issues	_____

DEVELOPING READING SKILLS

Understanding Text Organization

Chronological Order

To understand a reading that involves several different time periods, it is important to be able to put the important events into the correct time, or *chronological*, order.

Number the following events in the correct order. If it is not clear from the reading when an event occurred, write a question mark (?).

_____ a. Choi worked for six months as a child welfare worker.

_____ b. Choi studied home economics.

_1_ c. The Korean War occurred.

_____ d. Choi learned Japanese in order to study at a Japanese university.

_____ e. Choi discovered the field of clothing physiology.

_____ f. Choi started working for her former professors.

_____ g. Choi became a professor at Seoul National University.

_____ h. Choi got married.

Reading Tip: Writers do not always follow exact chronological order when telling a story. The story might move back and forth between different time periods. Pay attention to time words and the context to avoid confusion.

Making Inferences

Recognizing Point of View

It is important to understand how a writer feels or thinks about a topic. Often, writers do not state their opinions, or points of view, directly. Rather, the reader needs to infer a writer's point of view.

Circle the statement that best expresses the writer's point of view.

1. The writer admires Jeong-Wha Choi.

2. The writer thinks that all women should have careers.

3. The writer thinks that Jeong-Wha Choi should not have had children.

Summarizing

A. List the major points that the writer mentions in the first paragraph of the reading.

B. Use the information from Chronological Order and Recognizing Point of View, as well as exercise A above, to write a summary of the reading. Do not copy—paraphrase.

> **Writing Tip:** The first paragraph of a reading often previews the major points that will be discussed in the rest of the reading. When you summarize, make sure you include all of the major points.

BUILDING ON THE VOCABULARY

Using the Target Vocabulary in New Contexts

Complete the sentences with the target words in the box. Be careful. There are two extra words.

agricultural	former	resist	sweating
came up with	function	slip	unique
confirm	glove	stain	well-being
fate	interfere	suitable	

1. I washed the shirt many times, but I couldn't get rid of the coffee _____.

2. That coat is not _____ for this cold weather. Why don't you buy a heavier one?

3. Be careful. The sidewalk is icy. You could _____ and fall.

4. The way that I raise my children is not your concern. Please don't _____ in my personal life.

5. I know that I shouldn't eat ice cream because I'm on a diet, but I can't

_____. It's one of the really pleasurable things in my life.

6. I make more money now than at my _____ job. That was my main

motivation for taking the new job.

7. The incident wasn't your fault. You didn't do it intentionally, and anyway, your life is

not completely under your control. It was _____ that made it happen.

8. The best doctors care deeply about the _____ of their patients.

9. We have detected some unusual activity on your account. For security purposes,

could you please _____ your telephone number? Is it the same

number you have always had?

10. The economy of that country is based on _____ products,

particularly coffee, rice, and fruit.

11. It took them a long time, but eventually they _____ a name for their

company.

12. I don't understand your _____ here. What exactly do you do? Can

you tell me what some of your tasks are?

13. _____ helps to cool off your body. It is your body's natural physical

response. It provides protection from the heat.

Word Families: The Prefix *Inter-*

The prefix *inter-* means "between." Look at the sentence.

> I don't think you should **interfere** in their argument. You will only make things worse.

In this sentence, the word *interfere* means "come between."

Complete the sentences with the words below.

interaction	interpersonal	interstate
interlocking	interrelated	

Vocabulary Tip:
Word prefixes help you figure out the meaning of unfamiliar words. However, you still need to use the context to get a full understanding of the word's meaning.

1. That company has offices in both New York and California, so they

have to pay _____ taxes.

2. When you work on a jigsaw puzzle, you must put together the _____
   pieces.

3. This job calls for excellent _____ skills. If you have trouble forming
   good relationships with others, this job is not suitable for you.

4. Research has confirmed that the more _____ there is between
   teachers and students, the more the students learn.

5. Those two research fields are _____. What happens in one area of
   research always affects the other.

Word Grammar: Phrasal Verbs with *Come*

The phrasal verb *come up with* means "to think of an idea, plan, or reply." There are many phrasal verbs that are formed with the verb *come*.

Read the sentences. Think about the meaning of the **boldfaced** phrasal verbs. Then write answers to the questions.

a. The project was going well until last week. We **came up against** some unexpected problems.

b. They were close companions until that woman **came between** them. Now they never speak to each other.

c. I don't feel very well. I think I'm **coming down with** a cold.

d. I **came across** an article while I was reading the newspaper. I think it might interest you.

1. What difficulties have you **come up against** in learning English?

   _____

   _____

2. Has anything or anyone ever **come between** you and a friend? Explain.

   _____

   _____

3. What is the best thing to do if you feel that you are **coming down with** a cold?

   _____

   _____

4. When you are reading and **come across** a word that you are unfamiliar with, what should you do?

_____

_____

CRITICAL THINKING

A. Discussion

Share your ideas in a small group. As you talk, try to use the vocabulary below. Each time someone uses a target word or phrase, put a check (✓) next to it.

☐ come up with	☐ former	☐ suitable
☐ confirm	☐ function	☐ unique
☐ determined	☐ see the big picture	☐ well-being

1. Read these sentences from paragraph 2 of "A Woman's Fate" on page 219.

   "The only girl in a family of four children, Choi lost her father in the Korean War. Her mother went to work as a nurse to support her family."

   In the first sentence, what does "lost her father" mean? What words in the context help you to figure out that "lost" is not being used in the usual way?

2. Reread the first paragraph of "A Woman's Fate" on page 219. It previews the story of Jeong-Wha Choi by listing six topics. Identify each topic. Then ask and answer questions about each one by referring to the rest of the reading. For example, you might ask "Which war is the writer talking about? How did that war affect the story?"

3. How much of an influence did Choi's mother have on her life? How was Choi's relationship with her mother a bit unusual or surprising? Support your answers with specific information from the reading.

4. What women have had an influence on your life? How have they influenced you?

5. Jeong-Wha Choi is described as a scientist who is able to see the big picture and come up with solutions to everyday problems that other people often don't even notice. Using Choi's method, come up with an invention that will be useful in everyday life. When you are ready, present your invention to the class. Explain the problem that the invention solves, as well as the way that it functions. Be prepared to answer questions from the class.

> **Critical Thinking Tip:** When writers do not want to say something unpleasant directly, they use a **euphemism**. A *euphemism* is a word that is less direct than the unpleasant word. Its meaning can be inferred from the context.

B. Writing

Complete one or both of these writing topics. When you write, use at least five of the target words from the chapter. Underline the target words in your paper.

1. Imagine that you want to convince someone to produce an invention that you have come up with. Write a letter to possible investors (people who might give you money to produce the invention). Your letter should include the following information:

   - What problem the invention solves
   - Who the invention is designed for
   - How the invention functions
   - Why people will want to buy this invention

2. What was the most important invention of the past 100 years? Write an essay describing the invention, who invented it, and why it was so significant. Write the essay in your own words. Don't copy; instead, paraphrase. Cite your sources according to your teacher's instructions.

CHAPTER 17

The Father of Vaccination

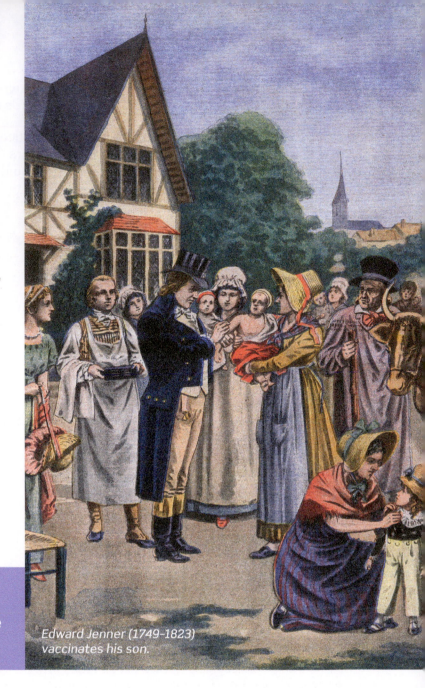

Edward Jenner (1749–1823) vaccinates his son.

GETTING READY TO READ

Talk with the whole class.

1. Put a check (✓) next to the diseases that you are familiar with. If you are not familiar with one of the diseases, ask your classmates or look it up in your dictionary.

   ☐ influenza (flu)   ☐ diabetes   ☐ chicken pox
   ☐ HIV (AIDS)   ☐ cancer   ☐ malaria

2. For some diseases, your doctor can give you medicine that will prevent you from catching the disease. This is called a vaccination. Which of the diseases above can be prevented with a vaccination? Circle them.

READING

Read to Find Out: What is smallpox?

Read the definitions beside the reading. Then read "The Father of Vaccination." If you see a new word, circle it, but don't stop reading. You can learn the word later.

The Father of Vaccination

1   In a small town in England, in the middle of the eighteenth century, an eight-year-old boy named Edward Jenner was intentionally **infected** with a deadly disease. He was then locked in a barn[1] with other children who had been similarly infected. There they remained until they either died or recovered. Fortunately for humanity, Jenner survived.

2   Child **abuse**? No—variolation. A common **practice** in the eighteenth century, variolation involved **deliberately** infecting a healthy person with the Variola virus that causes a terrible illness, smallpox. To infect the healthy person, doctors would take the pus[2] from a person sick with smallpox and intentionally inject[3] it into the healthy person.

3   Why would a doctor do this? Variolation was the only effective **means** of fighting smallpox, a deadly disease that was regularly killing between 10–20% of the population of Europe at that time. Among children, the death rate was even higher; one in three infants and children who caught smallpox died. Although almost everyone who was variolated caught the disease, the death rate among variolated children was only about 10%, as compared to more than 30% in children who caught the highly **contagious** disease directly from another person. And most importantly, almost everyone who survived variolation never caught the disease again.

4   It is possible that variolation saved Jenner's life, but he would never forget his terrible days in the barn. Perhaps that is what led him to choose a career in medicine. In 1761, at just thirteen, Jenner began his medical studies. By 1770, he was studying anatomy[4] and **surgery** under John Hunter at St. George's Hospital in London. With Hunter, Jenner was trained in the scientific method, which his instructor described simply as "Why think; Why not try the experiment?"

5   After two years in London, Jenner returned to his hometown. He was a popular doctor, due to his gentle personality and surgical skill. One common **request** from his patients was for variolation. Jenner performed the **procedure** many times, although he used a more humane method than the one that he had suffered through as a child.

6   In his medical practice, Jenner observed something unexpected: a small number of his variolated patients never developed smallpox. Because of his training in the scientific method, he wanted to understand why these particular individuals were able to resist the disease while all others, as expected, contracted a mild to severe case of the deadly disease. He discovered that the variolated patients who did not develop smallpox worked closely with cows and had all previously had cowpox. Coxpox is an illness passed from cows to humans. Jenner observed that some of the symptoms

[1] barn = a large farm building in which animals are kept

[2] pus = a thick yellowish liquid produced in an infected part of the body

[3] inject = give a drug by using a special needle that goes directly into someone's vein

[4] anatomy = the scientific study of the structure of human or animal bodies

of cowpox and smallpox were similar. However, while cowpox was a **mild** illness that did not lead to death, smallpox was a severe, life-threatening disease. He was also aware of a common belief that people who had had cowpox never got smallpox. Based on his observations, Jenner came up with a theory. He believed that cowpox not only protected **against** smallpox, but could be passed from one human being to another as a deliberate means of protection from the disease.

7   In May 1796, Jenner got the chance to test his theory. He learned that a young woman from a local farm, Sarah Nelmes, had cowpox. Jenner asked the parents of an eight-year-old boy named James Phipps for **permission** to conduct an experiment on their son. Jenner chose James because he had never had cowpox or smallpox. Jenner removed pus from Sarah's hand and spread it on scratches he had made on the boy's arms. As expected, the boy developed cowpox, but recovered rapidly. Jenner was now ready for the second, riskier stage of his experiment. On July 1, 1796, Jenner variolated Phipps with pus from a smallpox patient. Jenner and other scientists and **physicians** waited anxiously for the results.

8   In fact, James Phipps never caught smallpox. This was clear evidence to support Jenner's theory, but more data were needed. Jenner experimented successfully on thirteen more patients, and at the end of 1796 wrote a report describing his work for the Royal Society.[5] However, it was **turned down** for publication. According to those who **reviewed** it, Jenner's theory was too much of a challenge to the accepted medical beliefs of the time.

9   Jenner **ignored** the criticism and continued experimenting. In 1798 he published his own book based on twenty-three cases in which vaccination (named for the *vaccinnia* virus[6] of cowpox) resulted in lasting protection against, or immunity to, smallpox. Although many people continued to criticize Jenner, some well-known London physicians were starting to vaccinate their patients. By the beginning of the nineteenth century, the practice of vaccination had spread throughout the world.

10 Eventually, Jenner's contributions to science were formally recognized. However, he never made an attempt to get rich through his discovery. Instead, he spent much of his time working, without pay, to spread the good news about vaccination. In 1977, the last known victim of smallpox recovered. No new cases appeared, and in 1980, the World Health Assembly announced that "the world and its peoples" were **free of** smallpox.

[5] *the Royal Society* = a group of respected physicians and scientists in London who review the research of other scientists

[6] *a virus* = a very small living thing that causes diseases that can be passed from one person or animal to another

Quick Comprehension Check

A. Read these sentences **about the reading**. Circle T (true), F (false), or ? (can't determine the answer from the reading). If you circle T or F, write the number of the paragraph with the answer on the line.

1. When Edward Jenner was a boy, he caught smallpox.   T   F   ? ____

2. Jenner decided to become a doctor because of his terrible experience with smallpox as a child.   T   F   ? ____

3. Because of his early experiences, Jenner refused to variolate his patients.   T   F   ? ____

4. At first, Jenner's work on vaccination was not accepted by the medical community.   T   F   ? ____

5. Jenner discovered a cure for smallpox.   T   F   ? ____

6. Jenner's work led to the end of smallpox and the discovery of how vaccines work.   T   F   ? ____

B. Work with your class. Share your answers from part A. Go back to the reading to find the reason why a sentence is true or false. Correct the false sentences.

EXPLORING VOCABULARY

Thinking about the Target Vocabulary

Guessing Strategy: Signal Words for Contrast

Signal words show the relationship between ideas. For example, the signal words *but*, *while*, and *although* show that a writer is contrasting two words or ideas. If you understand the contrast the writer is making, it can help you guess the meaning of unfamiliar words. Look at the example.

__While__ cowpox was a mild illness that did not lead to death, smallpox was a severe, life-threatening disease.

In this sentence, the contrast is between a **mild** illness and a **severe**, life-threatening disease. In Chapter 9 you learned that *severe* means "very serious." From this sentence, you can see that *mild* is the antonym, or opposite, of *severe*. Therefore, *mild* means "not serious."

A. Read the sentences, and write a definition of the **boldfaced** target word.

1. While the editors usually accept articles from well-known writers, they might **turn down** an article if they do not agree with the writer's ideas.

   Turn down means _____.

2. For many years, women could work as nurses, but not as **physicians**.

   A physician is _____.

3. Although at first the doctors decided not to operate, they soon realized that **surgery** was the only way to save the patient's life.

   Surgery means _____.

4. The doctor told the patient to pay attention to his diet, but he **ignored** her advice.

   Ignore means _____.

Vocabulary Tip: There are several major categories of signal words. Learning the most common words in each category will help your reading comprehension. The major categories include: Condition *(if)*; Examples *(such as)*; Cause/Effect *(because)*; Adding information *(also)*; Contrast *(although)*; Similarity *(likewise)*; Time *(before)*; and Process *(first)*.

B. Look at the target words. Which ones are new to you? Circle them here and in the reading. The numbers in parentheses help you find the words in the paragraphs.

Target Words

vaccination (title)	contagious (3)	physicians (7)
infected (1)	surgery (4)	turned down (8)
abuse (2)	request (5)	reviewed (8)
practice (2)	procedure (5)	ignored (9)
deliberately (2)	mild (6)	free of (10)
means (3)	permission (7)	

C. Read "The Father of Vaccination" again. Look at the context of the new words. Can you guess their meanings?

D. Complete the word form chart. Fill in the shaded areas of the chart with the target words from the reading. Write the base form of the verbs and the singular form of the nouns.

NOUNS	VERBS	ADJECTIVES	OTHER
vaccination			

Understanding the Target Vocabulary

A. These sentences are **about the reading**. Complete them with the words in the box. Circle the words in the sentences that help you understand the meanings of the target words.

abuse	infected	practice	reviewing
contagious	means	procedure	turned down
deliberately	permission	request	vaccination
free of			

1. Before Jenner made his discovery, it was common medical _____ for doctors to intentionally give children smallpox. That was what most doctors did.

2. The doctors who gave children smallpox were not guilty of child _____. Rather, their motivation was to protect the children from dying of the disease.

3. The _____, called variolation, involved _____ putting a child into contact with the pus of a person who had the disease. It might seem hard to believe, but variolation was done intentionally.

4. Although they knew it was risky, parents asked for variolation because it was the only _____, or way, to protect their children from the disease.

5. Smallpox is a highly _____ disease. Sustained contact with anyone who had the disease was very risky.

6. However, not all children who were _____ with smallpox died. About two thirds recovered.

7. When physician Edward Jenner asked the Phipps family if he could use their son in an experiment, it was just a _____. They did not have to agree to it, but they did. They gave Jenner _____ to conduct the experiment.

8. As a result of those early experiments, Jenner eventually developed a medical procedure called _____.

9. However, Jenner's work was not immediately accepted. Indeed, when Jenner attempted to publish his research, he was _____ by the prestigious medical journals. They refused to publish his articles and even attempted to humiliate him.

10. The Royal Society didn't do a good job of _____ Jenner's research. They just looked at it quickly and decided that his ideas were too new.

11. Today, due to Jenner's work, the world is _____ the deadly

disease of smallpox.

DEVELOPING READING SKILLS

Understanding Reference

Referring to Previously Introduced Ideas

In Chapter 11, you learned that a reference word takes the place of a noun or noun phrase. Reference words are often pronouns, such as *he*, *she*, and *it*, but there are many other ways to refer back to a previous idea. Look at the **boldfaced** words in the sentences.

In his medical practice, Jenner observed something unexpected: a small number of his variolated patients never developed smallpox. Because of his training in the scientific method, he wanted to understand why **these particular individuals** were able to resist **the disease**.

In these sentences, the boldfaced words replace, or refer back to, something already mentioned in the text. The noun phrase *these particular individuals* refers back to *a small number of his variolated patients*, and *the disease* refers back to *smallpox*.

What do the **boldfaced** words refer to in the previous clause, sentence, or paragraph? Write your answers.

1. He was then locked in a barn with other children who had been similarly infected. **There** they remained until they either died or recovered.

   There = _____

2. With Hunter, Jenner was trained in the scientific method, **which his instructor** described simply as "Why think; why not try the experiment?"

   which = _____

   his instructor = _____

3. Jenner performed the procedure many times, although he used a less severe method than **the one** that he had suffered through as a child.

   the one = _____

4. In fact, James Phipps never caught smallpox. **This** was clear evidence to support Jenner's theory, but more data were needed.

   This = _____

> **Reading Tip:** If you have trouble understanding the relationship between ideas from one clause, sentence, or paragraph to the next, check to see if there are any words in the sentence that refer back to an idea previously mentioned.

5. By the beginning of the nineteenth century, the practice of vaccination had spread throughout the world. Eventually, Jenner's contributions to science were formally recognized. However, he never made an attempt to get rich through **his discovery**.

his discovery = _____

Understanding Major Points and Important Details

Complete the chart with information from the reading. Use notes—just short phrases, not sentences. If the reading does not contain the information, write a question mark (?). The completed chart should tell the story of Edward Jenner's life and work.

WHEN?	WHAT?	WHERE?	WHO?
Jenner-8 years old			
		St. George's Hospital, London	
1772–May 1796			
May–July 1796			
End of 1796			The Royal Society
1797–1798			
1798			
1798–beginning of 19th century			
1977			
	Announcement: smallpox eliminated	?	World Health Assembly

Reading Tip: When you read a narrative, use the reporting questions of *Who, What, When, Where, Why,* and *How* to check your comprehension of both main points and important details.

Writing Tip: In summarizing, always avoid copying directly from the reading. To help you, make a chart with the questions *Who, What, When, Where, Why,* and *How*. Answer the questions in your own words. Then write the summary from the chart.

Summarizing

Write a summary of the reading. Do not look back at the reading. Use the information in the chart as a guide.

BUILDING ON THE VOCABULARY

Using the Target Vocabulary in New Contexts

Complete the sentences with the target words in the box. Be careful. There are two extra words.

abuse	ignore	permission	reviewed
contagious	infected	practice	turned down
deliberately	means	procedure	vaccinations
free of	mild	request	

1. He was shocked and insulted when his boss turned down his _____ for a pay increase. He was sure that his boss would say "Yes."

2. For the well-being of the hospital staff, patients suffering from _____ diseases must be identified immediately and kept in a separate area.

3. The writer who _____ the movie was very critical of it. She did not recommend the movie.

4. I asked my boss for _____ to leave early, but he refused.

5. We don't have the _____ to pay for a prestigious university for our son. We have good jobs, but we are not rich.

6. He was _____ for the job. They told him he was not suitable because of his lack of experience.

7. Everyone should have a childhood _____ abuse. No child should be harmed intentionally.

8. That cut on your hand is _____. It's not getting better. You should ask a physician to look at it.

9. Could you please explain the _____ for getting a driver's license? It's more complex than I thought it would be.

10. Before you and your travelling companions leave the country, you must get all of the required _____. That way, you won't catch a contagious disease and bring it back with you.

11. Two government officials were accused of _____ of power. They insulted their employees and made them work extra hours without pay.

12. A police officer is not permitted to _____ harm a suspect, unless the suspect threatens the officer's life.

13. Regardless of how small an incident seems, school officials should never _____ bullying. If they don't do anything, the bullying will just get worse.

Word Families: Words with a Root and a Prefix

Some words contain both a root and a prefix. For example, the target word **procedure** contains the root *ced*, which means "go" or "move," as well as the prefix *pro-*, which means "according to." The definition of a *procedure* is "something that follows a set of rules"—in other words, something that goes or moves forward according to certain rules.

Read the sentences. Using both context and what you know about the meaning of the root *ced* and the prefixes *inter-* (between or among), *pre-* (before) and *re-* (back or again), write a definition of each **boldfaced** word. Then, compare your definitions with a partner's. When you are finished, look the words up in your dictionary.

1. If the parents cannot agree on whether or not their daughter should have surgery, her physician will have to **intercede**.

   intercede: _____

2. As we drove away from the coast, the sound of the ocean **receded**.

   recede: _____

3. Variolation, a dangerous medical procedure, **preceded** the far safer practice of vaccination.

   precede: _____

Word Grammar: Collocations with *Mild* and *Severe*

The adjective **mild** and its antonym **severe** are used in several common collocations.

Read the sentences. Think about the meaning of the **boldfaced** collocations. Then write answers to the questions. Use complete sentences.

a. There is going to be a **severe storm** tomorrow. If you can, stay at home.

b. My husband is very **mild-mannered**. He almost never gets angry.

c. Most American food has a very **mild taste**. I prefer food with a stronger flavor.

d. When the president announced his plan to raise taxes, he came up against **severe criticism**.

e. He's in such **severe pain** that he can't walk.

f. After the dentist removes the tooth, you might experience some **mild pain**.

1. What is the most **severe** storm you have ever experienced? Describe it.

_____

2. How does a **mild-mannered** person usually behave?

_____

3. Do you prefer food with a **mild** taste or a spicy taste?

_____

4. Have you ever received **severe** criticism for something you've done? Explain.

_____

5. What can you do to deal with **mild** pain? **Severe** pain?

_____

CRITICAL THINKING

A. Discussion

Share your ideas in a small group. As you talk, try to use the vocabulary below. Each time someone uses a target word or phrase, put a check (✓) next to it.

☐ abuse	☐ means	☐ procedure
☐ contagious	☐ mild	☐ request
☐ deliberately	☐ permission	☐ surgery
☐ free of	☐ physician	☐ turn down
☐ infect	☐ practice	☐ vaccination/vaccine

1. The reading contains a lot of information about smallpox. Review the reading carefully. What did you learn that could explain the following?

   • why Jenner and other children were locked in a barn after being variolated

   • why it is possible that variolation saved Jenner's life

   • why Jenner's patients wanted to be variolated

   • why Jenner's theory was finally accepted

2. In paragraph 4 of "The Father of Vaccination," the writer quotes John Hunter's description of the scientific method. Paraphrase Hunter's definition of the scientific method. Do you agree with that description? Why or why not? If you do not agree, how would you explain the scientific method?

3. The writer claims that Jenner's early experiences might have influenced his decision to become a physician. First, give an example from Jenner's life that shows how his childhood experience with variolation might have affected the way that he practiced medicine. Then, give an example from the reading that shows the influence that Jenner's early training in the scientific method had on his work.

4. One problem with testing new vaccines is that it is risky to use an untested vaccine on human beings. Today, there are laws that limit scientists' ability to conduct such experiments on human beings. However, those laws did not exist in Edward Jenner's time. Discuss the advantages and disadvantages of such laws. Are there any situations under which it might be permissible to allow experiments involving human beings? Explain your answer with specific examples.

5. What medical advances do you think will occur in your lifetime? Consider the following questions in your discussion: Which diseases will be cured? For which diseases will a vaccine be developed? Will life expectancy (how many years a human being, on average, lives) increase? By how many years?

> **Critical Thinking Tip:** Always look for evidence of a writer's claims. If you cannot find support for the claim, the information in the reading may not be reliable.

B. Writing

Complete one or both of these writing topics. When you write, use at least five of the target words from the chapter. Underline the target words in your paper.

1. Conduct research on vaccines that scientists are currently working to develop. Write a report on your findings. Write the report in your own words. Do not copy—paraphrase. Cite your sources according to your teacher's instructions.

2. Write an essay based on question 4 in the Discussion section above.

CHAPTER 18

A Nose
for Science

Luca Turin

LEARNING OUTCOME

❯ Learn about the theory of
scientist Luca Turin

GETTING READY TO READ

Talk with a partner.

1. Do you like to wear cologne?[1] If so, do you always wear the same kind? Are there any situations for which wearing cologne is not appropriate? Explain your answers.

2. What smells can you remember from your childhood?

3. Which sense is the most important to you—sight, hearing, speech, touch, taste, or smell? Which is the least important? Why?

[1] *cologne* = a liquid that smells like flowers or plants, which you put on your neck and wrists

Read to Find Out: How has Luca Turin's unusual hobby influenced his scientific career?

Read the definitions beside the reading. Then read "A Nose for Science." If you see a new word, circle it, but don't stop reading. You can learn the new word later.

A Nose for Science

1   In 1791, Marie Antoinette[1] escaped Paris with her husband, Louis XVI. Dressed as simple travelers, they left for Austria. But before they arrived, they were caught. How? The **legend** says that when the queen stepped down from her carriage[2] in a cloud of expensive **perfume**, everyone knew she must be **royalty**. No ordinary person could afford to wear anything that smelled so heavenly. The queen eventually paid for the mistake with her life.

2   This is just one of the many perfume **tales** that scientist Luca Turin enjoys retelling. Turin is a biophysicist[3] with an unusual hobby—collecting perfume. Turin has been **obsessed** by smell since he was a boy and he used to **entertain** himself by analyzing the **scents** of wild plants. He has an unusually sensitive nose and is very good at identifying different scents. Turin describes his excellent sense of smell in this way: "Every perfume I've ever smelled has been to me like a movie, sound and vision. . . . To me, smell is just as real as they are." When he was a young scientific researcher in Nice, France, Turin frequently visited local perfume shops, collecting rare **fragrances**. He was well known for his ability to smell a perfume and analyze it, immediately identifying the individual scents that it contained.

3   As he added to his perfume collection, Turin was also progressing in his scientific career. Although trained as a biologist, he considered the division of science into separate fields—biology, chemistry, and **physics**—to be artificial. He moved freely from one field to another, following a **path** determined only by his interest and intellect. In that way, he gained a wider range of knowledge than most scientists possess.

4   At the same time, Turin's fascination with perfume grew. One day he and some friends visited a large **discount** perfume store where Turin bought almost everything on the shelves. On the way home, he entertained his friends by describing the fragrances in language that was so **poetic** that they told him he should write a book.

5   He decided to do exactly that. In 1992, Turin's book was published as *Parfums: Le Guide* (*Perfume: The Guide*). In it, Turin skillfully critiques some of the world's most famous fragrances. For example, this is how he describes Rush, by Gucci: "It smells like an infant's breath mixed with his mother's hair spray.[4] . . . What Rush can do, as all great art does, is create a yearning,[5] then fill it with false memories of an invented past. . . ."

6   Turin's book was extremely popular among the **secretive** "Big Boys"—the seven large companies that control the world scent market. Turin's talent

[1] *Marie Antoinette* = wife of Louis XVI, the king of France from 1774 to 1792. They were both put in jail and killed during the French Revolution

[2] *a carriage* = a vehicle with wheels that is pulled by a horse, used in past times

[3] *a biophysicist* = a scientist who studies the natural forces that affect living things

[4] *hair spray* = a sticky liquid that is forced out of a special container in a stream of very small drops and that you put on your hair to make it stay in place

[5] *a yearning* = a strong desire or feeling of wanting something

at translating smell into words won him a rare invitation to visit their laboratories. There, Turin discovered that the widely accepted theory about how we are able to identify particular smells—by the shape of their molecules[6]—did not seem to work. Under this theory, it should be fairly easy for a chemist to "build" new molecules and accurately predict what they will smell like. But in fact, this is not the case. Each new smell the Big Boys create involves an **investment** of millions of dollars. That is because only a very small percentage of the new molecules possess the desired fragrance.

7   Now Turin had a new obsession: solving the mystery of smell. As a scientist with an extremely sensitive nose, an obsession with perfume, **access** to the Big Boys' laboratories, and a wide range of scientific knowledge, he was particularly well suited to the challenge. Within just three years, Turin believed that he had the answer. The key was not the shape of the molecules, but rather their vibrations.[7]

8   Turin sent a paper presenting his theory to a prestigious science journal and waited anxiously for a response. However, a few scientific reviewers recommended that the journal turn the paper down. Scientists who had based their careers on the old theory of smell also reacted negatively, and he was even accused of **fraud**, an accusation that turned out to be false.

9   What is Turin's explanation for this negative reaction from some in the scientific community? First of all, he is sharply critical of the **standards** for publication in science journals. He argues that the reviewers turned his paper down due to their narrow **focus** on just one field of science. Therefore, they couldn't make sense out of a complex theory involving biology, chemistry, and physics. He also believes that scientists do not have enough time to write scientific reviews. In an interview in 2013, Turin said, "These days people have nine-hundred emails per day, how much time is there to read, to think, to review a paper. Reviewing papers? Honestly, all of us have better things to do. But of course you have to do it, so the standard of review now is really, really low."

10 However, Turin has not given up on his theory, nor have many in the scientific community. Although his ideas remain controversial, he has continued to research and publish scientific papers. For nine years, he used his theory to create scent molecules to sell to companies that use scent in their products. He has also worked as a visiting professor at prestigious American and international universities and research institutes. He has conducted research for the Defense Advanced Research Projects Agency (DARPA), a U.S. government agency, on an "artificial nose" that would be much more sensitive than the human nose. Such a nose could be used in a wide range of fields, including medicine, where it could be used to identify cancer cells.

11 Turin's interest in the art of scent also remains strong. In 2006, he published a book about his work, *The Secret of Scent: Adventures in Perfume and the Science of Smell*. In 2008, he and his wife, Tania Sanchez, wrote another guide to perfume titled *Perfumes, the A–Z Guide*, which received excellent critical reviews in prestigious American and British publications.

[6] *a molecule* = the smallest unit into which any substance can be divided without losing its own chemical nature

[7] *a vibration* = a continuous, small shaking movement

Quick Comprehension Check

A. Read these sentences **about the reading**. Circle T (true), F (false), or ? (can't determine the answer from the reading). If you circle T or F, write the number of the paragraph with the answer on the line.

1. Turin's interest in smell led him to become a scientist. T F ? _____

2. Turin came up with a new theory about how we are able to distinguish different scents. T F ? _____

3. Turin's theory is widely accepted within the scientific community. T F ? _____

4. Turin thinks that the scientists who reviewed his theory did not treat him or his theory fairly. T F ? _____

5. Turin's scientific career ended when his paper was turned down. T F ? _____

6. Turin does not believe that his theory will ever be accepted by the scientific community. T F ? _____

7. Turin continues to be interested in both the art and the science of smell. T F ? _____

8. Turin now works for the Big Boys in the perfume industry. T F ? _____

B. Work with your class. Share your answers from part A. Go back to the reading to find the reason why a sentence is true or false. Correct the false sentences.

EXPLORING VOCABULARY

Thinking about the Target Vocabulary

Guessing Strategy: Signal Words for Cause and Effect

Words that express cause-and-effect relationships can help you guess the general meaning of unfamiliar words or phrases. Some examples of words that signal cause and effect are *so . . . that; that is; because; due to;* and *therefore.*

Look at the example.

> He described the fragrances in language that was **so poetic that** they told him he should write a book.

In this sentence, the cause-and-effect relationship expressed by *so . . . that* indicates that poetic language is good enough to be in a book, so you can infer that it is well written. The exact definition of *poetic* is "graceful, beautiful, and having deep feelings."

A. Read the sentences. Circle the cause-and-effect signal words. Then select the best definition or explanation of the **boldfaced** words.

1. Turin was so **obsessed** with coming up with a theory of smell that he couldn't think of anything else.

   When you are **obsessed** with a theory, you have difficulty

   a. coming up with a theory
   b. thinking of anything else

2. Each new smell the Big Boys create involves an **investment** of millions of dollars. That is because only a very small percentage of the new molecules possess the desired fragrance.

   An investment is

   a. money that someone puts into a business in order to make more money.
   b. a very small percentage of the total money someone puts into a business.

3. He argues that the reviewers turned his paper down due to their narrow **focus** on just one field of science. Therefore, they couldn't make sense out of a complex theory involving biology, chemistry, and physics.

   When you **focus** on just one field of science, you

   a. might have trouble understanding a theory in your own field.
   b. might turn down papers that contain complex theories involving several fields.

B. Look at the target words. Which ones are new to you? Circle them here and in the reading. The numbers in parentheses help you find the words in the paragraphs.

Target Words

legend (1)	entertain (2)	discount (4)	access (7)
perfume (1)	scents (2)	poetic (4)	fraud (8)
royalty (1)	fragrances (2)	secretive (6)	standards (9)
tales (2)	physics (3)	investment (6)	focus (9)
obsessed (2)	path (3)		

C. Read "A Nose for Smell" again. Look at the context of the new words. Can you guess their meanings?

D. Complete the word form chart. Fill in the shaded areas of the chart with the target words from the reading. Write the base form of the verbs and the singular form of the nouns.

NOUNS	VERBS	ADJECTIVES
legend		

Understanding the Target Vocabulary

A. These sentences are **about the reading**. Complete them with the words in the box. Circle the words in the sentences that help you understand the meaning of the target words.

access	focus	obsessed	poetic
discount	fraud	path	secretive
entertaining	investment	physics	standards

1. Scientist Luca Turin enjoys _____ people with interesting stories about perfume.

2. Turin is fascinated by different scents. In fact, you could say that he is _____ with smell.

3. One day, Turin went to a _____ perfume store. The prices were very low, and he bought almost every perfume there.

4. Turin is a scientist, but he is also a very artistic writer. His descriptions of perfume are remarkably _____ .

5. The makers of expensive perfume are so _____ that they almost never let anyone visit their labs.

6. Turin was given _____ to the laboratories of the perfume makers because they were impressed by his perfume guide.

7. Turin has used his knowledge of science, particularly biology, chemistry, and _____, to come up with a scientific theory of how we are able to smell.

8. Turin follows a different _____ from others. He doesn't follow the way other people do things. He comes up with his own way.

9. Some scientists do not believe Turin's theory, and one has accused him of deliberately changing or inventing data—in other words, scientific _____.

10. Turin believes his paper was turned down because a small number of powerful scientists have too much of an _____ in the old theory of smell. As a result, they don't want to admit that his theory might be correct.

11. According to Turin, the reviewers of his paper couldn't see the big picture due to their _____ on their individual fields of science.

12. Turin does not agree with the _____ that prestigious science journals use when they decide whether to publish a paper.

B. Read the paragraph and answer the questions.

One of France's most famous royal couples was King Louis XVI and his wife, Marie Antoinette. There are many stories about Marie Antoinette, but one tale is especially interesting. It involves her attempted escape from Paris during the French Revolution. According to the legend, Marie Antoinette and Louis XVI dressed in the clothes of simple travelers in order to escape from France. However, although Marie Antoinette's clothing was simple, her fragrance was not. Marie Antoinette and her husband were caught when someone smelled the expensive perfume that she was wearing. They knew that she was not an ordinary person, because only a member of royalty could afford such an expensive scent.

1. What are the three nouns in the paragraph that refer to smells?

_____, _____, _____

2. What are the two nouns in the paragraph that refer to a type of story?

_____ , _____

3. What is the adjective in the paragraph that means "relating to or belonging to a

king or queen"? _____

4. What is the noun form of the adjective in question 3? _____

DEVELOPING READING SKILLS

Understanding Purpose

To understand a text, it is important to understand *why* the writer wrote the text, or the writer's *purpose*. When you read, try to answer these questions about the information in a text:

- Why did the writer include this particular information?
- Why did the writer present the information in this particular order or in this particular way?

Complete the sentences. Circle a or b.

1. The writer includes the legend about Marie Antoinette

    a. to teach the reader some French history.
    b. to get the reader interested in the text.

2. The writer includes the quote from Luca Turin in paragraph 2

    a. to help the reader understand why Turin is so interested in smell.
    b. to convince the reader that smell is an important sense.

3. The writer includes information about Turin's perfume guide because

    a. it shows that Turin has a very sensitive sense of smell.
    b. it shows that Turin is both a poet and a scientist.

4. The writer of the text believes

    a. that Turin's theory of smell could be correct.
    b. that Turin should not have challenged the scientific community.

> **Reading Tip:** Often, writers do not state their purpose directly. The reader has to infer it.

Summarizing

A. Put a check (✓) next to the topics that should be included in a summary of the reading.

    ☐ a. the legend about Marie Antoinette's perfume

    ☐ b. Turin's visit to a discount perfume store

    ☐ c. Turin's perfume guide

    ☐ d. Turin's description of the fragrance Rush

> **Writing Tip:** The first step in writing a summary is to decide which information to include. Usually, a summary includes the main idea, the main points, and just enough detail to clarify the main points.

e. Turin's lifelong fascination with smell

f. Turin's scientific background

g. the shape theory of smell

h. Turin's theory of smell

i. other scientists' reaction to Turin's theory

j. Turin's opinion about why his theory is not accepted by many scientists

k. Turin's work history

B. Use both part A and your answers to the Understanding Purpose exercise to write a summary of the reading. Do not copy—paraphrase.

BUILDING ON THE VOCABULARY

Using the Target Vocabulary in New Contexts

Complete the sentences with the target words in the box. Be careful. There are two extra words.

access	fragrance	path	secretive
discount	fraud	physics	standards
entertain	investment	poetic	tales
focus	obsessed		

1. She is so _____ with detail that she can't see the big picture.

2. Originally, these gloves were priced at $100, but I got them at a 50 percent

   _____ .

3. The academic _____ for entering a prestigious university are very

   high. Fortunately, I have excellent grades.

4. The reviewer said the movie was wonderful. He said it would _____

   the whole family.

5. The former president of my company was accused of _____ . The

   company lost a lot of money while he was president. He and his family were

   humiliated by what happened.

6. That business is a good _____ . You will make a lot of money from it.

7. My _____ professor is the best scientist at the university.

8. _____ to that room is restricted. Only a few employees can enter.

9. Stay on the walking _____, and you won't get lost. It's easy to follow.

10. Your _____ should be on the main ideas. Don't worry about the details.

11. I don't understand why my son is suddenly so _____. What is he

    hiding?

12. You have such an original and _____ way of expressing yourself.

    How did you learn to speak so beautifully?

EXPANDING VOCABULARY

Word Families: Adjective suffixes

As you have seen in previous chapters, adjectives can have a variety of suffixes, such as *-ous, -ful, -ic, -al, -ed*, and *-ing*. Other adjective endings include the suffixes *-ive, -ant, -ent*, and *-ary*.

Complete the sentences with the adjectives below.

| fragrant | fraudulent | legendary | obsessive | secretive |

Vocabulary Tip: Learn to recognize the common suffixes for different parts of speech. Knowing an unfamiliar word's part of speech (noun, verb, adjective, adverb) may help you guess the meaning of the word.

1. The roses are wonderfully _____ this year. They have never smelled more heavenly.

2. There is no reason to be so _____. Everyone already knows what happened.

3. The _____ movie actor died yesterday at the age of eighty-two.

4. I'm concerned about you. You are becoming _____ about your work. Don't be such a perfectionist!

5. He was arrested for possessing _____ identification papers.

Word Grammar: Reflexive Pronouns

A **reflexive pronoun** is an object pronoun that is used when the subject and object of a verb are the same. Never use a reflexive pronoun if the subject and the object of the verb are different. Look at the examples.

Correct: *He used to entertain **himself** by analyzing the scents of wild plants.*

The reflexive pronoun *himself* is used **correctly** in this example because the subject (He) and object of the verb (himself) are the same.

Incorrect: *His **mother** entertained **himself** by telling him Greek legends.*

The reflexive pronoun *himself* is used **incorrectly** in this example because the subject (She) and object of the verb (himself) are different. The correct sentence would have to be: *His **mother** entertained **him***.

The reflexive pronouns in English are *myself, yourself, himself, herself, itself, themselves, yourselves, ourselves,* and *oneself.*

Answer these questions. Use the **boldfaced** verbs in your answers. Be careful. When you answer the questions, the pronouns may change.

1. What do you and your friends do to **entertain yourselves**? When your friends are busy, what do you do to **entertain yourself**?

   _____

   _____

2. Do you think teachers should try to **entertain their students**? Why or why not?

   _____

   _____

3. In which sports is it common for the players to **injure themselves**?

   Have you ever **injured yourself** when you were playing a sport?

   Have you ever **injured anyone else** when you were playing a sport?

   Explain what happened.

   _____

   _____

4. Are you someone who likes to **analyze yourself** and your behavior?

   Do you like it when other people try to **analyze you** and your behavior?

   _____

   _____

5. What famous people have **humiliated themselves**, in your opinion? Explain how they humiliated themselves.

   _____

   _____

CRITICAL THINKING

A. Discussion

Share your ideas in a small group. As you talk, try to use the vocabulary below. Each time someone uses a target word, put a check (✓) next to it.

☐ access	☐ invest	☐ poetic
☐ entertain	☐ legend/legendary	☐ secretive
☐ focus	☐ obsession/obsessive	☐ standard
☐ fraud/fraudulent	☐ physics	

1. Is the writer's attitude toward Luca Turin and his theory positive, negative, or neutral? Underline the words and phrases in the reading that support your answer.

2. Find the three examples of figurative language used in paragraph 1 of "A Nose for Science." Then talk about what the writer means. Remember that figurative language uses common words, but in a way that goes beyond the normal, literal meaning of the word.

   Figurative language (1st example) _____

      Writer's meaning _____

   Figurative language (2nd example) _____

      Writer's meaning _____

   Figurative language (3rd example) _____

      Writer's meaning _____

> **Critical Thinking Tip:** One way to identify a writer's attitude toward her subject is to pay attention to whether most of her words have positive, negative, or neutral connotations.

3. If you had the chance to interview Luca Turin, what questions would you ask him? Make a list.

4. "A Nose for Science" is about a scientist who has come up with a theory that is not accepted by some people in the scientific community. Look at the list of scientists below. First, match the scientists to their theories or discoveries. Then, circle those whose ideas were not accepted when they were first introduced. Finally, compare your answers to those of other groups.

Scientist	Theory or Discovery
_____ 1. Marie Curie	a. the theory of relativity
_____ 2. Charles Darwin	b. the theory of gravity
_____ 3. Albert Einstein	c. the theory of evolution
_____ 4. Galileo Galilei	d. the discovery of the relationship between bacteria and disease
_____ 5. Isaac Newton	e. the discovery of the elements radium and polonium
_____ 6. Louis Pasteur	f. the discovery that planets orbit (turn around) the sun

5. How do the following things smell to you? Complete the chart individually. Then share your answers with your group. Did any of your classmates' answers surprise you?

	WONDERFUL	GOOD	NEUTRAL	BAD	DISGUSTING
Freshly cut grass					
Horses					
Fresh fish					
Frying onions					
Leather					
A new car					
An infant					

B. Writing

Complete one or both of these writing topics. When you write, use at least five of the target words from the chapter. Underline the target words in your paper.

1. Choose one of the scientists your group discussed in question 4 above. Do some research on him or her and write a report. Include the following information in your report:

   - Background (nationality, education, family, etc.)
   - How he/she developed the theory or made the discovery
   - Research, experiments, evidence, etc., done to support the theory or discovery
   - Scientific and public reaction to the theory or discovery
   - When and how the theory or discovery was finally accepted

   Cite your sources according to your teacher's instructions.

2. Think of a smell that you associate with a particular memory of a person, place, or situation. Write a description of the memory. Use specific details and descriptive adjectives to make your description come alive.

UNIT 6

Checkpoint

LEARNING OUTCOME

> Review and expand on the content of Unit 6

LOOK BACK

A. Think About This

Think again about your responses in the *Think About This* exercise on page 217. After reading the chapters in Unit 6, are you interested in learning more about these topics? Check (✓) the ones that interest you.

- [ ] How the first human vaccination was developed
- [ ] How humans are able to distinguish so many different smells
- [ ] How perfumes are developed
- [ ] How scientists become interested in their fields
- [ ] How workers' clothing can help them do their jobs better
- [ ] How a scientific theory is tested

B. Remember the Readings

What do you want to remember most from the readings in Unit 6? For each chapter, write one sentence about the reading.

Chapter 16: A Woman's Fate

_____

Chapter 17: The Father of Vaccination

_____

Chapter 18: A Nose for Smell

_____

Read the text. Do not use a dictionary.

A New Way of Teaching Science?

1   There is concern among some in the scientific community that fewer and fewer young people are choosing careers in science and technology. Studies of university students confirm that this reduction in student numbers could soon lead to a shortage of new scientists. At a time when fascinating scientific discoveries are made almost every day, this apparent lack of interest in careers in science is quite striking. How can it be explained?

2   Experts who have reviewed the data believe that the key to the problem is in the way that science is taught. They claim that the teaching practices used in introductory science classes are suitable for only a small percentage of learners. For example, while most people are visual learners, most science professors use very few visual images in their teaching. Instead, they present information verbally, either through written words and formulas, or spoken words in lectures. This leaves the visual learners in the class without the means to make sense of the information.

3   But what about laboratory classes? Aren't they perfectly suited to visual learners? Maybe, but there's a problem. In a standard physics lab, for example, students usually focus on detailed procedures, rather than the big picture. They are given an experiment to perform, but have little opportunity to analyze what they are doing or explore how it relates to the larger theory and to their everyday lives.

4   What can be done to make science teaching meaningful to more students? Experts in science education believe that teachers need to focus on the educational well-being of all of the students in their classes. To that end, they should come up with methods and tasks that will be effective for a wider range of learners.

Quick Comprehension Check

A. Read these sentences **about the reading**. Circle T (true), F (false), or ? (can't determine the answer from the reading). If you circle T or F, write the number of the paragraph with the answer on the line.

1. Scientists are worried that students who graduate from universities with science degrees are not well trained.   T   F   ?   ____

2. The way that science is taught in schools is not effective for the majority of the students.   T   F   ?   ____

3. Science teachers often use visual images that confuse their students.   T   F   ?   ____

4. In most science lab classes, students have a chance to understand theories and relate them to their individual experiences. T F ? _____

5. Overall, science teachers are not very interested in the well-being of their students. T F ? _____

B. Go back to the reading to find the reason why a sentence is true or false. Correct the false sentences.

Guessing Meaning from Context

Find a word or phrase in the text that matches each of the definitions below. The numbers in parentheses are the paragraphs where you can find the word or phrase.

Definition	Word or Phrase
1. pictures that describe ideas (2)	_____
2. with words rather than pictures (2)	_____
3. a series of numbers or letters that represent a mathematical or scientific rule (2)	_____
4. for that purpose (4)	_____

Understanding Inference and Applying Information

Use inference and apply what you have learned to answer these questions.

1. Does the writer of the text imply that visual images are more important in the teaching of science than in other subjects? Explain.

   _____

   _____

   _____

2. Give two or more specific examples of visual images that science teachers could use in class to make science easier for visual learners.

   _____

   _____

   _____

Summarizing

Write a summary of the text. Remember, do not copy—paraphrase.

EXPANDING VOCABULARY

A. Read the sentences, and write the meaning of the **boldfaced** phrasal verbs.

1. On the night the restaurant opened, there were so many customers that they had to **turn** people **away**.

   _____

   _____

2. Don't worry about him. He's always late. He'll **turn up** eventually.

   _____

   _____

3. Has anyone **turned in** a set of keys? I think I lost mine somewhere in the building.

   _____

   _____

4. You should be proud of your son. He's **turned into** a fine young man.

   _____

   _____

5. I liked my boss at first, but after a few weeks, his negative attitude **turned** me **off**.

   _____

   _____

B. Answer these questions in complete sentences. Use the **boldfaced** phrasal verbs.

1. When was the last time you were **turned away** from a restaurant or other public place?

   _____

   _____

2. What would you do if you were waiting for a friend and he never **turned up**?

_____

_____

_____

3. If you found $100 in an empty classroom, would you **turn** it **in**? Why or why not?

_____

_____

_____

4. At what temperature does water **turn into** ice?

_____

_____

_____

5. What kinds of movies **turn** you **off**?

_____

_____

_____

Word Families: Prefixes, Suffixes, and Roots

When you learn a new word, check to see if it contains a word part—a prefix, suffix, or root. Then, use your understanding of the meaning of the word to help you guess the meaning of the word part. The next time you see a word that contains that word part, it will be easier for you to guess its meaning.

A. The words *physics* and *physician* both contain the root *phys*. The word *unique* contains the prefix *uni-*, and the word *agricultural* contains the prefix *agr-*. Use your understanding of the meanings of the words to write the meanings of the word parts.

1. The root *phys* means _____.

2. The prefix *uni-* means _____.

3. The prefix *agr-* means _____.

B. Working with a partner, answer the questions. Make sure you use the **boldfaced** words in your answers.

1. How often do you go to your doctor for a **physical**? _____

2. What is a **unisex** bathroom? Are there **unisex** bathrooms in public places in your city?

   _____

3. Would you like to live in an **agrarian** community? Why or why not?

   _____

PLAYING WITH WORDS

Look back at the lists of target vocabulary on pages 222, 234, and 246. In a small group, write as many target words and phrases as you can under each category. Be ready to explain your answers. Some words might fit under more than one category, and some words might not fit under any category.

SUCCESS AND FAILURE	HEALTH	SCIENTIFIC RESEARCH	SMELL	MONEY
prestigious	vaccination	confirm	fragrance	prestigious

BUILDING DICTIONARY SKILLS

Idioms

Dictionary Entries for Idioms

An **idiom** is a group of two or more words that has a special meaning that is different from the ordinary meaning of the separate words. For example, the phrase *see the big picture* is an idiom. Most dictionaries do not have separate entries for idioms. Instead, they can be found under the entry for a key verb or noun in the idiom.

A. Read the dictionary entries, and circle the idioms.

1.

> **pic·ture¹** /ˈpɪktʃɚ/ *n* **1** IMAGE [C] a painting, drawing, or photograph: *a **picture of** Nelson Mandela* | ***Draw/paint a picture of** your house.* | *a group of tourists **taking pictures** (= taking photographs)* | *Leo's **picture** (=photograph of him) is in the newspaper.* **2** SITUATION [singular] the general situation in a place, organization, etc.: *The **political picture** has greatly changed since March.* | *You're missing the **big/bigger/wider picture** (=the situation considered as a whole).* **3** DESCRIPTION [C usually singular] a description that gives you an idea of what something is like: *To get a better **picture of** how the company is doing, look at sales.* | *The book **paints a clear picture** of life in Ancient Rome.* **4** BE IN/OUT OF THE PICTURE *informal* to be involved or not be involved in a situation: *With his main rival out of the picture, the mayor has a chance of winning the election.* **5** ON A SCREEN [C] the image that you see on a television or in a movie: *Something's wrong with the picture.* **6** GET THE PICTURE *(spoken)* to understand something: *I don't want you around here anymore, get the picture?* **7** MOVIE [C] *(old-fashioned)* a MOVIE: *Grandma loved going to the pictures.*

2.

> **mean³** *n* **1** MEANS [plural] a method, system, object, etc. that is used as a way of achieving a result: *We'll use any means we can to raise the money.* | *My bicycle is my **main means** of transportation.* | *The oil is transported **by means of** (=using) a pipeline.* **2** MEANS [plural] ECONOMICS the money or income that you have: *They don't have **the means** to buy a car.* | *Try to live **within** your **means** (=only spending what you can afford).* | *a man **of means** (=who is rich)* **3** BY ALL MEANS *(spoken)* used to mean "of course" when politely allowing someone to do something or agreeing with a suggestion: *"Can I invite Clarence?" "Oh, by all means."* **4** BY NO MEANS *(formal)* not at all: *The results are by no means certain.* **5** A MEANS TO AN END something that you do only to achieve a result, not because you want to do it: *This job is just a means to an end.* **6** THE MEAN MATH the average amount, figure, or value → MEDIAN, MODE: *The mean of 7, 9, and 14 is 10.*

3.

> **free¹** /fri/ *adj* **1** NOT RESTRICTED allowed to live, exist, or happen without being controlled or restricted: *Students are **free to** choose the activities they want to work on.* | *The media is **free from** governmental control.* | *the right to **free speech*** **2** NO COST not costing any money: *I won free tickets to the concert.* | *Admission is free for children.* **3** NOT CONTAINING STH not having any of a particular substance: *sugar-free bubble gum* | *The water is **free from** chemical pollutants.* **4** NOT BUSY not busy doing other things: *Are you **free for** lunch?* | *Hansen does volunteer work in her **free time**.* **5** NOT BEING USED not being used at this time: *Excuse me, is this seat free?* **6** FEEL FREE *(spoken)* used in order to tell someone that s/he is allowed to do something: *Feel free to ask me any questions after the class.* **7** NOT A PRISONER not a prisoner or slave: *Muller will be free in three years.* | *The UN demanded that the three hostages be **set free** (=be given their freedom).* **8** NOT SUFFERING not suffering or not having to deal with something bad: ***free of** danger* | *Patients undergoing the treatment are now **free from** cancer.* | *a happy and trouble-free life.*

B. Complete each sentence with an idiom from the dictionary entries in part A.

1. If you have any problems, _____ to give me a call. I'll be happy to help you.

2. Now that his former girlfriend is _____, he is free to date someone else.

3. Some students study just because they enjoy it, but for many students, studying is _____ .

Vocabulary Self-Test 2

Circle the letter of the word or phrase that best completes each sentence.

1. She was seriously _____ in a car accident.

   a. ignored   b. bitter   c. injured   d. ashamed

2. I don't believe in _____. I think that with hard work, you can make anything happen.

   a. function   b. fate   c. controversy   d. motivation

3. I love reading about European _____. Tales about English kings and queens are particularly interesting.

   a. royalty   b. scents   c. species   d. virtue

4. I have tried to _____ her behavior, but I just can't understand her.

   a. turn down   b. recognize   c. come up with   d. make sense of

5. Put on your _____. It's cold outside.

   a. gloves   b. stains   c. legends   d. perfume

6. How did you _____ your car? Did you have an accident?

   a. injure   b. distinguish   c. possess   d. damage

7. You should never touch a _____ animal.

   a. ashamed   b. puzzled   c. wild   d. mild

8. The _____ of the first public school in the United States was in 1635.

   a. establishment   b. frequency   c. increase   d. security

9. When his wife died, he never thought he would recover from his _____.

   a. grief   b. well-being   c. humiliation   d. honor

10. I need to _____ this into English. Can you help me?

    a. calculate   b. accuse   c. greet   d. translate

11. I don't appreciate his jokes. They just aren't _____ to me.

    a. disgusting   b. moody   c. humorous   d. cheerful

12. I need to know the _____ meaning of that word. It is important that I translate it correctly.

    a. precise   b. suitable   c. former   d. striking

13. When you go to a job interview, it is important to wear the _____ clothing.

    a. particular   b. deliberate   c. proper   d. artificial

14. I will always _____ the smell of that perfume with my mother. It reminds me of her.

    a. reveal   b. focus   c. entertain   d. associate

15. That vase looks heavy, but it isn't because it's _____.

    a. mutual   b. sustained   c. hollow   d. endless

16. Receiving a Nobel Prize is a great _____ for any scientist.

    a. shame   b. observation   c. honor   d. legend

17. Children who are learning how to read usually start by reading _____.

    a. out loud   b. in contrast   c. eventually   d. out of sight

18. The price of a new car _____ from $10,000 to $40,000.

    a. measures   b. ranges   c. resembles   d. calculates

19. If a police officer stops you, you should not _____. You must do exactly what he says.

    a. possess   b. analyze   c. focus   d. resist

20. Oranges are usually sweet, but this one is _____.

    a. contagious   b. mild   c. suitable   d. bitter

21. I'd like to help you fix the sink, but I left my _____ at home.

    a. surgery   b. tools   c. piles   d. discount

22. It was a _____ that she died so young.

    a. rage   b. fraud   c. tragedy   d. witness

23. Are you angry with him? You didn't _____ him when he came in.

    a. greet   b. confirm   c. ignore   d. abuse

24. It is a _____ opportunity. You will never have such a good opportunity again.

    a. royal   b. unique   c. poetic   d. mild

25. I tried to talk to him, but he completely _____ me.

    a. ignored   b. infected   c. invested   d. reviewed

26. He is _____ to find her. He won't stop searching until he does.

    a. disgusted   b. reserved   c. puzzled   d. determined

27. Her _____ with money is destroying her life. It's the only thing she ever thinks about.

    a. discount   b. function   c. mood   d. obsession

28. I can't go on the trip. My mother won't give me _____.

    a. physician   b. standard   c. permission   d. request

29. What _____ are you wearing? It smells heavenly!

    a. stain   b. fragrance   c. legend   d. flash

30. Some children closely _____ their parents. Others do not look like their parents at all.

    a. detect   b. interpret   c. raise   d. resemble

31. You should not _____ directly at the sun. It is harmful to your eyes.

    a. gaze   b. accuse   c. injure   d. sweat

32. It feels good to _____ when you first wake up in the morning.

    a. entertain   b. stretch   c. slip   d. gesture

33. If your _____ is always on the details, you might not be able to see the big picture.

    a. interference   b. investment   c. possession   d. focus

34. She and her sister have a close _____. They understand and respect each other.

    a. access   b. bond   c. companion   d. gesture

35. She's a _____ woman. Everyone who meets her remembers her.

    a. striking   b. mild   c. sustained   d. well-being

36. Please don't walk on the grass. Stay on the _____.

    a. theme   b. journal   c. task   d. path

See the Answer Key on page 265.

Vocabulary Self-Test Answer Key

Below are the answers to the Vocabulary Self-Tests. Check your answers, and then review any words you did not remember. You can look up the word in the Index to Target Vocabulary on pages 266–267. Then go back to the reading and exercises to find the word. Use your dictionary as needed.

Vocabulary Self-Test 1, Units 1-3 (pages 126–128)

1. b	13. c	25. c
2. a	14. d	26. c
3. a	15. d	27. a
4. a	16. b	28. d
5. d	17. d	29. b
6. b	18. c	30. a
7. a	19. c	31. d
8. b	20. c	32. b
9. d	21. c	33. c
10. c	22. a	34. a
11. b	23. a	35. b
12. d	24. b	36. c

Vocabulary Self-Test 2, Units 4-6 (pages 262–264)

1. c	13. c	25. a
2. b	14. d	26. d
3. a	15. c	27. d
4. d	16. c	28. c
5. a	17. a	29. b
6. d	18. b	30. d
7. c	19. d	31. a
8. a	20. d	32. b
9. a	21. b	33. d
10. d	22. c	34. b
11. c	23. a	35. a
12. a	24. b	36. d

Index to Target Vocabulary

injustice, 56
instruction, 88
insult, 68
intellectual, 197
intend, 112
intentional, 68
interact, 26
interfere, 219
interpret, 155
investment, 244
involve, 3
journal, 175
key, 175
knowledge, 14
laboratory, 14
lack, 45
lead to, 99
legal, 155
legend, 243
likely, 45
literature, 56
live, 26
make sense of, 176
make up, 143
meaningful, 197
means, 231
measure, 186
mild, 232
mood, 143
moral, 4
motivation, 155
muscle, 143
mutual, 186
mystery, 14
observe, 131
obsessed, 243
official, 45
operation, 111
originality, 4
out loud, 143
out of sight, 197
particularly, 131
path, 243
pattern, 45
peer, 57
perfectionist, 56
performer, 26
perfume, 243
permission, 232
personality, 27
physical, 68
physician, 232
physics, 243
pick on, 68
pile, 197
pleasurable, 186
poetic, 243

poison, 112
popularity, 3
possess, 197
practice, 231
precise, 175
prescribe, 111
pressure, 56
prestigious, 219
prevent, 88
procedure, 231
progress, 111
proof, 15
proper, 143
protest, 197
provide, 3
publish, 57
puzzled, 197
rage, 155
raise, 186
range, 154
rapid, 4
realize, 87
recognize, 132
recover, 111
reduce, 46
regardless of, 187
related, 3
release, 186
remarkable, 14
replace, 88
reportedly, 3
request, 231
resemble, 186
reserved, 143
resist, 219
restrict, 99
reveal, 132
review, 232
rhyme, 26
risk, 99
royalty, 243
scale, 175
scent, 243
scratch, 26
secretive, 243
security, 155
see the big picture, 219
self-esteem, 68
sensitive, 56
severe, 111
shame, 131
shortage, 100
slip, 220
species, 175
spinning, 26
stain, 220
stand by, 15

stand, out 26
standard, 244
stay up, 45
stretch, 198
striking, 186
structure 175
suffer, 111
suitable, 219
surgery, 231
survey, 68
survive, 56
sustained, 186
sweat, 220
system, 175
tale, 243
talented, 3
task, 187
technique, 26
tend to, 56
the deaf, 176
the wild, 198
theme, 175
theory, 14
threatened, 15
tool, 154
tragedy, 155
trait, 87
translate, 131
turn down, 232
unique, 219
universal, 131
vaccination, 231
vehicle, 155
victim, 68
violent, 68
virtue, 143
visual, 176
well-being, 220

REFERENCES

Associated Press. "Scientists growing ears, bone, skin to heal wounded troops." New York Daily News. (September 10, 2012). Retrieved from http://www.nydailynews.com/life-style/health/scientists-growing-ears-bone-skin-heal-wounded-troops-article-1.1155785

Berman, J. "Dogs Can Recognize Human Emotional Expressions." Voice of America News. (February 12, 2015). Retrieved from http://www.voanews.com/content/dogs-can-recognize-human-emotional-expressions/2640772.html

"Bullying Statistics." Retrieved June 15, 2015 from http://www.bullyingstatistics.org/content/school-bullying-statistics.html

Dooley, J. J. & Pyzalski, J. & Cross, D. "Cyberbullying Versus Face-to-Face Bullying: A Theoretical and Conceptual Review." Hogrefe Publishing Zeitschrift für Psychologie / Journal of Psychology. (2009) Vol. 217(4):182–188. Retrieved from http://icbtt.arizona.edu/sites/default/files/cross_set_al_cyber_vs_face-to-face.pdf

Ekman, P. Retrieved April 27, 2016 from http://www.paulekman.com

Foreman, J. "A conversation with: Paul Ekman; The 43 facial muscles that reveal even the most fleeting emotions." The New York Times. (August 5, 2003) Retrieved from http://www.nytimes.com/2003/08/05/health/conversation-with-paul-ekman-43-facial-muscles-that-reveal-even-most-fleeting.html

Georgakopoulos, T. "Luca Turin: On Smell And The Future Of Science A discussion in Athens." Space & Anthropology. (October 22, 2013). Retrieved from https://medium.com/space-anthropology/on-smell-and-the-future-of-science-991a6cf2872a#.nyx6tbmi5

Gladwell, M. "The Naked Face." Annals of psychology, The New Yorker – Archive. (August 5, 2002)

Goldberg, C. "Why we need to talk now about the brave new world of editing genes." WBUR Boston NPR News Station. (May 22, 2015). Retrieved from http://www.wbur.org/commonhealth/2015/05/22/crispr-edit-genes-designer-babies

"Growing Up Gifted." The Canadian Press. (2000)

Healey, M. "Gaze helps dog-human bond." Los Angeles Times. (April 16, 2015). Retrieved from http://azdailysun.com/news/science/gaze-helps-dog-human-bond/article_6dcc6742-34fc-511f-b5ff-1ea20f4b9c86.html

Hines, H. N. "Traditional Bullying and Cyber-bullying: Are the Impacts on Self-concept the Same." A Thesis Submitted to the Faculty of the Graduate School of Western Carolina University in Partial Fulfillment of the Requirements for the Degree of Specialist in School Psychology. Western Carolina University Cullowhee, North Carolina. (2011). Retrieved from http://libres.uncg.edu/ir/wcu/f/Hines2011.pdf

Ledford, H. "Bitter fight over CRISPR patent heats up." Springer Nature. (January 12, 2016). Retrieved from http://www.nature.com/news/bitter-fight-over-crispr-patent-heats-up-1.17961

Matsumoto, D. & Hwang, H. S. "Reading facial expressions of emotion." Psychological Science Agenda, American Psychological Association. (May 2011). Retrieved from http://www.apa.org/science/about/psa/2011/05/facial-expressions.aspx

Minthe, C. "Interview: Message in a Bottle." Vogue Magazine. (July 27, 2013). Retrieved from https://en.vogue.me/archive/interview-message-in-a-bottle-luca-turin/

"Nagyvary Violins." Retrieved June 15, 2015 from http://nagyvaryviolins.com

Nguyen, T. C. "Will Japanese Researchers Grow Human Organs Inside Pigs?" Smithsonian Magazine. Retrieved from http://www.smithsonianmag.com/innovation/will-Japanese-researchers-grow-human-organs-inside-pigs-180949396/?no-ist

O'Sullivan, M. "Emotion, Lies, and Wizardry" Transcript from: Ask a Scientist Lecture Series (October 12, 2005). Retrieved from www.askascientistsf.com

Regalado, A. "Engineering the Perfect Baby." MIT Technology Review. (March 5, 2015). Retrieved from http://www.technologyreview.com/featuredstory/535661/engineering-the-perfect-baby/

Scully, A. & Newhouse, M. & Murray, P. & Bates, S. "Traditional Bullying vs. Cyber Bullying." Retrieved on June 15, 2015 from https://sites.google.com/site/cyberbullyingawareness/traditional-bullying-vs-cyberbullying

Slezak, M. "Dogs Tap into Human Bonding System to Tap into Our Hearts." New Scientist. (April 16, 2015). Retrieved from http://www.newscientist.com/article/dn27363-dogs-tap-into-human-bonding-system-to-get-close-to-our-hearts.html#.VXbQTinF_wx

Skirble, R. "Common Hormone Plays Role in Canine-Human Bond." Voice of America News. (April 16, 2015). Retrieved from http://www.voanews.com/content/hormone-canine-human-bond/2722840.html

"The Annual Bullying Survey." 2015. Retrieved June 15, 2015 from http://www.ditchthelabel.org/research-papers/the-annual-bullying-survey-2015/

Tucker, N. "Don't Believe the 'Lie to Me' Hype: Even Trained Eyes Have a Hard Time Spotting Untruths" Washington Post. (February 15, 2009). Retrieved from http://www.washingtonpost.com/wp-dyn/content/article/2009/02/12/AR2009021204220.html?hpid=artsliving

"Violence Prevention Works! Safer Schools, Safer Communities." Retrieved June 15, 2015 from http://www.violencepreventionworks.org/public/index.page

Zehnder, I. "What are the differences between 'traditional' bullying and 'cyberbullying?'" Seattle Family Examiner. (November 15, 2010.) Retrieved from http://www.examiner.com/article/what-are-the-differences-between-traditional-bullying-and-cyberbullying